Wholeheartedly English: A Life of Learning

Festschrift for
Johannes-Peter Timm

Cornelsen

Herausgegeben von Claudia Finkbeiner

Druck: Lengericher HD
ISBN 3-464-37130-1
Bestellnummer 371301

Gedruckt auf säurefreiem Papier, umweltschonend hergestellt aus chlorfrei gebleichten Faserstoffen.

Contents

Preface 7

Publications by Johannes-Peter Timm 10

Tabula Gratulatoria 16

English in a multilingual world

Werner Hüllen
A world language is born: English as a national and as *the* world language 21

Gerhard Bach
Europeans and languages: Assessing the multilingual divide 35

Peter Doyé
Education for plurilingualism 51

Wholeheartedly English right from the beginning

Werner Bleyhl
Foreign language acquisition at the primary school starting in grade one. The new Baden-Württemberg curriculum 73

Gerhard W. Schnaitmann
Early foreign language learning in first grade elementary school. Results from a school experiment in Baden-Württemberg with the European project DINOCROC 94

Language learning in a cooperative, holistic, task-oriented, student-centred way

Claudia Finkbeiner
Foreign language practice and cooperative learning 109

Renate Löffler
"Brainlinking": Holistic learning and learner orientation 123

Liesel Hermes
"Do they love each other?" Learner autonomy in university literature courses 137

Joachim Appel
Student-centred approaches and teachers' experiential knowledge 149

Grammar and spoken discourse

Wolfgang Butzkamm
Grammar in action – The case for bilingual pattern drills 163

Uwe Multhaup
A processing view of teaching English grammar 176

Christina Lausevic
Spoken discourse: From linguistics to pedagogy 196

Content and language integrated learning

Sylvia Fehling
Language awareness in content and language integrated learning 213

Heike Rautenhaus
Teacher students practising task-oriented foreign language exercises 222

Helmut J. Vollmer
Project orientation in content and language integrated learning 235

Learning languages through songs and media

Willis Edmondson
Elvis analysed 255

Wilfried Brusch
Discovering Shakespeare: A media-integrated approach 267

Wilfried Gienow & Karlheinz Hellwig
Are pop and rock songs "simple forms"? A genre study with some implications for the process-oriented approach to foreign language learning 281

Preface

Wholeheartedly English: A Life of Learning is dedicated to Prof. Dr. Johannes-Peter Timm, Heidelberg, Germany, in honour of his scholarly contributions to foreign language research and teaching of English as a foreign language.

Johannes-Peter Timm looks back on a rich life as a professor. In the winter semester of 1970/71 he began his work as an assistant professor for English at the University of Education – Pädagogische Hochschule – Heidelberg. In 1974 Timm was appointed Professor of English Language, Literature and Language Teaching in Heidelberg where he taught and conducted his research until September 2000. More than 30 years after the beginning of his career, we are celebrating Prof. Dr. Johannes-Peter Timm's 60th birthday and his scholarly achievements in the field of foreign language teaching and research.

Johannes-Peter Timm was born in Baden-Baden on November 7, 1942, and grew up in Villingen, Black Forest. From 1962 until 1967 he studied English, French, Pedagogy and Philosophy at the University of Freiburg and at the University of Bristol in England. Timm was a student of Herbert Pilch and Hermann Heuer and was influenced by Helmut Lüdtke and Hugo Friedrich. Graduating in 1969, he worked as an assistant for Andreas Digeser at the University of Education – Pädagogische Hochschule – Lörrach.

From the 70s on, Timm's focus of research lay in applied linguistics with a special interest in grammar instruction. He met Harald Gutschow, Berlin, and a long-lasting correspondence evolved.

In 1976, Timm began working on his doctoral dissertation in the field of Teaching English as a Foreign Language with Prof. Dr. Werner Hüllen as his mentor and "doctor father". Johannes-Peter Timm's doctoral dissertation deals with a pragmatic communicative concept of English language grammar for communication-oriented teaching. The dissertation built on his previous work of the 70s which focused on a rational and controlled foreign language teaching methodology following Corder's premise: *What we cannot describe we cannot teach systematically.* This premise was an important foundation of Timm's orientation towards a cognitive model of teaching grammar.

In the mid 80s, Timm moved towards a more holistic methodology of teaching, undoubtedly influenced by his year at a secondary school in Neckargemünd in 1985/86. Major research projects focused on students' interim grammar, the effectiveness of awareness, the efficiency of 'operational rules' for learner-oriented language awareness, the consistency of learners' interlanguage, 'fuzzy sets' in English grammar as well as didactic concepts of learner orientation.

Timm was one of the founding members of the German Association for Foreign Language Research (Deutsche Gesellschaft für Fremdsprachenforschung – DGFF) established in 1989. He served on its board until 1991, and again from 1993 to 1995.

Timm's professional development can be described as moving from a rational and planned teaching methodology to a holistic, "intuitive" and learner-oriented one. Within this approach, students are considered as independent and active learners making use of the foreign language and learning material in order to construct their knowledge of and competence in the target language. The foreign language environment, material and activities play a fundamental role in enhancing learners' experience, abilities, interests and needs. Authenticity and holism are decisive factors towards a content-oriented, interactive foreign language learning process in which the subject matter is no longer mediated but becomes a meaningful trigger of learners' expectations and experience.

Wholeheartedly English follows this approach. The authors contributing to this book have been professionally connected with Johannes-Peter Timm for a long time. They express their most sincere admiration for Johannes-Peter Timm and congratulate him warmly on his 60th birthday.

Wholeheartedly English: A Life of Learning consists of six parts:

I. "English in a multilingual world" with articles by Werner Hüllen, Gerhard Bach and Peter Doyé.

II. "Wholeheartedly English right from the beginning" with contributions by Werner Bleyhl and Gerhard W. Schnaitmann.

III. "Language learning in a cooperative, holistic, task-oriented, student-centred way" with articles by Claudia Finkbeiner, Renate Löffler, Liesel Hermes and Joachim Appel.

IV. "Grammar and spoken discourse" with articles by Wolfgang Butzkamm, Uwe Multhaup and Christina Lausevic

V. "Content and language integrated learning" with contributions by Sylvia Fehling, Heike Rautenhaus and Helmut J. Vollmer.

VI. "Learning languages through songs and media" with essays by Willis Edmondson, Wilfried Brusch and Wilfried Gienow & Karlheinz Hellwig.

Wholeheartedly English: A Life of Learning highlights the importance of continuity: it draws a line from Johannes-Peter Timm's academic beginning with Werner Hüllen as the mentor and tutor to the editor of this book and her doctoral students, thus connecting four academic generations: Werner Hüllen ⇨ Johannes-Peter Timm ⇨ Claudia Finkbeiner ⇨ Sylvia Fehling and Markus Knierim.

I want to express my deepest thanks to Werner Hüllen for contributing the opening essay to this Festschrift and all the authors who so patiently and willingly cooperated.

My thanks include both my doctoral students, Markus Knierim and Sylvia Fehling, who contributed actively in the whole organization from the very first planning to the final printing. Last but not least, *Wholeheartedly English* would not have happened if it were not for the strong support of Michael Ferguson, Cornelsen Publishers, to whom I express my deepest thanks.

This book is dedicated to Prof. Dr. Johannes-Peter Timm. It reflects his methodological perspectives and invites the readers to explore the possibilities that are given in a more open and holistic approach to foreign language teaching.

Claudia Finkbeiner — Kassel, November 2002

Publications by Johannes-Peter Timm

Monographs and works edited by Timm

(1979). *Pragmatisch-kommunikative Grammatik im Englischunterricht. Theorie und Praxis der Unterrichtsplanung*. München: Hueber.

with G. Bach (Eds.). (1989, 1996 rev. ed.). *Englischunterricht. Grundlagen und Methoden einer handlungsorientierten Unterrichtspraxis*. Tübingen: Francke.

with G. Bach (Eds.). (1989). *Fremdsprachenunterricht im Wandel*. Heidelberg: Pädagogische Hochschule/Institut für Weiterbildung.

with H. J. Vollmer (Eds.). (1993). *Kontroversen in der Fremdsprachenforschung. Kongressdokumentation des 14. Kongresses für Fremdsprachendidaktik, Essen 1991*. Bochum: Brockmeyer.

(Ed.). (1995). *Ganzheitlicher Fremdsprachenunterricht*. Weinheim: Deutscher Studien Verlag.

(Ed.). (1995). *Workshop: Grammar* [Special issue]. *Der Fremdsprachliche Unterricht – Englisch, 29*(3).

(Ed.). (1998, 2001 rev. ed.). *Englisch lernen und lehren. Didaktik des Englischunterrichts*. Berlin: Cornelsen.

Articles in periodicals and essay collections, textbook development

(1971). Kurzgutachten Englisch. In Schuldezernat der Stadt Mannheim (Ed.), *Schule – aber wie? Vol. 2: Kurzgutachten zur Kommissionsarbeit der Orientierungsstufe* (pp. 113-133). Mannheim.

(1971). 'La fille que j'aimerons ... La fille que j'aimera' – Über die Subjektivität der Personen in Jacques Brels Chanson 'La Bourrée du Célibataire'. *Die Neueren Sprachen, 70*, 63-68.

(1972). Linguistische Grundlegung einer Didaktik des Englischunterrichts. Rezension von W. Hüllen, *Linguistik und Englischunterricht 1* (Heidelberg: Quelle & Meyer, 1971). *Englisch, 7*, 88-93.

(1972). Strukturalistische und transformationelle Syntax: Möglichkeiten und Probleme im Englischunterricht. *Zeitnahe Schularbeit, 25* (6/7), 1-96.

(1973). Rezension von János S. Petöfi, *Transformationsgrammatiken und eine ko-textuelle Texttheorie. Grundfragen und Konzeptionen* (Frankfurt/M., 1971). *International Review of Applied Linguistics, 11*, 177-182.

(1974). Integrierte Gesamtschule Mannheim-Herzogenried: Methodenkonzept und Curriculumentwurf Englisch für die Orientierungsstufe (Hauptgutachten). In Schuldezernat der Stadt Mannheim (Ed.), *Schule – aber wie? Vol. 3a: Gutachten zu Sachbereichen und Curriculumentwürfe zu Fachbereichen der Orientierungsstufe* (pp. 323-446). Mannheim.

with T. Moston et al. (1978). *English in action. Vol. 1H.* München: Langenscheidt-Longman.

(1980). Pragmatisch-kommunikative Grammatik im Englischunterricht. Theorie und Praxis der Unterrichtsplanung [Pragma-Communicative Grammar in the Teaching of English. Theory and Practice of Instructional Design]. *EASG*, 139-142.

(1981). Sprachliche „Konzepte“ und „Regeln“ in der Interimsgrammatik deutscher Schüler – „Hervorlockungstests“ und methodische Folgerungen für den Englischunterricht. In W. Kühlwein & A. Raasch (Eds.), *Sprache: Lehren und Lernen. Kongressberichte der 11. Jahrestagung der Gesellschaft für Angewandte Linguistik GAL e.V., Darmstadt 1980. Vol. 2* (pp. 99-103). Tübingen: Narr.

(1982). Wh-Fragen im Englischunterricht: Eine Untersuchung zur Effizienz von operationellen Regeln als Mittel für eine lernerbezogene Bewusstmachung. In C. Gnutzmann et al. (Eds.), *Fremdsprachendidaktiker-Kongress Hannover 1981: Nachpublikation* (pp. 91-107). Hannover: C.T.

(1985). Bemerkungen zur Rezeption der Forschung in den revidierten Lehrplänen Englisch in Baden-Württemberg. In K.-R. Bausch et al. (Eds.), *Forschungsgegenstand Richtlinien. Arbeitspapiere der 5. Frühjahrskonferenz zur Erforschung des Fremdsprachenunterrichts* (pp. 151-159). Tübingen: Narr.

(1986). Interdependenzen in der Unterrichtsforschung. In K.-R. Bausch et al. (Eds.), *Lehrperspektive, Methodik und Methoden. Arbeitspapiere der 6. Frühjahrskonferenz zur Erforschung des Fremdsprachenunterrichts* (pp. 159-169). Tübingen: Narr.

(1987). Operationelle Regeln für den Englischunterricht. In W. Lörscher & R. Schulze (Eds.), *Perspectives on language in performance. Studies in linguistics, literary criticism, and language teaching and learning* (2 vols.) (pp. 1398-1417). Tübingen: Narr.

(1987). Plädoyer für ein ganzheitliches Sprach- und Methodenkonzept im Fremdsprachenunterricht der Sekundarstufe I. In K.-R. Bausch et al. (Eds.), *Sprachbegriffe im Fremdsprachenunterricht. Arbeitspapiere der 7.*

Frühjahrskonferenz zur Erforschung des Fremdsprachenunterrichts (pp. 190-197). Tübingen: Narr.

(1988). Fortschritte auf dem Weg zur kommunikativen Freiheit des Individuums. In K.-R. Bausch et al. (Eds.), *Fortschritt und Fortschritte im Fremdsprachenunterricht. Arbeitspapiere der 8. Frühjahrskonferenz zur Erforschung des Fremdsprachenunterrichts* (pp. 127-134). Tübingen: Narr.

(1989). Das institutionelle Lernumfeld 'Schule': Teufel oder Beelzebub eines handlungsorientierten Fremdsprachenunterrichts? In K.-R. Bausch et al. (Eds.), *Der Fremdsprachenunterricht und seine institutionellen Bedingungen. Arbeitspapiere der 9. Frühjahrskonferenz zur Erforschung des Fremdsprachenunterrichts* (pp. 122-127). Tübingen: Narr.

(1989). Fehlerkorrektur zwischen Handlungsorientierung und didaktischer Steuerung. In G. Bach & J.-P. Timm (Eds.), *Englischunterricht. Grundlagen und Methoden einer handlungsorientierten Unterrichtspraxis* (pp. 161-186). Tübingen: Francke.

(1989). The consistency of interlanguage in task-bound second-language production. *Applied Linguistics, 7*, 86-107.

(1989). Wandlungen im Selbstverständnis eines Angewandten Linguisten. In G. Bach & J.-P. Timm (Eds.), *Fremdsprachenunterricht im Wandel* (pp. 35-42). Heidelberg: Pädagogische Hochschule.

with G. Bach (1989). Was ist "handlungsorientierter Englischunterricht"? In G. Bach & J.-P. Timm (Eds.), *Englischunterricht. Grundlagen und Methoden einer handlungsorientierten Unterrichtspraxis* (pp. 1-21). Tübingen: Francke.

(1990). Handlungsorientierte Lehrerbildung für einen handlungsorientierten Fremdsprachenunterricht. In A. Abele (Ed.), *Neuere Entwicklungen in Lehre und Lehrerbildung. Symposion '90 – Heidelberg 1990* (pp. 124-127). Weinheim: Deutscher Studien Verlag.

(1990). Zur Integration von Wissenschaft und Praxis in der Ausbildung von Fremdsprachenlehrern. In K.-R. Bausch et al. (Eds.), *Die Ausbildung von Fremdsprachenlehrern: Gegenstand der Forschung. Arbeitspapiere der 10. Frühjahrskonferenz zur Erforschung des Fremdsprachenunterrichts* (pp. 175-181). Bochum: Brockmeyer.

(1991). Englischunterricht zwischen Handlungsorientierung und didaktischer Steuerung. *Die Neueren Sprachen, 90*(1), 46-65.

(1991). Englischunterricht zwischen Handlungsorientierung und didaktischer Steuerung (Ein Nachtrag). *Die Neueren Sprachen, 90*(5), 559-563.

(1991). Handlungsorientierte Lehrerbildung für einen handlungsorientierten Fremdsprachenunterricht. *Praxis des neusprachlichen Unterrichts, 38*(2), 123-128.

(1992). Auswahlbibliographie zum Themenheft *Vom Umgang mit Fehlern. Der fremdsprachliche Unterricht – Englisch, 26*, 11.

(1992). Fehler und Fehlerkorrektur im kommunikativen Englischunterricht. *Der fremdsprachliche Unterricht – Englisch, 26*, 4-10.

(1992). Wie effizient ist handelndes Lernen im Fremdsprachenunterricht. *Fremdsprachenunterricht, 45*(7), 373-378.

(1993). Freiräume organisieren für handelndes Lernen. Schulisches Fremdsprachenlernen und -lehren im Spannungsfeld von Steuerung und Offenheit. In K.-R. Bausch et al. (Eds.), *Fremdsprachenlehr- und -lernprozesse im Spannungsfeld von Steuerung und Offenheit. Arbeitspapiere der 13. Frühjahrskonferenz zur Erforschung des Fremdsprachenunterrichts* (pp. 161-168). Bochum: Brockmeyer.

with H. J. Vollmer (1993). Einleitung. In J.-P. Timm & H. J. Vollmer (Eds.), *Kontroversen in der Fremdsprachenforschung. Kongressdokumentation des 14. Kongresses für Fremdsprachendidaktik, Essen 1991* (pp. 1-5). Bochum: Brockmeyer.

with H. J. Vollmer (1993). Fremdsprachenforschung: Zur Konzeption und Perspektive eines Wissenschaftsbereichs. *Zeitschrift für Fremdsprachenforschung, 4*(1), 1-47.

with H. J. Vollmer (1993). Fremdsprachenlernen in interkultureller Perspektive: Kontext, Konzepte, Kontroversen. In: J.-P. Timm & H. J. Vollmer (Eds.), *Kontroversen in der Fremdsprachenforschung. Kongressdokumentation des 14. Kongresses für Fremdsprachendidaktik, Essen 1991* (pp. 7-37). Bochum: Brockmeyer.

with H. Barthel & H. J. Vollmer (1993). Der Beitrag der früheren DDR zur zukünftigen Fremdsprachenforschung. In J.-P. Timm & H. J. Vollmer (Eds.), *Kontroversen in der Fremdsprachenforschung. Kongressdokumentation des 14. Kongresses für Fremdsprachendidaktik, Essen 1991* (pp. 543-566). Bochum: Brockmeyer.

(1995). Auswahlbibliographie zum Themenheft „Workshop: Grammar". *Der Fremdsprachliche Unterricht – Englisch*, *29*(3), 13.

(1995). Dem „Sprachgefühl" auf der Spur: Fuzzy Concepts in der englischen Grammatik. In L. Bredella (Ed.), *Verstehen und Verständigung durch Sprachenlernen? Dokumentation des 15. Kongresses für Fremdsprachendidaktik, Gießen 1993* (pp. 225-235). Bochum: Brockmeyer.

(1995). Die „Fuzziness" der Sprache als Begründung für einen ganzheitlich-funktionalen, erfahrungsorientierten Grammatikunterricht. In J.-P. Timm (Ed.), *Ganzheitlicher Fremdsprachenunterricht* (pp. 120-148). Weinheim: Deutscher Studien Verlag.

(1995). Ganzheitlichkeit als Anliegen. In J.-P. Timm (Ed.), *Ganzheitlicher Fremdsprachenunterricht* (pp. 11-14). Weinheim: Deutscher Studien Verlag.

(1995). Grammatiklernen im Kontext verschiedener Lern- und Methodenkonzepte. *Der Fremdsprachliche Unterricht – Englisch*, *29*(3), 4-12.

(1995). Wortschatz erwerben: Lebenswelten strukturieren – Wortschatz vermitteln: „Natürliche" Lernkontexte anbieten. In K.-R. Bausch et al. (Eds.), *Erwerb und Vermittlung von Wortschatz im Fremdsprachenunterricht. Arbeitspapiere der 15. Frühjahrskonferenz zur Erforschung des Fremdsprachenunterrichts* (pp. 183-191). Tübingen: Narr.

(1996). Fehlerkorrektur zwischen Handlungsorientierung und didaktischer Steuerung. In G. Bach & J.-P. Timm (Ed.), *Englischunterricht. Grundlagen und Methoden einer handlungsorientierten Unterrichtspraxis*, pp. 167-191.

(1996). Neue Perspektiven: Konsequente Schülerorientierung. In G. Bach & J.-P. Timm (Eds.), *Englischunterricht. Grundlagen und Methoden einer handlungsorientierten Unterrichtspraxis* (pp. 268-284). Tübingen: Francke.

with G. Bach (1996). Handlungsorientierung als Ziel und als Methode. In G. Bach & J.-P. Timm (Eds.), *Englischunterricht. Grundlagen und Methoden einer handlungsorientierten Unterrichtspraxis* (pp. 1-21). Tübingen: Francke.

(1997). A Stairway to Heaven? In R. Gäßler & W. Riethmüller (Eds.), *Künstlerisches Wirken. Kunst und Künstlertum in Gesellschaft, Kultur und Erziehung* (pp. 314-329). Weinheim: Beltz/Deutscher Studien Verlag.

with J. Siebold (1997). Zur Arbeit der Sektion 1: Sprach- und Textarbeit zwischen Prozess- und Gegenstandsorientierung. In M. Wendt & W. Zydatiß (Eds.), *Fremdsprachliches Handeln im Spannungsfeld von Prozess und Inhalt. Kongressdokumentation des 16. Kongresses für Fremdsprachendidaktik, Halle 1995* (pp. 65-71). Bochum: Brockmeyer.

(1998). Entscheidungsfelder des Englischunterrichts. In J.-P. Timm (Ed.), *Englisch lernen und lehren. Didaktik des Englischunterrichts* (pp. 7-14). Berlin: Cornelsen.

(1998). Grammatiklernen: Die Entwicklung praktischer Sprachkenntnisse. In J.-P. Timm (Ed.), *Englisch lernen und lehren. Didaktik des Englischunterrichts* (pp. 299-318). Berlin: Cornelsen.

(1998). Pop- und Rocksongs als „Lernschrittmacher". In J.-P. Timm (Ed.), *Englisch lernen und lehren. Didaktik des Englischunterrichts* (pp. 178-184). Berlin: Cornelsen.

(1998). Zur Rolle von Kognitionen in einem lernorientierten Fremdsprachenunterricht. In K.-R. Bausch et al. (Eds.), *Rolle und Funktion des Begriffs 'Kognition' bei der Erforschung des Lehrens und Lernens fremder Sprachen. Arbeitspapiere der 18. Frühjahrskonferenz zur Erforschung des Fremdsprachenunterrichts* (pp. 168-178). Tübingen: Narr.

with W. Bleyhl (1998). Wortschatz und Grammatik im Kontext. In J.-P. Timm (Ed.), *Englisch lernen und lehren. Didaktik des Englischunterrichts* (pp. 259-271). Berlin: Cornelsen.

(1999). Unterrichtsmaterialien für einen lernorientierten Fremdsprachenunterricht. In K.-R. Bausch et al. (Eds.), *Die Erforschung von Lehr- und Lernmaterialien im Kontext des Lehrens und Lernens fremder Sprachen. Arbeitspapiere der 19. Frühjahrskonferenz zur Erforschung des Fremdsprachenunterrichts* (pp. 218-225). Tübingen: Narr.

(2001). Fremdsprachenlernen in einem „integrierten Sachfach- und Fremdsprachenunterricht". In K.-R. Bausch et al. (Eds.), *Neuere curriculare und unterrichtsmethodische Ansätze und Prinzipien für das Lehren und Lernen fremder Sprachen. Arbeitspapiere der 21. Frühjahrskonferenz zur Erforschung des Fremdsprachenunterrichts.* Tübingen: Narr.

(in press). Fremdsprachenlernen in einem „integrierten Sachfach- und Fremdsprachenunterricht". *Praxis des neusprachlichen Unterrichts.*

Tabula Gratulatoria

Rüdiger Ahrens
Würzburg

✧

Wolfgang Alberts
Koblenz

✧

Joachim Appel
Ludwigsburg

✧

Johann Aßbeck
Regensburg

✧

Gerhard Bach
Bremen

✧

Werner Bleyhl
Ludwigsburg

✧

Petra Bosenius
Köln

✧

Wilfried Brusch
Hamburg

✧

Wolfgang Butzkamm
Aachen

Peter Doyé
Braunschweig

✧

Willis Edmondson
Hamburg

✧

Sylvia Fehling
Kassel

✧

Michael Ferguson
Berlin

✧

Claudia Finkbeiner
Kassel

✧

Wolfgang Gehring
Würzburg

✧

Wilfried Gienow
Potsdam

✧

Claus Gnutzmann
Braunschweig

✧

Detlev Gohrbandt
Koblenz-Landau

✧

Lucille Grindhammer
Hamburg

✧

Helga Haudeck
Ludwigsburg

✧

Karlheinz Hellwig
Hannover

✧

Liesel Hermes
Koblenz-Landau

✧

Alfred Hornung
Mainz

✧

Werner Hüllen
Essen

✧

Ingrid Kerdelhué
Kassel

✧

Ingrid Kerkhoff
Bremen

✧

Werner Kieweg
München

✧

Eberhard Klein
Erfurt

✧

Friederike Klippel
München

✧

Markus Knierim
Kassel

✧

Doris Kocher
Freiburg

✧

Evelyn Köhnke
Bad Bederkesa

✧

Frank G. Königs
Marburg

✧

Reinhard Kuhnert
Schwäbisch Gmünd

✧

Norbert Lademann
Potsdam

✧

Christina Lausevic
Newcastle upon Tyne, UK

✧

Eva Leitzke-Ungerer
Rostock

✧

Renate Löffler
Reutlingen

✧

Christiane Lütge
Hannover

✧

Nikola Mayer
Bremen

✧

Andreas Müller-Hartmann
Heidelberg

✧

Uwe Multhaup
Wuppertal

✧

Mario Oesterreicher
Nürnberg

✧

Sigrid Paul-Hoffmann
Koblenz

✧

Roland Petersohn
Jena

✧

Horst Raabe
Bochum

✧

Heike Rautenhaus
Oldenburg

✧

Thomas Rist
Landau

✧

Ute Römer
Köln

✧

Gisela Schmid-Schönbein
Koblenz-Landau

✧

Gerhard W. Schnaitmann
Stuttgart

✧

Rainer Schulze
Hannover

✧

Hellmut Schwarz
Mannheim

✧

Catherine Anne Schwerin
Hamburg

✧

Felicitas Tesch
Berlin

✧

Helmut J. Vollmer
Osnabrück

✧

L. Weidner-Golletti
Heidelberg

✧

David R. Whybra
Hildesheim

✧

Rüdiger Zimmermann
Marburg

English in a multilingual world

A world language is born: English as a national and as *the* world language

Werner Hüllen

Das Englische ist in seine heutige Rolle als Weltsprache über zwei historische Bewegungen hineingewachsen. Zum einen dehnte es sich aus seiner verhältnismäßig isolierten insularen Situation ab etwa 1530 auf dem europäischen Kontinent aus, wo es als Handelssprache, Sprache der Reformation, Sprache der Wissenschaften und schließlich als Sprache einer kulturell und politisch besonders fortschrittlichen Nation geschätzt wurde. Zum anderen gelangte es mit dem Britischen Empire in viele Teile der Welt. Zu Zwecken globaler Kommunikationsanliegen kehrt Welt-Englisch heute, vorwiegend über die amerikanische Variante, nach Europa zurück und trifft hier, wie auf einen vorbereiteten Boden, auf die älteren Kenntnisse des Englischen als einer Nationalsprache.

The English language grew into its present role as a world language through two historical movements. First, it started to spread on the European continent after about 1530, leaving its comparatively isolated insular situation. It was appreciated as a language for trade, as language of the Reformation, as language of sciences, and finally as the language of a culturally and politically progressive nation. Second, it was transferred into many parts of the world by the British Empire. For the purpose of globally conceived communication it returns today, mainly in its American variety, to Europe as a world language and finds here, like a well-prepared soil, the older knowledge of English as a national language.

1. Interest of topic

English is *the* world language of the 21st century. The development which led to this fact has been visible at least since the end of World War II. It is the first time in human history that one language has been credited with being the authoritative means of communication everywhere. Naturally, this pertains only to the communicative events which are of interest everywhere. This is why national languages are not touched in their indigenous rights at all. There were, of course, eras in the past with far-reaching and boundary-crossing languages like Latin or French, like Russian or Chinese. But, as the examples show, they covered only one region at their time, not the world at large. For the individual speaker this may not have made a real difference. If he or she moved only within a region, this region was "the world", and the regional language, functionally speaking, was in fact a world language. The emergence of a total world language is, therefore, bound to the emergence of communicative events which are of potential interest and importance for, literally speaking, everybody.

In order to understand this development an historiographical reconstruction of the ways which led to the present state is required. The *raison d'être* of teaching English in our schools in the comprehensive way in which this is done is, not totally but partly, determined by the same fact. This is why, also in the didactic context, a look back into history is highly advisable (Hüllen, 2000). It underpins what teachers are doing every day in their classes and which curricular decisions determine their guidelines and textbooks. This is the interest of the topic to be treated in the following. One of the guiding ideas is that English established itself on the continent as other languages did, that its role as a world language, however, was (and still is) imported from outside Europe. Consequently, there is a "European English" and an "international English" to be taught side by side.

2. From the island to the continent

Richard Mulcaster (c.1530-1611) was a nationally-minded humanist who, besides caring for Latin, cared for the cultivation of his national language, English. This was not to be taken for granted during his lifetime, when the classical languages had a higher reputation than any vernacular. He deliberated on English orthography in his book *The first part of the elementarie* of 1582, to which a "Peroration" was appended which dealt with English and its use, in particular in the sciences. He wrote:

> [The English tongue] is of small reatch, it stretcheth no further than this Ila[n]d of ours, naie not there ouer all. What tho? Yet it raigneth there, and it serues us there, and it wold be clean brusht for the wearing there. Tho it go not beyond sea, it will serue on this side. [...]. But our state is no Empire to hope to enlarge it by comma[n]ding ouer countries. What tho? Tho it be neither large in possession, nor in present hope of great increase, yet where it rules, it can make good

> lawes, and as fit for our state, as the biggest can for theirs, and oftimes better [...]. (Mulcaster [Reprint], 1970, p. 256; see Viereck, 1983, p. 9)

This diagnosis was just as correct for the period before 1582 as it was wrong for the period after that year. Above all, the life of the English language was determined by the fact that it was spoken on an island, i.e. that it had no linguistic neighbours. It had to contend with the remains of Celtic languages in Scotland, Ireland, Cornwall, the Isle of Man, and Wales, all of which it was able to suppress, together with their indigenous cultures, and which it was able to render completely extinct in the Isle of Man, Scotland (with small exceptions), and Cornwall. Otherwise English had no stimulating (or interfering) linguistic neighbours, as was the rule for the languages on the continent. A special case is, however, French because of its temporary supremacy in language use after the conquest of 1066 (Kibbee, 1991). After this date the learning of French became important for people with a certain status in society. Since the end of the 12th century a chain of textbooks originated in which French was taught, at first via Latin and then via English. They are associated with the names of Alexander Nequam (1157-1217; *De utensilibus*), John of Garland (fl. 1230; *Dictionarius*) und Walter de Bibbesworth (fl. 1277-1283). The rhymed textbook (without a title) of the last-mentioned author launched a chain of similar ones called *Femina* and *La Manière*, which appeared at the beginning of the 15th century and which aimed at teaching French with the help of useful dialogues to children of noble families. They (the families) were indeed the first to be involved with the English claims on French territory. These textbooks are in principle nothing else but word-lists turned into dialogues (Kibbee, 1991; Stein, 1997; Hüllen, 1999).

A keen interest in the languages of the continent originated in England, where political and economic interests already existed. Besides French, this applied to what we today call Dutch or Flemish (as a rule called Low Dutch in the 17th century). French and Low Dutch were the languages which facilitated the cloth trade around the towns of Antwerp and Bruges. This becomes obvious in the dialogues in French and English (1483) published by William Caxton (c.1420-1491). In them England's first printer adapted a textbook which had originated in Bruges around 1340 and which was popular even as late as 1500 under the title *Livre des Mestiers* and *Gesprächsbüchlein* in the area between Cologne and Amsterdam, where Low German and Dutch dialects, French and English competed with each other (Hüllen, 1995). This country between the rivers Rhine and Meuse, united by commerce and a fairly homogeneous culture, is an early example of a polyglot but culturally unified area in which the learning of foreign vernacular languages (besides Latin of course) was of high importance. Here, English was present for the first time as a foreign language on the continent. An intense motivation for Dutch speakers to learn English came into being which has lasted till today (Loonen, 1991; Noordegraaf & Vonk, 1993). All the textbooks mentioned so far are renowned as examples of practical methods of teaching vernaculars, different from the methods of teaching Latin.

Towards the end of the 15th century and in the course of the 16th, English was to spread all over the continent. We learn this from the selection of languages in polyglot textbooks of vernaculars which became very popular at that time. They testify to the spirit of the Renaissance, in which not only the classical but also the national languages gained new attention all over Europe.

There is a manuscript of 1424 called *Liber in volgaro* (Pausch, 1972). It is attributed to an otherwise unknown Master George of Nuremberg and was obviously written in the *Fondaco dei Tedesci*, a German trade centre in Venice. It contains Italian-German word-lists arranged by topic, above all nouns and adjectives, but also grammatical paradigms, mostly of verbs, and finally lists of situational expressions and dialogues.

Related to the *Liber in volgaro*, although not directly depending on it, is the first printed textbook of living foreign languages, again in Italian and German, *Introito e porta* (1477). It too was published in Venice, the author being one Adam of Rotweil. Just as the earlier *Liber in volgaro*, the book is part of the tradition of *nomenclators*, i.e. encyclopaedically arranged dictionaries which juxtaposed Latin and vernacular lexemes. It contains lists of Italian and German words and expressions, but no dialogues. The noteworthy fact is that *Introito e porta* became the point of departure for a wide filiation of dictionaries as textbooks with various titles which gradually, up to 1600, covered all the known languages of Europe and among them English (Bart, 1984). Eighteen editions of the Italian-German version were succeeded by a Catalan-German one. There then followed: a Latin-German-Czech (Bohemian) version (three languages), eight editions of a Latin-Italian-

French-German version (four languages), 13 editions of a Latin-Italian-French-Spanish-German version (five languages), 34 editions of a Latin-French-Spanish-Italian-English-German version (six languages) plus five more which contain Czech and Hungarian instead of Spanish and English, five editions of a Latin-Dutch-French-Spanish-Italian-English-German version (seven languages) and finally 11 editions with Greek plus the other languages mentioned (eight languages).[1]

It is noteworthy for historiographers that in this book-family all the languages which were thought important at that time in Europe are represented by an identical corpus of words and in parallel arrangement. "Parallel" means the typographical order but also the mental presence of languages, which was obviously presupposed. These books took the place of the Latin-based *nomenclators* which were to be found all over Europe, and they confirmed that, in terms of culture, Europe was still a unity. It was not a Latin unity any more, but a cultural unity constituted by the parallel arrangement of its linguistic varieties. Moreover, it is exciting that, from 1530 on, English is part of this linguistic variety. It is still marginal compared to the two German and the Romance languages, but it is now present on the continent.[2] In identical prefaces the polyglot textbooks gave as reasons for learning foreign vernaculars the communicative needs of commerce and of travel. This means that the knowledge of English must have been useful in these two contexts. Otherwise nobody would bother to introduce this insular language to potential continental learners.

Very much of the same significance is a series of textbooks called *Colloquia et dictionariolum* by Noel of Berlaimont, an otherwise unknown language teacher from Antwerp. They consist of alphabetical dictionaries and dialogues. They started with a French-Flemish edition in 1530 and, by 1700, had been published in more than 100 editions with up to eight languages (Verdeyen, 1925, 1935; Hüllen, 1999). Here, too, English appears for the first time in an edition of six languages in 1576.

---

1 References in Hüllen (1999).

2 *Oberdeutsch* and *Niederdeutsch* counted as two languages, not only linguistically but also politically. *Niederdeutsch* (Low Dutch) embraced Low German, but also what today is called Dutch and Flemish. *Oberdeutsch* was called *Alemannisch*. The English word High Dutch (*Hochdeutsch*) refers to the dialects of Saxony and Thuringia, which slowly developed into the German standard dialect.

This means that two polyglot regions of Europe – the region between the German town of Augsburg and the Italian town of Venice, and the region around and between the German town of Cologne and the Dutch town of Antwerp, both of them areas with lively commercial traffic – started traditions of foreign-language teaching in which English established itself among other foreign languages on the continent. We find it there from 1530 on.

With the beginning of the 17th century the extra-European history of the English language started, thus increasingly defining its role as a world language rather than a continental one, which however must be seen in its own light (see below). Among the countries of the European continent, England gained a reputation as a safe haven for religious refugees from the war against the Huguenots as well as from the Thirty Years' War. In the other direction England's interest slowly transcended the area of the Dutch language and turned towards those countries which counted as domains of the Reformation. So English became the language either of the reformed or of the heretics. This consolidated the already good relations between England and the Calvinistic Netherlands. In the 18th century England entered the normal linguistic competition of European languages in so far as its literature and its scientific writings were read.[3] At least for the northern part of Germany the alliance between the English monarchy and the house of Hanover had a further impact. However, in the 18th century French established itself in western and central Europe and German in its eastern and south-eastern parts as languages of regional importance. English could not prevail against them. Two clear spheres of influence emerged: French dominated the countries of the Romance languages, Poland and the European part of Russia as a language of intercultural communication, German did the same in the countries of the Germanic languages and of the Austro-Hungarian monarchy. English was not a regional language then, but merely a foreign vernacular among others.

---

3 For the reception of English literature in Germany see Oppel, 1971, and also the contributions 92-96 in Ahrens, Bald, and Hüllen (1995, pp. 345-375). For the teaching and learning of English in Germany during the 18th and 19th centuries see Klippel (1994) with further references. For English as the new foreign language of the 18th century see Fabian (1985).

3. From the island into the world

The history of English as a world language runs parallel to the development of the British Empire (Viereck, 1983). It started in 1607 with the foundation of Jamestown and the settlement of the so-called New England states, which represented the beginning of the settlement of the whole of the North American continent. It found some rather strong competition from French in Louisiana, Maine and Quebec. This competition also occurred in the Carribean, which was firmly occupied by the English around 1640. In 1651 the first state on the African continent, Gambia, was colonised by the English.

With the territorial government over Bengal, the English started to gain the upper hand in India against Portugal, the Netherlands and France after 1765. In 1788 a colony of prisoners was founded in Port Jackson, Australia. The settlement of New Zealand followed in and after 1792. Many other important years could be given, in particular those of the conquest of strategic places and islands (1704 Gibraltar, 1796 Ceylon (Sri Lanka), 1797 Trinidad, 1897 Hong Kong). All of them mark political events with commercial and military backgrounds of different kinds. For the growth of English as a world language they merely mean that one national European language was transported to many areas of the world and remained there. The fact that this happened cannot be explained by political or military facts alone (see below). Speech communities sprang up which are nowadays allocated to four different types (Görlach, 1995):

(1) The speech community of native speakers resulting from massive immigration and permanent settlement in the USA and Canada, Barbados, parts of South Africa (the Cape-Province and Natal), Australia, New Zealand, and Malta. The establishment of these communities was completed by 1850.

(2) The speech community of standard-language speakers, in which English is spoken alongside dialects not recognised as standard, as in Scotland, or alongside pidgin and Creole languages, as in the Caribbean or West Africa.

(3) The speech community of second-language speakers, whose distribution is almost identical with the British Empire in the 19th century and, consequently, is to be found in African countries –

Nigeria, Ghana, Kenya, Zambia, Zimbabwe (the former Rhodesia), South Africa – as well as in Asian countries (Pakistan, India, Bangladesh, Singapore) and in Papua New Guinea. Typologically, countries like Egypt, Sudan, Iraq and Burma belong to this group, but the presence of English in these countries is much less obvious than in the ones mentioned before. Somalia, Tanzania and Malaysia extricated themselves from this group by adopting their own national languages after the end of the Empire (Somali, Swahili and Bahasa Malaysia), but linguistic reality did not always follow these political decisions. English is still an important means of communication in these countries.

The speech communities of standard-language and second-language speakers have in common that they use standard English parallel to the common vernaculars. English is used in this way because it is thought of as superior in the fields of legislation or administration and also for the highly reputed activities of religion, literature and the sciences.

(4) The speech community of foreign-language speakers who learn English in schools and use it for special purposes, frequently only for reading.

All in all there are said to be around 600 million speakers of English. But the number of foreign-language speakers, who are included here, is quite uncertain. 340-350 million native speakers is, however, a safe guess. (Other sources say that there may be as many as 1.6 billion English-speakers in the world.)

Beside the politically-motivated transport of English to the various countries mentioned above, certain general and social circumstances account for the establishment of the speech communities 1-3. The most important factor is how much the life of the indigenous population was bound to the use of English as a result of military occupation, general administration, jurisdiction, education and religious practice (e.g. missionary activity), etc. This happened most of all where such institutions did not exist on the basis of a native language or where they were rendered complicated because of their diversity. The period of occupation and its acceptance by the native people play an important role too. This does not mean that the acceptance of political circumstances was a prerequisite for the spread of English in these cases. India is a good example of the success of English as a second language in spite of widespread politically motivated resistance on the part of the native speakers of the country (Fishman, 1977).

4. Globalisation of communication

The fourth type of speech community, the foreign-language speakers, uses English neither as a result of natural (or almost natural) language acquisition nor in a variety which has geographical boundaries. It is almost the negation of these normal circumstances which marks their language use. It originates because there is a widespread need for communication which is identical in far-flung parts of the world with a comparable standard in culture and technology. We can call this by the modernistic term "globalisation of communication". As such, it is nothing entirely new. It existed already in the Middle Ages with the "global" Church or the influential chancelleries of empires. It also came into being where people pursued aims which transcended linguistic boundaries, like in the Hansa, the regions of Southern Germany/ Northern Italy or the Netherlands already mentioned.

The modern phenomenon of the widespread use of English as a first foreign language in many countries of the world was, of course, stimulated by its presence there as the language of Empire. In Europe, where this was not the case, a knowledge of English as one foreign language among others was certainly helpful. Yet the growth of the world language English had other reasons besides. It first became visible towards the end of the 19th century as a result of the English supremacy in the industrial revolution and in navigation. Its spread increased dramatically as a result of the two World Wars, in particular the last one, and the steadily growing influence of the United States, from which the British, in America's shadow as it were, also profited. This newest development, therefore, did not come from the national origin of English, but from one of its colonial offshoots.

Note that the two World Wars were also global technical enterprises which presupposed effective communication – irrespective of local languages – around the whole globe. In this respect, the following so-called Cold War was something very similar. After that, space exploration grew into a similar dimension. Finally, we can all observe modern technical developments which require not only the globalisation of industrial production, but also of the communication preceding it. For worldwide mail and for maritime traffic global communication was already established at the beginning of this century. But now we have aviation, space travel, various industries like car production and electronics, the world of the press and media, and following global armament a certain degree of global disarmament, tourism, etc.

In all these activities with their concomitant communicational needs the USA has been leading in tone and language since 1950. There is no denying this fact. Whoever wants to dispute this role – like Japan in electronics and the car industry, or Europe in the aviation industry – must do so in English.

In many respects there is a parallel influence from the United States in cultural matters, which is not to be taken for granted. From history we know that the cultural achievements of a small conquered country often proved superior to the culture of the conqueror, as was the case, for example, in classical Greece and Rome. Even in scientific disciplines which have no direct contact with politics, like linguistics, we find a clear American superiority since 1950. However, we must not forget the less obvious impact of British sciences, for example medicine, biology and chemistry, which have been able to benefit from the advantage of the one language. This does not mean that scientific work has only been done in the United States, it does mean, however, that it must be written in English, or at least using a terminology which can be easily anglicised if it aims to catch global attention. A writer who does not follow this rule risks losing his or her reputation. This says nothing about the standard of the scientific work, only something about the echo it is likely to evoke. Neither does it say that the contents and methods were dictated by America. The message is simply that academic and scientific discourse takes place, on a global scale, either in English or not at all. It is more the supremacy of a language than of a country that we encounter here.

Of course, reality is somewhat more complex than this. Besides anglophone disciplines – like physics, chemistry, medicine – we have near-anglophone disciplines – like sociology, linguistics, historiography – and, what is more, polyglot ones – like archaeology, musical theory and theology (Skudlik, 1990). In spite of this, the general dominance of the English language as a means of communication in the first two groups of disciplines cannot be in doubt.

Whatever was said about the four types of speech community and of academic and scientific discourse was meant to be descriptive. A lot of opposition has been voiced against the power of these facts. Note that all this is not entirely new in cultural history. The hegemony of Vulgar Latin in the area of the Roman Empire, later the hegemony of Italian in the Eastern and of Catalan in the Western Mediterranean, the hegemony of Spanish in Western Europe and South America, of Portuguese in South America and South-East Asia, of French in Europe and Central Africa, of Russian in Eastern Europe and Central Asia, and, finally, of German in Northern, Central, and South-Eastern Europe depended on comparable developments and circumstances, even if these were of regional and not of global compass, as they are today. The fact that after the loss of Latin as the language of intellectuals in Europe attempts were made again and again to construct an artificial world language (Hüllen, 1989), clearly shows the need for a universal means of communication able to promote global understanding.

5. Linguistic identification vs. linguistic communication

Our historical and structural deliberations have aimed to show how a special constellation of historical developments and present-day communicative needs have led to the linguistic situation in which we find ourselves today. We also indicated that this constellation is by no means unique in European history. All this gives us a chance to pursue a coherent language policy in Germany, if we do it with great care. The differentiation between English as a national language and as a world language is of great importance in this context.

There is no linguistic insight of greater impact on German thinking about language than Herder's and Humboldt's statement that languages have to be understood and evaluated as the expression of their cultures, that acquiring one's own language means finding one's own culture and learning a foreign language means finding a foreign one. Since the middle of the last century all pedagogical programmes which referred to language learning have depended on this principle. Again and again Humboldt's sentence was quoted:

> Die Erlernung einer fremden Sprache, auf die richtige Art benutzt, ist daher die Gewinnung eines neuen Standpunkts in der bisherigen Weltansicht, da jede das ganze Gewebe der Begriffe und der Vorstellungsweise eines Theils der Menschheit enthält. (Humboldt, 1968[Reprint], vol. V, p. 388)

It is deeply irritating that the existence of English as a world language seems to refute this generally accepted opinion. Certainly, English culture in all its European and non-European variants is transported into the world with the help of the English language, but this language also became the means of expression for quite different cultures which frequently turned aggressively against the Anglo-Saxon one. This entails that

> [e]in Erlernen des Englischen als „neutralem Werkzeug“ zwecks Zugang zu internationaler Kommunikation, besonders auf den Gebieten von Wissenschaft, Technik und Handel, [...] keine Identifizierung mit britisch-amerikanischen Werten, Lebensart, politischen Überzeugungen und Glaubensbekenntnissen [erfordert]. (Görlach 1995, p. 25)

But does this not mean that, following Humboldt, we are making the wrong use of a foreign language?

Obviously Humboldt's deep insight that languages are bound to their cultures no longer does full justice to the present-day situation of global communication. Today, we see a difference between a language of identification and a language of communication (Hüllen, 1992), a difference which corresponds to English as a national language and as a world language. Both can be one's first, a second or a foreign language, although it is the normal case that the "mother tongue" is the language of cultural identification. According to this differentiation you can learn and use English as a language of identification with a particular culture, or alternatively as a language of communication for the rather neutral purposes of information. Historical facts underpin this contention and show that worries about a mono-culture arising in the wake of English as a world-language go back to a mistaken impression of English as the language of a European national culture. These differentiations are, of course, valid for all other languages – e.g. French, Spanish, Russian – although it is obviously a special property of English that it can move away more easily from its national origins than other languages can.

The two dichotomies outlined above – national language vs. world language and language of identification vs. language of communication – have their clearest impact in processes of linguistic (grammatical, lexical, stylistic, etc.) standardisation. Admittedly, it is irritating that there seems to be hardly any expert reflection on this problem in the British Isles. Language criticism is shunted away to "language corners" in newspapers, although occasionally they are of a high standard. Generally, the sociolinguistic axiom is accepted that language norms are not of a linguistic but of a social nature.

However, there is much controversy about "the standard-language question" (Crowley, 1989; Harris, 1989; Cameron, 1995; Honey, 1997). Whatever its results and in spite of all the reservations about a linguistic hegemony, we should not forget that the old dream of mankind of possessing a universal language as a means of universal communication has never been so near.

References

Ahrens, R., Bald, W.-D., & Hüllen, W. (Eds.). (1995). *Handbuch Englisch als Fremdsprache (HEF).* Berlin: Erich Schmidt.

Bart, A. R. (1984). *Antichi vocabulari plurilingui d'uso popolare: la tradizione del "Solenissimo Vochabulista".* Alessandria: Edizioni dell'Orso.

Cameron, D. (1995). *Verbal hygiene.* London: Routledge.

Crowley, T. (1989). *The politics of discourse. The standard language question in British cultural debates.* London: Macmillan.

Görlach, M. (1995). Die Ausbreitung des Englischen als Weltverkehrssprache. In R. Ahrens, W.-D. Bald, & W. Hüllen (Eds.), *Handbuch Englisch als Fremdsprache (HEF)* (pp. 23-26). Berlin: Erich Schmidt.

Fabian, B. (1985). Englisch als neue Fremdsprache des 18. Jahrhunderts. In D. Kimpel (Ed.), *Mehrsprachigkeit in der deutschen Aufklärung* (pp. 178-196). Hamburg: Felix Meiner Verlag.

Fishman, J. A., et al. (Eds.) (1977). *The spread of English. The sociology of English as an additional language.* Rowley, Mass.: Newbury House.

Harris, R. (1989, April 24). The worst English in the world? *University of Hongkong Supplement to the Gazette,* Vol. XXXVI, 1, 37-46.

Honey, J. (1997). *The story of standard English.* London: Faber and Faber.

Hüllen, W. (1989). *"Their Manner of Discourse". Nachdenken über Sprache im Umkreis der Royal Society.* Tübingen: Narr.

Hüllen, W. (1992). Identifikationssprache und Kommunikationssprache. Über Probleme der Mehrsprachigkeit. *Zeitschrift für germanistische Linguistik, 20*(3), 298-317.

Hüllen, W. (1995). A close reading of William Caxton's dialogues: "...to lerne shortly frenssh and englyssh". In A. H. Jucker (Ed.), *Historical pragmatics. Pragmatic developments in the history of English* (pp. 99-124). Amsterdam: Benjamins.

Hüllen, W. (1999). *English dictionaries 800-1700. The topical tradition.* Oxford: Clarendon.

Hüllen, W. (2000). Ein Plädoyer für das Studium der Geschichte des Fremdsprachenunterrichts. *Zeitschrift für Fremdsprachenforschung, 11*, 31-39.

Humboldt, W. v. (1968). *Wilhelm von Humboldts Werke* (Ed. A. Leitzmann) Vol. V. Berlin: de Guyter. (Original work published 1905/1906)

Kibbee, D. A. (1991). *For to speke Frenche trewely. The French language in England, 1000-1600: Its status, description and instruction.* Amsterdam: Benjamins.

Klippel, F. (1994). *Englischlernen im 18. und 19. Jahrhundert. Die Geschichte der Lehrbücher und Unterrichtsmethoden.* Münster: Nodus.

Loonen, P. L. M. (1991). *For to learne to buye and sell. Learning English in the Low Dutch area between 1500 and 1800. A critical survey.* Amsterdam/Maarssen: APA.

Mulcaster, R. (1970). *The first part of the elementarie.* Menston: Scolar Press. (Original work published 1582)

Noordegraaf, J., & Vonk, F. (1993). *Five hundred years of foreign language teaching in the Netherlands 1450-1950.* Amsterdam: Stichting Nerlandistiek VU (Münster: Nodus).

Oppel, H. (1971). *Englisch-deutsche Literaturbeziehungen.* 2 vols. Berlin: Erich Schmidt.

Pausch, O. (1972). *Das älteste italienisch-deutsche Sprachbuch. Eine Überlieferung aus dem Jahre 1424 nach Georg von Nürnberg.* Wien: Hermann Böhlau.

Skudlik, S. (1990). *Sprachen in den Wissenschaften. Deutsch und Englisch in der internationalen Kommunikation.* Tübingen: Niemeyer.

Stein, G. (1997). *John Palsgrave as Renaissance linguist.* Oxford: Clarendon Press.

Verdeyen, R. (1925, 1935). *Colloquia et dictionariolum septem linguarum.* Gedrukt door Fickaert te Antwerpen in 1616. Op nieuw uitgegeven door Prof. Dr. [...]. I. Antwerpen, 's Gravenhage: Nederlandsche Boekhandel / M. Nijhoff 1926; II: Id. 1915; III: Antwerpen: Solvijnstraat, 70, 1935. Vereeniging Der Antwerpsche Bibliophilen, Uitgave Nr. 39, 40, 42.

Viereck, W. (1993). Englisch als Weltsprache. In W. Viereck, S. Köppl, J. Schmied, & E. Schneider (Eds.), *Englisch. Formen und Funktionen einer Weltsprache* (pp. 9-26). Ausstellung des Lehrstuhls für englische Sprachwissenschaft und Mediävistik der Universitätsbibliothek. Universität Bamberg.

Europeans and languages: Assessing the multilingual divide

Gerhard Bach

In einem Weißbuch der Europäischen Kommission über die Lerngesellschaft „von morgen“ hieß es Mitte der 1990er Jahre: „Wir alle können drei Sprachen lernen“, denn in vielen europäischen Ländern ist es für viele Menschen „normal, drei Sprachen zu verwenden.“ Diese Aussage wird von zwei jüngst veröffentlichten *Eurobarometer*-Umfragen über „Die Europäer und die Sprachen“ bzw. „Junge Europäer 2001“ nicht gestützt. Die Ergebnisse der beiden Umfragen werden in diesem Beitrag vorgestellt und miteinander verglichen. Dabei geht es primär um fremdsprachendidaktisch relevante Bereiche, die im Zentrum heutiger bildungspolitischer Interessen stehen, vor allem im Hinblick auf die (fremd-)sprachlichen und kommunikativ-strategischen Kompetenzen, mit denen junge Menschen, die morgen Europa mitgestalten wollen, heute erwerben müssen.

In 1995 the European Commission issued a “White Paper” on “Teaching and learning: Towards the learning society.” The paper claims that in many European countries “it is quite normal for most people to be able to use three languages” (European Commission, 1995, p. 1). This blatantly optimistic assessment is challenged by two surveys conducted more recently in the 15 EU member nations, the results of which are detailed in this essay. A comparison of these results reveals encouraging as well as disturbing details on language competence among Europeans, their general communicative competence and social skills, and their interests and concerns, at large, in languages as part of the self-definition of an expanding Europe. To complement these findings, the essay then focuses on consequences and suggestions for teaching and learning foreign languages inside and outside instructional perimeters.

1. Europeans and their language(s)

In 1995 the European Commission introduced its “White Paper” on “Teaching and learning: Towards the learning society” with the (unsupported) claim that “we can *all* learn to speak three languages” (European Commission, 1995, p. 1). The text continues in unfettered optimism:

> In many countries it is quite normal for most people to be able to use three languages. In the European Union, such people are well placed to take full advantage of European citizenship and of the single market. They are better able to move between countries for educational, professional or other reasons. Their linguistic skills are attractive to employers. (ibid.)

Half a decade later, in early 2001, the public media shocked their audiences with reports relating to a survey conducted by the European Commission concerning Europeans and their (foreign) language skills, later published as *Eurobarometer 54*. The shocking part of the news was that, language-wise, most nations among the 15 member states of the European Union had little to boast about. The survey revealed that nearly half of Europe's population speak no other language than their mother tongue, the UK leading with 65.9%, followed by Portugal (56.3%) and Spain (53.4%), and France (50.7%). Germany, generally assumed to be more upscale about the foreign language skills of its population, fared little better: 42.8% confessed to possessing no foreign language skills, and an almost equal percentage (39%) among the citizens of the new German states generally questioned the usefulness of knowing foreign languages (against the 22% EU-15 average). In contrast, the Scandinavian nations as well as Luxembourg and the Netherlands boasted 60% to 80% foreign (i.e. English) language skills.

Skills in a *second* foreign language lagged behind even more drastically: 74% of European citizens do not have *second*-foreign-language skills. Such numbers do reveal in rather chilling terms the fact that Europeans have a long way to go in their desire to develop into a community of nations where linguistic boundaries will no longer be an obstacle to mutual understanding.

As would be expected, the media's interpretation of the survey concentrated on what appeared to be the downside of the results. Of course, one can reverse this bleak outlook for Europe by simply turning these numbers around. 53% of Europeans say that they *can* speak at least one European language in addition to their mother tongue. The primary language known and spoken as a *foreign* language is English (40.5%); other languages that can boast a double-digit percentage in this category are French (19.2%) and German (10.3%) (see Table 1). Overall, the language most often spoken in Europe as a *first* foreign language is English (32.6%), followed by French (9.5%), and German (4.2%). As expected, English predominates Europe as the *lingua franca* of international communication.

Juggling these numbers, while permitting an either negativist or positivist summary conclusion, will satisfy self-fulfilling premonitions, but little more. To address the issue more conclusively, one needs to look beyond surface numbers and interpret the underlying spectrum of individual results both from a statistical/quantitative and a demographic/qualitative position. It is worthwhile, therefore, to take a new look at the findings of the 2001 *Eurobarometer* survey. Thus, in our analysis, we will firstly analyze the results of the seven individual sectors of *Eurobarometer 54*, with particular emphasis on the issues concerning monolingualism and multilingualism. Secondly, we will then approach these findings from a demographic perspective, and interpret the results with respect to age, length of education, and professional status. In a third step, we will further narrow down these results by comparing them to that age group which will determine the course of a multilingual and multicultural Europe in the near future – the younger generation aged 15 to 24. Here we will use the results of "Young Europeans in 2001", a survey carried out shortly after *Eurobarometer 54* was made public.

Such a comparison will reveal a number of issues today's generation of younger Europeans is about to face – demands concerning multilingual skills, general communicative skills, and skills instrumental for "survival" in the workplace. These issues, in turn, will directly impact upon the field of foreign language instruction inside and outside the boundaries of formal schooling. There is a certain urgency to address such issues in an educational market where, as the results of the 2001 PISA study suggest, the need for reform is imminent, at least very much so in Germany. A particular relevance here exists for the educational sector which, increasingly, is turning into a highly competitive marketplace, in which Germany is threatened to take a back seat unless educational policy makers turn around, define strategically necessary objectives and agree to enforce (and solidly budget) efficient educational programs.

This is where, in the larger matrix of transnational, intercultural, and socio-economic issues, "Europakompetenz" as the binding metaphor of Europe's future generation would have to be addressed (which cannot be done here due to limits of space). It is a term denoting a set of key skills broadly related to successful linguistic, social, political, and economic interaction among European citizens. Beyond these vague parameters, "Europakompetenz" as yet awaits particular definition and description.[1] Interestingly, our research suggests that corresponding terms in English or French are not widely used. "*European competence*" is as much a construct by way of translation as would be "*competence europeenne*". It will only be a matter of time, though, to see terminological equivalencies appear in other European languages, particularly in English as Europe's emergent *lingua franca*.

2. *Eurobarometer 54*: Europeans and languages

This survey was conducted in the 15 member states in December 2000, at the request of the European Commission's Education and Culture Directorate-General. In each member state, a representative sample of the national population aged 15 years and older was investigated. The survey captured opinions on a wide range of language in general and second/foreign languages in particular, in seven pre-defined areas:

1. Mother tongue and other languages
2. Foreign languages known, spoken, and perceived usefulness
3. Use of foreign languages
4. Learning or improving languages
5. Motivation to learn languages
6. Importance of speaking a foreign language
7. Difficulties of learning a foreign language

The following summary will briefly outline the major results in each category, highlighting those factors deserving closer interpretation.

---

1 This is an area in pressing need of more intensive research. Dethloff's (1993) early account investigates "Europakompetenz" merely as a *concept* defined by social, political, and educational parameters. The first critical empirical study to address "Europakompetenz", by Finkbeiner (1995), compared the factors considered indispensable for Europe's future generation and workforce ("Schlüsselqualifykationen") to the initial response to such claims found among German school-age respondents. "Europakompetenz" as a knowledge-based and skills-based category of individual behavior is being researched in a project at the University of Bremen and results will be available soon (Bach & Hiddessen, 2002).

2.1 Mother tongue and other languages

In each member state the language cited most often as the mother tongue is the national language (or one of the national languages in states home to more than one). The highest rates are found in Portugal (100%), followed by Italy and Greece (99% each). In expansion of previous surveys, four new items were introduced into the list of languages, namely Irish, Luxembourgish, Turkish and sign language. While this had no significant immediate effect on the overall results for the 15 EU member states, the inclusion of these four languages highlights the fact that a significant proportion of the Irish population regards Irish as its mother tongue (14%) and that 62% of Luxembourgers regard Luxembourgish as their mother tongue. The main results, as collated in Table 1, reveal the distribution (in percent of total European population) of individual languages spoken in the Union either as mother tongue or as a foreign language. The predominance of certain languages, and English in particular, over others documents the inequality of European nations, irrespective of population numbers, geopolitical position, or economic status.

Table 1. Language Skills of Europeans
EU responses to the questions: "What is your mother tongue?" and "What other languages do you know?" + Total of these. (Source: INRA, 2001)

		Percentage for whom this is mother tongue	Percentage who speak as a foreign language	Total who speak as mother tongue or as a foreign language
English	EN	15.9	40.5	56.4
Français	FR	16.0	19.2	35.2
Deutsch	D	23.3	10.3	33.6
Italiano	I	16.0	3.0	19.0
Español	ES	10.5	6.6	17.1
Nederlands	NL	5.5	1.0	6.5
Elinika	GR	2.9	0.5	3.4
Português	PO	2.8	0.5	3.3
Svenska	SV	2.3	1.0	3.3
Dansk	DK	1.5	0.4	1.9
Suomi	FIN	1.4	0.1	1.5
Gaeilgel	Irish	0.2	0.4	0.6
Lëtzebuergesch	L	0.1	0.1	0.2

2.2 Foreign languages known and perceived usefulness

In addition to their mother tongue, the language most frequently known by Europeans is English (41%), with French (19%), German (10%), Spanish (7%) and Italian (3%) taking a "backburner" position. A small group of nations stands out from among the average. Denmark, Sweden, and the Netherlands score in the 80-percent range in the ability to communicate in English as a foreign language; citizens of Belgium, Luxembourg and, to a lesser degree, the Netherlands, score more highly in the ability to communicate in two or more languages aside from their mother tongue. In the United Kingdom and in Ireland, the two nations trailing the other nations in overall foreign language skills, French is the foreign language most frequently known (UK: 22%, Ireland: 25%). German as a foreign language is most frequently known in the Netherlands (68%), Denmark (42%) and Sweden (36%).

Eurobarometer 54 further asks about the perceived usefulness of foreign languages within the EU-15 context. A great majority of Europeans believe that knowing one or several foreign languages is generally useful and/or would be useful for them in particular (72% positive responses). This tendency displays a common concern, even among those who do not speak a language other than their mother tongue. Europeans were also asked *which two languages* they thought were most useful to know apart from their mother tongue. In all 15 member states, English is considered the most useful language to know (75%), followed by French (40%), German (23%) and Spanish (18%).

2.3 Use of foreign languages

The survey distinguishes between *knowing* a foreign language and *using* it. English is the first foreign language most *used for purposes of communication* by Europeans (33% on average, with the Scandinavian countries again reporting the highest scores). It is the language most likely used on such occasions as trips abroad (47%), watching films, particularly in countries where films are not dubbed (23%). It should be considered more than incidental that this latter category correlates positively with the percentage given for English as the first foreign language (33%); another correlation apparently exists when we consider that those countries where films on television are not dubbed –

such as Denmark, Sweden, and the Netherlands – are those countries rating highest in English-as-a-foreign-language skills. English predominates written correspondence as much as face-to-face communication with foreign clients, business partners, and visitors. Second in this overall category comes French with an EU-15 average of 10%, and German and Spanish follow in third and fourth places with a reported EU-15 average of 4% and 3%.

2.4 Learning languages or improving foreign language skills

The vast majority of Europeans have learned or are in the process of learning a foreign language at an age that, in most countries, corresponds to the secondary school level. The fact that close to two thirds of all Europeans have learned or begin learning a foreign language at about the age of ten or thereafter, shows that foreign language learning is basically delimited to secondary level education. It forces a significant portion of EU-15 citizens not privileged by such educational backing to seek language instruction and language exposure outside of institutional educational settings. This further suggests that foreign-language skills are significantly related to age and level of education (for details, see the following section on demographics). Also, foreign language education at the primary school level is not sufficiently utilized throughout the European Community; it is a potential as yet largely wasted.

2.5 Motivation to learn languages

Asked what would encourage them to learn another foreign language (also in addition to the ones they already know), respondents cited the following factors: holidays abroad (47%), personal satisfaction (37%), perceived use in the workplace (26%), ability to better understand people from other cultures (24%), and improved job opportunities in their own country (22%). At the other end of the spectrum, these are the factors that would most discourage people from learning or improving a foreign language (first or other): lack of time to study (34%), general lack of motivation (31%), cost (cited particularly in southern European countries), and negative self-perception: 22% of respondents claim that they are "not good at languages". While linguists might question an individual's ability to judge his or her language-learning ability (or even the innate absence of such a capacity), educators here need to ask themselves whether this perceived lack in skill is a result of such instruction where languages are considered merely an object of study rather than a means of communication.

2.6 Importance of speaking a foreign language

In this category as well as in the next, respondents were presented with a series of statements and asked whether they tended to agree or disagree. The results are encouraging when it comes to what Europeans consider to be *important concerns*, but, at least in part, discouraging when *actual capabilities* are addressed. While 71% agree that everyone in the European Union should be able to speak one European Union language in addition to their mother tongue, *only 53% actually do so.* While close to 70% agree that everyone in the European Union should be able to speak English, *only 41% actually are able to.* The *lingua franca* debate among (foreign language) educators, and the fears of some that English might become the predominant means of communication in the EU (a given factor for many already today), both are worthy of concern to little more than one third of all Europeans: a mere 38% of respondents agree with the statement that the enlargement of the European Union to include new member countries means that we will all have to start speaking a common language; 47% disagree, while 15% are undecided. More disturbing, to professionals in education, science, and business alike, might be the division over the question whether everyone in Europe should be able to speak two EU-languages in addition to their mother tongue. While 32% agree, a majority of 53% disagree, with 14% undecided. Combined with the results concerning the percentage of foreign languages actually spoken, this is a clear signal to the authors of the "White Book" on "Teaching and learning: Towards the learning society" that the Union's goals for EU citizens to be proficient in two other languages aside from their mother tongue is yet a very distant goal requiring pragmatic incentives.

2.7 Difficulties of learning a foreign language

Such incentives are an even greater urgency for that group of Europeans who do *not* speak a foreign language *at all*. A large majority of respondents from this group think that learning an additional language would be too difficult for them (65%) and too time-consuming (64%). Even if they had a chance, 54% of all respondents among this group would not wish to learn another language, and an even larger group (63%) do not believe that competence in another language would give them better employment prospects.

3. The demographic divide: *Eurobarometer 54* in focus

The *Eurobarometer 54* results represent across-the-board findings irrespective of age, educational background, and professional status: the "voice" of the 15-year old high-school drop-out is heard equally and without distinction from that of the 25-year-old university student, the 35-year-old office clerk, and the early retiree at 55. Therefore, as was pointed out earlier, while statistically valid, the information that 47% of all Europeans surveyed speak no other language besides their mother tongue bears little value beyond its media hype and politics-for-the-moment appeal. *Eurobarometer 54* does contain a wealth of critical information, much of this, however, is not readily available since the results of the survey are presented in summary fashion only. A demographic breakdown would reveal a different reality behind the "47% of Europeans are monolingual" pronouncement; namely, that the tendency to know other languages in addition to the mother tongue clearly *diminishes with age* and *increases with length and level of education*. Thus, according to the fine print in the survey, 66% of the 15 to 24-year-olds say of themselves that they are conversant in English, as compared to 53% of the 25 to 39-year-olds, 38% of the 40 to 54-year-olds, and just 18% of those over 55. Furthermore, the same pattern applies across the spectrum of EU languages, at least for the major language groups, including French, Spanish, and German. This reveals a much more positive outlook for Europe's immediate future: Nearly two thirds of Europe's workforce of tomorrow already today speaks English as a foreign language!

Since the structure of *Eurobarometer 54* allows for a breakdown of the major results according to (1) age, (2) length of education, and (3) level of education/professional status, a critical interpretation of these results can help educators develop important guidelines in policy making. As detailed below, these three factors have been found to have an impact in all seven categories, irrespective of whether we take them individually or group them together.

3.1 Age

The tendency to know other languages in addition to the mother tongue diminishes with age. Older persons are less likely to know another language; the better-educated are more likely to know another language; those who know more than one foreign language are likely to know English. The younger age-groups are more likely to regard knowledge of foreign languages as very useful or fairly useful. Thus, 87% of 15-24 year-olds share this view, as compared to 78% of 25-39 year-olds, and 76% of 40-54 year-olds. The number of persons claiming a good level of English also decreases with age, and increases with the length of study and the level of education achieved (see below). 38% of citizens between 15 and 24 years of age consider themselves as having a good level, as compared with 25% of those above 55 years of age. However, if correlated with the level of education, only 18% of persons who ended their education by age 15 claim to have a good level of English, compared with 39% of those whose education continued up to the age of 20 or beyond.

3.2 Length of education

Here a simple equation rules: the longer the duration of education, the greater the likelihood of knowing another language. Knowledge of another language is therefore proportionally highest among post-primary level students (78% of secondary and higher education students), among managers (67%) and white-collar workers (59%), and lowest among pensioners (17%) and house persons (27%). The level of education is also a significant factor when usefulness is addressed. The longer Europeans have stayed in education, the more they feel that knowing foreign languages is or would be very useful or fairly useful to them personally. A mere 56% of those who ended their education by the age of 15 agree with this view, as compared to 87% among those who remained in education until age 20 or beyond. A similar signature is found where English as a foreign language is correlated with the length of education. The increase in duration correlates positively with the self-evaluative claim of a very good knowledge of English.

3.3 Level of education/professional status

The one variable of major importance across all categories is the level of education, usually interconnected with the individual's professional status, and this regardless of age. Thus, the higher the level of education, the greater the likelihood of speaking one or more foreign languages. In socio-professional terms, managers most frequently claim to have very good English (27%), a marked contrast to manual workers (8%). The level of education is also a significant factor when related to length of school-based education. As was noted above, the length of educational exposure correlates with the conviction that knowing foreign languages is actually or very likely considered a personal benefit.

4. Young Europeans and languages

If the major variable in assessing language competence is age in combination with length and level of education, it is important to take a closer look at how younger Europeans (aged 15 to 24) respond to the challenges Europe will have them face in the future if not already at present. Shortly after *Eurobarometer 54* results were made public the European Commission conducted another survey focussing on questions dealing with young people's views of social involvement, their concerns about employment and job opportunities, about changes in the workplace and in education, and the importance of knowing languages as a basic skill for successful participation in the European "experiment". The survey followed the guidelines established for *Eurobarometer* surveys in general.

Changes in attitudes over earlier similar surveys (1990, 1987, 1982) reflect changes in education and the workplace as influenced by new technologies. Nearly half of all respondents (43%) claim to use the new media regularly – computers, video games, and the Internet. The increase over a four-year span has doubled. The demographic divide between boys and girls, however, is still the same. Girls, more often than boys, enjoy going shopping (55% as compared to 22%), reading (49% to 31%), and dancing (31% to 16%), while boys outdistance girls in practicing sports (63% to 37%) and using computers (53% to 33%). For both groups, the primary (social) activities are meeting friends (74%), watching TV (69%), and listening to music (66%).

What the survey most clearly reveals is the increasing presence of new information technologies and the impact they have in young Europeans' daily lives. 80% of respondents use mobile phones on a regular basis, more than half now use a PC at least once a week (56%), followed by the Internet (37%), and e-mail (31%). The usage rates vary greatly from north to south: The information society appears to be more advanced in the northern EU countries. Since these countries (including Luxembourg, but excepting the UK), are also the ones scoring high on multilingual skills, it would be worthwhile to study a possible interdependence between these factors. The most likely downside to increasing "mobility" on the Internet is the fact that nearly half of all Europeans aged 15 to 24 have not traveled to another European country within the two years prior to the survey. The results here are the same as in 1997, so physical mobility for at least 44% of Europe's younger generation is not a priority – at least as far as travel within Europe is concerned.

Languages, however, have fared better. Whereas in 1990 60% of young Europeans claimed to speak a foreign language, this ratio has increased to 69% in 2001. Clearly, in comparison to the percentage across all ages (53%) younger Europeans are making major strides. And yet, when it comes to foreign language skills in a second and third foreign language, Europe is still a far cry from its self-professed goals, even among the younger Europeans. A breakdown of the 69% total reveals a sharp decline: 47% of all Europeans aged 15-24 speak just one, 16% speak two, and a mere 6% speak three or more foreign languages.

Not surprisingly, the language most widely used as a foreign language is English. Slightly more than half of Europe's youth (54%) whose mother tongue is not English claim to be conversant in English. Again, in the course of ten years and more there has been a marked increase: In comparison, the numbers for 1992 (42%) and 1987 (43%) clearly show that young Europeans today are on their way to adopting English as their *lingua franca*. Conversely, the interest in learning other languages beyond English has made no gains. If there is an interest at all, Europe's youth would prefer to learn Spanish (29%) over French (21%) and Italian (20%).

While these numbers might suggest that many Europeans even of a younger age consider languages a valuable but not necessarily strategic skill, this is not corroborated by their responses to the questions concerning skills and qualities required of a young person in order to succeed in the job market. Here the category of languages leads the list (44%), closely followed by information technology skills (43%), a sound general education (40%), and good communication skills (39%). There is a significant change over the responses of four years earlier, as Table 2 reveals.

Table 2. *Most useful qualities to find a good job (in percent)*
(Source: Adapted from INRA, 2002)

2001			1997
Command of foreign languages	44	43	Good general education
Information technology skills	43	40	Command of foreign languages
Good general education	40	38	Communication skills
Communication skills	39	32	Information technology skills

These four categories not only play a major role for younger Europeans to find employment, they also affect their attitudes towards foreigners and the evolution of Europe into a multi-ethnic and culturally diverse union of nations. As the *Eurobarometer 54* poll reveals, many Europeans think foreign-language skills are very important for Europeans to establish peaceful relations amongst each other, but few will invest time, money, and energy to study foreign languages, particularly those that do not speak any as yet. The survey among younger Europeans again reflects that language skills play a significant part in how they perceive foreigners in their own country and what the best way to integrate minorities in their own societies would be.

Again, from a demographic viewpoint, education and language skills are decisive factors in opinion making. The higher the level of education and the better the language skills, the greater is the tolerance level that is displayed towards foreigners. Education, languages, and exposure to other cultures through travel are important factors to help reduce xenophobia and racism, to enhance the willingness to integrate minorities (ethnic, religious, sexual) and people with disabilities and illnesses.

5. Bridging the multilingual divide

For younger Europeans, looking towards their Europe of the future, three core factors signify success: the ability to work (57%), live (51%), and study (42%) wherever they choose to move within the European Union. They are aware that these privileges come at a price – the skills mentioned above. They also expect policy makers to prioritize EU-wide employment opportunities. Europeans aged 15 to 24 appear well-informed about the opportunities EU programs offer, but they also expect the educational sector to assist them in making full use of these programs.

For the educator, the results of both surveys discussed here reveal the primary need to implement better and more diversified language education programs. No matter what the issue – integration, diversity, equal opportunity, employment, residency, travel – language skills in English *and* one or more other languages will be required. German educators need to be aware of the fact that school-based foreign language instruction in this country lags behind EU-wide developments in several respects. While nationwide programs are being developed to establish foreign languages in the primary grades, Germany still does not meet EU-wide standards. Although there is no conclusive "hard" evidence proving a correlation between starting age, length of foreign language study, and achievement level, experiential "soft" evidence supports this supposition, particularly in educational settings where foreign languages in the primary grades are curriculum-integrated and progression in the secondary grades is continuous. In most German states, no such curricula exist as yet. Similarly, efforts need to be increased to expand the curricula to include a diversity of languages already in the primary grades – such as Spanish and French alongside English.

Parallel to these efforts, policy makers and language educators in Germany need to implement bilingual programs into the secondary school programs as part of the regular curriculum. Models such as "languages across the curriculum" or "content and language integrated learning" need to move beyond the trial stage. This, however, necessitates more pronounced efforts to coordinate subject matter instruction ("Sachfachdidaktik") and foreign language instruction ("Fremdsprachendidaktik") to integrate individual objectives and methodologies.

Foreign language educators and policy makers across Europe will need to make a decision soon in order to face an already widespread reality called "ELFE": English as *lingua franca* in Europe. Not only has English become Europe's (and the world's) most widespread means of communication; it has also become de-nativized to the extent that the number of non-native speakers of English worldwide exceeds that of native speakers by a ratio of four to one. Such diversification has produced a number of Englishes which sometimes bear little relation to the Englishes "owned" by their native speakers, whether – to name just a few examples – in the United States, India, Britain, or South Africa. One of these variants is an emerging "Euro-English" as the *lingua franca* of its residents – called ELFE by its researchers and proponents (see Jenkins & Seidlhofer, 2001). The question to be resolved here is to what extent ELFE should be accepted as a norm and thus find its way into the EFL curriculum.

For language policy makers in Europe all of this implies redefining the complex issue of protecting lesser used languages against the predominance of English as Europe's *lingua franca* without denouncing its impact on our daily lives. The claim that English has become the "international shark" about to devour other EU languages, is, as Walsh (2001) says, a simplistic notion. Research such as the surveys discussed above has shown that the links between identity, education, language, and socio-economic status are significant, and that it is likely that these links ensure the survival of minority languages. The EU at large needs to establish and clarify further criteria to guide the Union as it increases its membership in order to ensure an equitable language policy so that communication between members of different languages can occur on an equal basis.

References

Bach, G., & Hiddessen, S. (2002). *Europäer und Sprachen: Kompetenzprofile von Mehrsprachigkeit.* Kolloquium Fremdsprachenunterricht (KFU). Frankfurt: Verlag Peter Lang.

Dethloff, U. (1993). *Interkulturalität und Europakompetenz.* Tübingen: Stauffenburg.

Eurobarometer 54. (2001). *Europeans and languages: Executive summary.* Retrieved March 1, 2002, from the World Wide Web: http://europa.eu.int/comm/education/barolang_en.pdf and additional tables and graphs: http://www.education.gouv.fr/discours/2001/langue.pdf

European Commission. (1995). *Towards the learning society: White Paper on education and training, teaching and learning.* COM(95) 590. Retrieved March 1, 2002, from the World Wide Web: http://europa.eu.int/en/record/white/edu9511/index.htm

European Commission. (2001). *Towards a Europe of knowledge: White Paper on youth 2001.* COM(97) 563. Retrieved March 1, 2002, from the World Wide Web: http://europa.eu.int/comm/education/youth/ywp/index.html

Finkbeiner, C. (1995). *Englischunterricht in europäischer Dimension: Zwischen Qualifikationserwartungen der Gesellschaft und Schülereinstellungen und Schülerinteressen. Berichte und Kontexte zweier empirischer Untersuchungen.* Bochum: Universitätsverlag Dr. Brockmeyer.

INRA. (2001). *Europeans and languages* (Eurobarometer 54 Special). Report produced by INRA (Europe) for the Education and Culture Directorate-General, February 2001. Retrieved March 1, 2002, from the World Wide Web: http://europa.eu.int/comm/education/languages.html

INRA. (2002). *Young Europeans in 2001: Results of a European opinion poll.* Retrieved March 1, 2002, from the World Wide Web: http://europa.eu.int/comm/education/youth/studies/eurobarometer/exec_summ_en.pdf

Jenkins, J., & Seidlhofer, B. (2001). Be proud of your lingua franca. *Learning English* [The Guardian Weekly TEFL Supplement], *April* 19-26, 2.

Walsh, J. (2001). Minority voices show strong instinct for survival. *Learning English* [The Guardian Weekly TEFL Supplement], *April* 19-26, 4.

Education for plurilingualism

Peter Doyé

Einer der anspruchsvollsten Pläne zur Verbesserung des Fremdsprachenlernens in Europa zielt auf die Einführung mehrsprachiger Erziehung. Alle jungen Europäer sollen künftig die Gelegenheit erhalten, im Laufe ihrer Schulzeit mindestens zwei Fremdsprachen zu erlernen. Ob dieser Plan realistisch ist, und – wenn akzeptiert – wie er umgesetzt werden kann, ist Gegenstand dieses Artikels.

Eine solide theoretische Grundlage des Planes liefern das lernpsychologische Konzept des Transfer und speziell die Erkenntnisse über den Transfer vom Erlernen einer Fremdsprache zu dem einer anderen. Ein Beispiel für die Anwendung solcher Erkenntnisse bietet die Deutsch-Italienische Schule in Wolfsburg.

One of the most ambitious plans for the promotion of foreign language teaching and learning in Europe aims at the implementation of plurilingualism. All young Europeans should be offered the opportunity to achieve communicative competence in at least two foreign languages. Whether this plan is realistic and, if accepted, how it can be realized, is the topic of the following article.

Theoretical support for the practicability of the plan can be drawn from the application of the psychological concept of transfer and from a critical examination of the kind of transfer that takes place between the learning of one language and the subsequent learning of another. The German-Italian School in Wolfsburg is an example of how this concept can be put into practice.

1. Introduction

Only 30 years ago politicians and educators in Europe were still discussing the question whether all pupils in institutions of general education should learn *one* foreign language. In the meantime this question has been answered positively by most European governments. They have integrated foreign language teaching and learning into the curricula of practically all their schools and have made one foreign language compulsory for everybody. It has become what is now called a core subject or foundation subject of the curriculum (see for example the National Curriculum of England and Wales; DES, 1990).

But one foreign language is no longer enough. Towards the turn of the century more and more European politicians became aware of the necessity of taking a decisive further step. They realized that the progress of European integration was generating new educational needs which can only be met by developing a strategy for intensifying and diversifying language learning all over the continent.

The initiative for the *new* plan – like many other important proposals – came from the Council of Europe. In 1998 the Committee of Ministers recommended to all member countries "to promote widespread *plurilingualism* by encouraging all Europeans to achieve a degree of communicative ability in a number of languages" (Committee of Ministers, 1998).

To put these ideas into practice is certainly a difficult task. If the recommendations are to become reality, a number of essential conditions have to be fulfilled, the most important of which is an appropriate methodology.

2. The lack of coordination as a handicap

Traditionally, the teaching of several foreign languages – where it does exist – takes place in an uncoordinated manner. The languages are taught without any reference to one another, although the advantages of close cooperation are so obvious.

Coste, Moore und Zarate have complained about the general lack of coordination and consider it responsible for the unsatisfactory results of plurilingual education so far:

> Dans la presque totalité des systèmes éducatifs, y compris quand ces derniers font une place importante à l'apprentissage de langues étrangères, la juxtaposition de connaissances distinctes (langue par langue) l'emporte sur la mise en place d'une compétence plurilingue intégrée. (Coste, Moore & Zarate 1997, p. 33)

The uncoordinated juxtaposition of contents is not a characteristic trait of language teaching alone. In most secondary schools, the subjects are taught as if they had nothing to do with each other, even where their relationship is close. Biology and chemistry, geography and history, music and art are taught as if they did not have anything in common. The main reason for this is the widespread compartmentalization of knowledge in our modern world. Many of our secondary school teachers do not look beyond the horizon of their own subjects any more. In their training at university or college they have studied one or two subjects and have become specialists in them. Rarely do they take an overall view of the educational process as a whole and regard their special subjects from the point of view of their contribution to the general task. But the unavoidable specialization does not justify uncoordinated juxtaposition. It would be unfair to leave the difficult task of reintegration to the pupils alone. On the contrary: valuable help can be given by teachers who are aware of their potential role as coordinators of knowledge.

All this is particularly true of language teaching. An integrated approach is required. For its realization it is not necessary to entrust the teaching of several languages in one class to one and the same teacher. (The number of teachers who teach more than one modern language is decreasing anyhow.) What is needed is good coordination.

In England Eric Hawkins made the widely-discussed proposal to build a bridge between English (the mother tongue) and foreign languages by introducing a course in "awareness of language". This course would equip the pupils with a general understanding of the nature of language, its forms and functions and its role in their lives and should thus lay a common ground for the teaching of individual languages (Hawkins, 1981, p. 237). For teacher education Hawkins suggested a course of studies that "would enable teachers of both English and foreign languages to play their part in a coherent programme of language education" (Hawkins, 1981, p. 281).

In Germany, foreign-language experts – most of them from Romance languages – have proposed a new branch of foreign-language pedagogy and called it *Mehrsprachigkeitsdidaktik*. In their seminal work with the same title, *Mehrsprachigkeitsdidaktik*, Meißner and Reinfried explain the desirability of this new discipline, outline its theoretical foundations and delineate its essential components: "Verarbeitung eines kognitiven Lernbegriffs; Nutzung des aus einer L1 bis Ln verfügbaren sprachlichen und kulturellen Vorwissens; Vernetzung vor- und nachgelernter Sprachen und Berücksichtigung vorhandener Mehrsprachigkeit" (Meißner & Reinfried, 1998, p. 20).

One year later, the *Deutsche Gesellschaft für Fremdsprachenforschung* dedicated its 18th congress to the topic of *"Mehrsprachigkeit und Mehrkulturalität"* and thus laid a fruitful foundation for further development (Aguado & Hu, 2000).

3. A useful concept: *transfer*

The most useful psychological concept for a theory of plurilingualism is the notion of transfer. By "transfer" psychologists understand "the process whereby experience on one task has an effect (either *positive* or *negative*) on performance on a different task subsequently undertaken. The underlying notion is that the knowledge or skill acquired in the first task either facilitates or interferes with carrying out the subsequent task" (Reber, 1985, p. 785).

In their classical work on learning, Hilgard and Bower list transfer among the six central issues which all theories have to include. For them the question "Does learning one thing help you to learn something else?" is one of the essential problems confronting learning theories.

> This is the problem of formal discipline, as it used to be called, or of transfer of training, to use a more familiar contemporary designation. Some transfer must occur or there would be no use in developing a foundation for later learning. Nobody denies that it is easier to build a vocabulary in a language after you have a start in it, or that higher mathematics profits from mastery of basic concepts. The question is really one of how much transfer takes place, under what conditions, and what its nature is. (Hilgard & Bower, 1966, p. 7)

Negative transfer is often called "interference".

Transfer exists in all spheres of life. Let us take two illustrative examples, one from sport and one from music! Children who have learnt to play table tennis profit from their skill when they start playing tennis because of positive transfer; but they also have to unlearn certain habits like holding the racket, as the manner of hitting the ball is very different in the two disciplines. In music, the fact that a person has learnt to play one instrument often facilitates the mastery of another; at the same time, the previously acquired skill can interfere with the learning of the second instrument, depending on the degree of commonality of the two processes.

The same is true of language learning. Here, too, positive as well as negative transfer occurs. Most obvious is the transfer from L1 to L2. Children who begin learning a second language tend to transfer the knowledge and competence which they have acquired in their first language and profit as well as "suffer" from it at the same time. Their familiarity with a linguistic system and with grammatical categories that L1 and L2 have in common is certainly of great help. In addition, the knowledge of a basic vocabulary that is similar in the two languages can be a great advantage. On the other hand, the danger of interference is always pending: the learners interpret similarity as equality and accordingly make many mistakes. German teachers of English can quote hundreds of examples of such misinterpretation.

On the phonological level, pupils often pronounce English sounds that are similar to certain German sounds in the same way as they are used to, for example, /oʊ/ like /oː/ as in "home" or /eɪ/ like /eː/ as in "station".

On the graphic level, similar words of the English language are often spelt like their German equivalents, for instance, "assistant" as "assist*e*nt"; "committee" with only one m, t, or e; "marmalade" as "marm*e*lade".

On the semantic level, words whose form resembles words of the German language are considered as congruent in their content. For example, "also", "become", "brave", "circle", "gymnasium", "receipt", "spend", "warehouse". These are the so-called false friends.

The concept of transfer in language learning has been well-known in contrastive linguistics for a long time. The famous "contrastive analysis hypothesis" is based on the assumption that in learning a second language the pupils – consciously or unconsciously – transfer habits they have acquired in the acquisition of their mother tongue. Fries first formulated this hypothesis (Fries, 1945) and Lado based his theory of a correlation of difference and difficulty on it.

> Since the learner tends to transfer the habits of his native language, we have here the major source of difficulty or ease in learning the structure of a foreign language.... Those structures that are different will be difficult because when transferred they will not function satisfactorily in the foreign language and will therefore have to be changed. (Lado, 1957, p. 59)

The idea of a close correlation between difference and difficulty has been heavily criticized as mono-causal in that it disregards other potential reasons for learners' problems in the acquisition of second and further languages such as concentration, motivation, memory, instructional input, complexity of the task – in short all factors of language learning beyond the relationship of the two systems (Odlin, 1989). This criticism is certainly well-founded. What is *not* justified is the rejection of the early theories of transfer because of a disagreement about the appropriate scientific approach. That those early researchers conceive the phenomenon of transfer in terms of "habits" and not of "cognitive structures" – as many of their successors do – is a matter of theoretical orientation, and to denounce them as "behaviorists" and therefore deny them their competence to explain the complex processes of transfer is not acceptable. The up-to-date cognitivist approach to transfer is not more justified than the earlier stimulus-response approach.

Hilgard and Bower have convincingly argued against all one-sidedness in the psychology of learning:

> The stimulus-response theorist and the cognitive theorist come up with different answers to the question, What is learned? The answer of the former is "habits"; the answer of the latter is "cognitive structures". The first answer appeals to common sense: we all know that we develop smooth-running skills by practicing them; but if we locate a store from one starting point, we can find it from another. A smooth-running skill illustrates a learned habit; knowing alternate routes illustrates cognitive structure ... The stimulus-response theorist is satisfied that he can deduce from the laws of habit formation the behavior that the cognitive theorist believes supports his interpretation. Hence we cannot choose between the theories by coming up with "decisive" illustrations of what we learn, for both groups of theorists will offer explanations of all our examples. (Hilgard & Bower, 1966, p. 9)

The consequence: also in foreign language pedagogy we should avoid one-sidedness in our attempts to understand the various processes of language learning (see Odlin, 1989). It is very plausible that one of the opposing theories can explain certain kinds of phenomena better, and that the second can explain others more adequately. Educational practice has anyhow followed an eclectic path for a long time: phenomena of transfer on the phonological level are usually interpreted in terms of habits, whereas those on the syntactic level are conceived in terms of cognitive structures. This practice is theoretically well-founded.

One essential modification of the early theories of transfer seems to be necessary, however. Later investigations into the functioning of transfer have shown that it can no longer be conceived as a one-way process. Transfer obviously takes place in both directions: from a previous task to a subsequent task and vice versa. Not only do habits or cognitive structures that have been acquired earlier influence those that follow in time; later acquisitions can retro-actively influence earlier ones as well. It is for this reason that Meißner, Reinfried and others speak of *Vernetzung*.

3.1 Forms of positive transfer

Whether positive transfer takes place or not, depends on a number of conditions. The most important of these is that the two tasks have something in common. Deese and Hulse have coined the term "task commonality" and stated that "transfer is only possible when two tasks require something in common in order to meet some satisfactory standard of performance" (Deese & Hulse, 1967, p. 357). Their theory is based on the concept of identical elements proposed by Thorndike (1913), who was the first researcher to examine the relationship between the two tasks in question. He had found that transfer depended essentially on the degree to which the tasks contained elements that are identical.

Task commonality is of high educational relevance because of the curricular and methodological consequences that can be drawn from it. Unfortunately it is often misunderstood as the congruence of contents only. Educators look at the objects that have to be learnt from the aspect of whether they contain identical elements. They examine, for instance, how closely related two languages are and how many common lexical and grammatical items they contain. On this basis they ask to what extent a student of Ly will profit from his previous study of Lx because of the relatedness of the two languages. However reasonable such a question may be, it has to be complemented by another one; for the commonality may well be one of a congruence of the operations required in the process of learning the two languages. In other words, the learning of Lx might not facilitate the learning of Ly for the reason that the two systems contain identical elements, but because in the learning of Lx the pupils acquire techniques and strategies that are useful also in the learning of Ly. In short: one has to consider and distinguish two kinds of commonality and therefore two forms of possible transfer.

The dispute about Latin as a "key" to other languages is a classic example, as the protagonists argue along two lines. First of all, they maintain that Latin as the "European mother tongue" provides the learner with a bulk of lexical and grammatical information upon which he can draw when studying a further language – a Romance language in particular. If this argument is rejected for logical reasons (why should a learner follow the historical development of languages?), the protagonists base their plea upon a second argument, namely that by learning Latin the pupils gain insights and habits that are helpful in the study of any following language; and as Latin is such a complex, but clear language, the profit in terms of operational knowledge is great. Hausmann has convincingly demonstrated that both arguments are equally invalid (Hausmann, 1995); however, our present intention is not to examine their justification, but to illustrate the different ways of arguing in view of two possible forms of transfer.

For the purpose of further clarification it might be helpful to use the distinction introduced by Gilbert Ryle (1949) who spoke of *declarative knowledge*, which he contrasted with *procedural knowledge*. Declarative knowledge is factual knowledge, knowledge about which a person can make a declaration. Procedural knowledge is practical knowledge, knowledge about how to do something. Ryle liked to refer to the two kinds of knowledge by the phrases "knowing that ..." and "knowing how ..." (ibid.). This distinction has become common usage in language learning theory (Dechert, 1983; Færch & Kasper, 1983; Grotjahn, 1997).

Positive transfer between two languages can take place either in terms of declarative knowledge or in terms of procedural knowledge, or both. It can occur because the languages have linguistic elements in common, or because in their acquisition the learner has to make the same operations.

If the two languages to be learnt are closely related, the students can transfer their declarative knowledge as well as their procedural knowledge. If not, they can only profit from their procedural knowledge. But this second chance is often underestimated. If the teaching of languages takes this opportunity into consideration right from the start, in other words, if the languages are not taught in isolation but in coordination, then the learners can very well profit from their acquired procedural knowledge

This, however, presupposes that the learners become aware of their own operations. And it is for this reason that the present concern about *learning awareness* is so important. The Common European Framework of Reference includes, besides the three traditional competences to be acquired in each language learning process – *savoir* (declarative knowledge), *savoir-faire* (procedural knowledge) and *savoir-être* (existential competence) – a fourth one, namely *savoir-apprendre*, which includes learning awareness and all the techniques and strategies that are used in language learning (Conseil, 1998, p. 41). Figure 1 summarizes and illustrates the whole spectrum of forms of transfer.

Figure 1. Forms of transfer

Declarative knowledge		Procedural knowledge	
Linguistic items	Linguistic rules	Techniques	Strategies
such as words, phrases, structures	such as phono-logical, grammatical, pragmatic rules and their application	such as using available media and handling materials for the acquisition, storage and retrieval of linguistic items	such as organizing one's learning, making effective use of opportunities for learning

It seems useful to subdivide (the transfer of) declarative knowledge as well as procedural knowledge into two further categories each, as both comprise specimens that are characteristically different from each other.

The subdivision in the domain of declarative knowledge is plausible: to learn a language means to learn words and phrases and sentences, but also to learn under which conditions to use them, that is, the rules for their application. Both kinds are indispensable and support one another.

But also in the domain of procedural knowledge a distinction seems helpful: there are on the one hand the technical operations that are necessary for an effective acquisition of the language, such as making use of a dictionary, of a grammar book and of technological media or registering in folders, notebooks and files what has been learnt (Rampillon & Zimmermann, 1997); on the other hand there are the strategies that allow a successful management and control of the learning process (Holec, Little, & Richterich, 1996)

Transfer of declarative knowledge is restricted to (closely) related languages, whereas transfer of procedural knowledge can take place between all languages – irrespective of their relationship – because of its general nature. In concrete terms this means, for example, that the similarity in vocabulary between Spanish and French as opposed to Turkish and French makes the acquisition of French vocabulary easier for Spanish-speaking than for Turkish-speaking students. Nevertheless this latter group can profit from their previous acquisition of Turkish in procedural terms, if in the process of their learning Turkish they have also acquired helpful techniques and strategies that they might use when learning French (see also Batley et al., 1993, p. 30).

3.2 Transfer from L2 to L3

In the preceding chapters the phenomenon of transfer was treated on a general level or with reference to the relationship between L1 to L2. We will now concentrate on the relationship between L2 and further languages, L3 in particular.

What do we know about the transfer from L2 to L3? Publications on programmes and practices of transfer from a second to a third language are numerous. They fall into three categories:

(1) Theoretical reflections on the possibilities of transfer between two foreign languages.
Examples: Reinfried (1998): French – Italian or Spanish
Klein (2000): English – Spanish

(2) Anecdotal reports on experiences with programmes of transfer between two foreign languages.
Examples: Becker (1998): French – Italian
Jaspaert & Lemmens (1989): French – Dutch

(3) Research reports on experiments in the teaching of two foreign languages based on transfer.
Examples: Hufeisen (1993): English – German
Huber & Lasagabaster (2000): Spanish – English
Meißner & Burk (2001): French – Spanish

Most of these works treat particular cases of transfer in specific educational contexts, but some of them draw conclusions that are of general interest for our understanding of the phenomenon of transfer. A particularly interesting example is the research report by Huber and Lasagabaster (2000) on an experiment in the Basque country, where Spanish and Basque are official languages and English is taught from the fifth form on as an L3. They found that the level of competence in L2 – in most cases Basque on the basis of Spanish as L1 – strongly influenced the achievement in English, and they concluded, in accordance with the threshold-level hypothesis (Cummins, 1976), that only those learners who have reached an appropriate level of proficiency in both previous languages – L1 and L2 – will profit from it when learning an L3. This conclusion is certainly daring, but also plausible. If it can be confirmed by further research, this might have a great impact on the development of a general theory of transfer (see Meißner & Burk, 2001)

Another potentially important contribution to such a theory could come from the so-called European Schools as they have been specifically designed as plurilingual/pluricultural institutions. One of their principal aims is to introduce their pupils to at least two languages other than their own and to make them familiar with at least two other cultures of the European community. There are two different kinds of European Schools: The first consists of the official schools of the European Community (Baetens Beardsmore, 1993). They form a network of nine schools in six European countries, that is, in places where supra-national European institutions are situated. They are attended by approximately 12,000 children who study in nine subsections covering all the official languages of the member states. The schools attempt to guarantee the development of the children's first languages and their national identity, but also strive to promote a European identity through instruction for all pupils in at least three languages. A characteristic trait of these schools is formal instruction in L2 and L3 and their coordination (for details see Baetens Beardsmore, 1993).

The second group is formed by those schools which in the 1990s, independently of one another, but based on the same educational philosophy, were founded in 12 different regions/cities in central Europe, for example, in Berlin, Copenhagen, Vienna and Wolfsburg (Doyé, 1997). Their common denominator is that they want to give children growing up in areas where another language community is present, the opportunity to be educated together with children of that other community, to learn their language and to become familiar with their culture. In the first four years, that is, in the primary school, the teaching is done in the two languages that are represented by the children (and teachers) at the individual school, for instance, in the *Staatliche Europaschule Berlin* French and German, Russian and German, Spanish and German, Turkish and German (Doyé, 1999). In the fifth form English is added as L3 and is taught through formal instruction. A similar organization is practiced in the Italian-German School in Wolfsburg, which will be described in the following section.

3.3 An example

L1:	German Italian	L2:	Italian German	L3:	English

> La Scuola Italo-Tedesca di Wolfsburg è frequentata, rispettivamente per il 50 % circa, da bambini di lingua tedesca ed italiana, compresi quelli di famiglie miste italo-tedesche. I bambini imparano assieme il tedesco e l'italiano dal prímo giorno di scuola. La scuola si pone l'obiettivo di attribuire ad ambedue le lingue culture, per quanto possibile, la medisima importanza. (Riccò & Sandfuchs, 1996, p. 11)

From their fifth form on they learn English as their L3. They may not have reached an equally high level of proficiency in the two previous languages – L1 and L2 – by then, but enough communicative competence to use them effectively in everyday situations and, above all, a fairly high degree of language awareness. Through constant confrontation with Italian and German they become aware of the differences and similarities of the two languages, their ways of expressing comparable ideas through different lexical and structural devices.

When they reach the fifth form, they have acquired a whole repertoire of declarative and procedural knowledge in and through learning Italian and German. It is upon this repertoire that the teachers of English build their programme. They have already developed a sophisticated strategy to exploit all opportunities for transfer from language to language and from L1 and L2 to L3 in particular.

In our report we will use the categorization proposed in section 3.1 above:

A. Declarative knowledge	1. linguistic items 2. linguistic rules
B. Procedural knowledge	1. techniques 2. strategies

A1. Transfer of linguistic items

To promote positive transfer of linguistic items, the teachers show their pupils the relationship between the three languages. A typical example is this: The children of a sixth form (second year of English) compile – under the guidance of their teacher – all the words they know in a certain area and thus accomplish a survey of the similarities and differences between the basic vocabularies in the three languages:

Italiano	Deutsch	English
famiglia	Familie	family
isola	Insel	island
lampada	Lampe	lamp
matematica	Mathematik	mathematics
nord	Norden	north
ottobre	Oktober	October
passegiero	Passagier	passenger
cioccolata	Schokolade	chocolate
scuola	Schule	school

The teachers also, of course, point to the traps that are to be avoided, the false friends that might lead to negative transfer, for example,

caldo	vs.	kalt	vs.	cold
camera	vs.	Kamera	vs.	camera
ovest	vs.	Ost	vs.	east

A2. Transfer of linguistic rules

We will cite one example each from phonology, grammar and pragmatics.

Phonology: In learning Italian, the German pupils had of necessity to acquire clear concepts of vowels and consonants, in the same way as the Italian pupils did when learning German. Now, in the beginning stages of learning English, both groups can apply their knowledge as soon as they are confronted with phonological problems. The author was therefore not too surprised to hear an Italian girl express the rule for the formation of the indefinite article in English in a remarkably clear manner: "Se un sostantivo comincia con una vocale, diciamo *an*. Se un sostantivo comincia con una consonante, diciamo *a*."

Grammar: In studying Italian, the German pupils had become familiar with the concept of adverb to a degree they could never have reached by learning their mother tongue only. They could now transfer this knowledge to English. And they could use their knowledge of the rule that in Italian *-mente* is added to adjectives in order to form adverbs when building English adverbs by a corresponding procedure, namely by adding *-ly* to the respective adjectives.

Pragmatics: Through learning Italian and German in parallel, both groups of pupils became aware of the different ways in which speech acts such as requests, apologies or thanks can be performed and profit from it when starting to learn English, for example, how in Italian or German a polite request is formulated and with which illocutionary force. Questions like when and how do speakers use *prego, bitte* and *please* can be very illuminating.

B1. Transfer of techniques

The teachers of the *Scuola Italo-Tedesca* have also found efficient devices for the transfer of procedural knowledge, and these have become essential components of their work. Two examples of customary techniques are the following:

(1) In the English classes there are always Italian-English and German-English dictionaries at hand which the children can use when they feel a need for it. They do this on the basis of having used German-Italian dictionaries in the primary school and having learnt how to consult them effectively.

(2) The pupils also apply their knowledge of how to store their linguistic knowledge appropriately in all kinds of media – in fold-

ers, files, notebooks, sometimes even computers – in order to remember it and have it easily available. They have learnt the principal techniques of storage and retrieval in their first four years when learning Italian or German respectively and can now transfer their procedural knowledge to the study of English. This applies to the storage of useful syntactic structures, of important semantic fields, of surveys of relevant speech acts as well as thematic collections.

B2. Transfer of strategies

In this fourth category, the efforts of the teachers are in perfect accordance with another general aim of the *Scuola Italo-Tedesca*: the education for autonomy. Autonomous learners are persons who can make the significant decisions in their learning process by themselves: decisions about objectives, contents, methods, techniques and materials. They are ready to take responsibility for their learning and capable of organizing it (Holec, Little, & Richterich, 1996; Holec & Huttunen, 1997). Autonomous learning is self-directed and differs essentially from traditional other-directed learning. The teachers of the Wolfsburg school have made it a principle of their education to convince their pupils of the need to assume responsibility for their own learning and to equip them with the capacity to plan and manage it.

It is in this respect that their education for autonomy coincides with one of the principles of an education for plurilingualism. Both require the capacity for decision-making and independent action and therefore the development and exercise of learning strategies. In most classes of the primary section of the *Scuola Italo-Tedesca* the teachers – in their German and Italian lessons – have already equipped their children with appropriate strategies, and the secondary section can build on them. Some of the teachers practice *offenen Unterricht* in their English lessons as often as possible and try to consolidate the pupils' procedural knowledge wherever they can. They ask the pupils to work independently within weekly frameworks and timetables and to decide freely when and where they want to learn what. Thus the learners are obliged to develop and apply strategies of their own and to take responsibility for their learning (see Wolff, 1998).

4. Consequences for language teaching policy

What are the consequences of our reflections on the theory and practicability of transfer in the preceding chapters? Two kinds of consequence may be drawn: methodological and curricular (see Königs, 1999).

The *methodological* consequences comprise all the measures that teachers can take to help pupils to profit from their previous experience with language(s). The guiding principle for these measures is *to encourage and support positive transfer and to discourage and restrain negative transfer* (see Meißner & Burk, 2001). A great many procedures have been proposed and tried out. The above-described teaching method practiced at the German-Italian School is just one example, although very typical, of the attempt to integrate all that is known so far about the possibilities of transfer in language learning.

The *curricular* issue gives rise to two questions: Which languages should be taught? In which order? The first question can be specified as follows: Should "language distance" (Odlin, 1989) play a part in the choice of the languages to be taught or not? There seems to be general agreement that one of the two foreign languages that all young Europeans are to learn should be English because of its global importance and irrespective of its distance to the other two languages. But language distance comes into play with the third language. Here the experts disagree about whether a language should be taught that is closely related to the mother tongue of the learners or one from another language family.

Posner (1991) favours the second alternative. He suggests that

> … each European school should teach the following languages:
> a. the student's mother tongue
> b. the world language English
> c. a language from a language family that does not include the student's mother tongue: a Romance or Slavic language for Germans, a Germanic or Slavic language for French, a Germanic or Romance language for Poles etc. Posner, 1991, pp. 133-134)

For Posner language distance is of lesser importance than the chance of gaining another view of the world and getting access to further groups of people by learning a language that is significantly different from the mother tongue of the learners.

Rieder (2001) takes the opposite view. He recommends choosing a language from the same family as the learners' mother tongue, i.e. another Romance language for speakers of French, Italian or Spanish, another Slavic language for speakers of Polish or Russian, another Germanic language for speakers of Dutch or Danish. He proposes the following: "[Man sollte] die Kenntnisse einer romanischen, germanischen, slawischen Sprache ... nutzen, um eine andere Sprache derselben Familie zu verstehen" (Rieder, 2001, p. 8). He speaks of "*Verstehen*" as he is of the opinion that it would be unrealistic to aim at full competence in the third language, including also the productive skills. Thus he is a representative of a group of educationists who favour the model of *polyglot dialogue,* in which intercomprehension is made possible on a much wider scale: If all young Europeans – after building a solid foundation in L1 and L2 – learn to understand an L3, this multiplies the chances of Europe-wide understanding (see Batley et al., 1993, p. 29).

The second question concerns the order in which the languages are to be taught. Until recently it was taken for granted that English, because of its global importance, should be the L2 in all European schools. After the educational reform in most European countries – one foreign language in the primary school, (at least) one in the secondary school – this would mean that all primary school children would have to learn English before they get access to any other language.

At present educationists are beginning to realize that this would lead to unnecessary uniformity and would certainly not be in accordance with the endeavour to achieve linguistic diversification. The acknowledgement of English as an indispensable world language does not imply that it has to be taught first. Königs speaks of good arguments for delaying the learning of English as a foreign language precisely because of its status as a global language (Königs, 1999, p. 255). The most important of these arguments is that if English is learnt and taught as a *lingua franca*, there is the danger that it will be conceived as culture-free and therefore not suited for intercultural education.

> Das Englische öffnet nicht für Sprachenvielfalt und Mehrsprachigkeit, sondern führt zu einer frühen Beschränkung, da die Lerner das Englische als universelles Kommunikationsmittel kennen lernen, ... als *lingua franca*, losgelöst von einzelnen Kulturen. (Baur & Chlosta, 1999, p. 29)

The adherents of this argument therefore urge us to consider alternative ways of organizing the language curricula, for example, the one practiced in Berlin or Wolfsburg with Spanish or Italian or Russian as L2 and English as L3.

All this is not meant as a rejection of English as the first foreign language altogether, but as an appeal to keep the door open for alternative curricular arrangements. Why should German children living near this country's western border not start with Dutch and those along the eastern border not with Polish? *Waarom niet? Czemu nie?*

References

Aguado, K., & Hu, A. (Eds.). (2000). *Mehrsprachigkeit und Mehrkulturalität.* Berlin: Pädagogischer Zeitschriftenverlag.

Batley, E., Candelier, M., Hermann-Brennecke, G., & Szepe, G. (1993). *Language policies for the world of the twenty-first century.* Paris: Unesco and FIPLV.

Baur, R., & Chlosta, C. (1999). Begegnung mit Sprachen – Reform oder Konkurs. In U. Gerling, E. Thürmann, & A. Nieweler (Eds.), *Wege zur Mehrsprachigkeit* (pp. 25-34). Soest: Landesinstitut für Schule und Weiterbildung.

Baetens Beardsmore, H. (Ed.). (1993). *European models of bilingual education.* Clevedon: Multilingual Matters.

Becker, N. (1998). Interferenzprobleme (Französisch – Italienisch) in der Mehrsprachendidaktik und ihre Behebung. In F.-J. Meißner & M. Reinfried (Eds.), *Mehrsprachigkeitsdidaktik. Konzepte, Analysen, Lehrerfahrungen mit romanischen Fremdsprachen* (pp. 179-197). Tübingen: Narr.

Committee of Ministers. (1998). *Recommendation no. R6 concerning modern languages.* Strasbourg: Council of Europe.

Conseil de la coopération culturelle. (1998). *Un cadre européen commun de références.* Strasbourg: Conseil de l'Europe.

Coste, D., Moore, D., & Zarate, G. (1997). *Compétence plurilingue et pluriculturelle.* Strasbourg: Conseil de l'Europe.

Cummins, J. (1976). The influence of bilingualism on cognitive growth. *Working Papers on Bilingualism, 9,* 1-43.

Dechert, H. (1983). How a story is done in a second language. In C. Færch & G. Kasper (Eds.), *Strategies in interlanguage communication* (pp. 175-195). London: Longman.

Deese, J., & Hulse, S. H. (1967). *The psychology of learning.* New York: McGraw-Hill.

DES. (1990). *National Curriculum of England and Wales.* London.

Doyé, P. (1997). Bilinguale Grundschulen. *Zeitschrift für Fremdsprachenforschung, 8*(2), 161-195.

Doyé, P. (1999). *The intercultural dimension.* Berlin: Cornelsen.

Færch, C., & Kasper, G. (Eds.). (1983). *Strategies in interlanguage communication.* London: Longman.

Fries, C. (1945). *Teaching and learning English as a foreign language.* Ann Arbor: University of Michigan.

Grotjahn, R. (1997). Strategiewissen und Strategiegebrauch. Das Informationsverarbeitungsparadigma als Metatheorie der L2-Strategieforschung. In U. Rampillon & G. Zimmermann (Eds.), *Strategien und Techniken beim Erwerb fremder Sprachen* (pp. 33-76). Ismaning: Hueber.

Hausmann, F. J. (1995). Altsprachlicher Unterricht und Fremdsprachenunterricht. In K.-R. Bausch, H. Christ, & H.-J. Krumm (Eds.), *Handbuch Fremdsprachenunterricht* (3rd ed.) (pp. 91-95). Tübingen: Francke.

Hawkins, E. (1981). *Modern languages in the curriculum.* Cambridge: Cambridge University Press.

Hilgard, E., & Bower, G. (1966). *Theories of learning.* New York: Appleton-Century-Crofts.

Holec, H., Little, D., & Richterich, R. (1996). *Strategies in language learning and use.* Strasbourg: Council of Europe.

Holec, H., & Huttunen, I. (Eds.). (1997). *Learner autonomy in modern languages.* Strasbourg: Council of Europe.

Huber, E., & Lasagabaster, D. (2000). Die kognitiven Auswirkungen der Zweisprachigkeit. *ITL Review of Applied Linguistics, 129-130,* 191-224.

Hufeisen, B. (1993). DaF-Unterricht bei Lernenden mit Englisch als erster Fremdsprache. *Neusprachliche Mitteilungen aus Wissenschaft und Praxis 46*(3), 167-174.

Jaspaert, K., & Lemmens, G. (1989). Linguistic evaluation of Dutch as a third language. In M. Byram & J. Leman (Eds.), *Bicultural and trilingual education* (pp. 30-56). Clevedon: Multilingual Matters.

Klein, E. (2000). Auf dem Wege zur Dreisprachigkeit: Inferenzen und Interferenzen bei der Perzeption der Phonetik und des Wortschatzes bei deutschen Lernern des Englischen (L2) und des Spanischen (L3). In K. Aguado & A. Hu (Eds.), *Mehrsprachigkeit und Mehrkulturalität* (pp. 135-143). Berlin: Pädagogischer Zeitschriftenverlag.

Königs, F. (1999). To know English or not to know English: Some thoughts on the hegemony of English from a methodological point of view, with special reference to German as a Foreign language. In C. Gnutzmann (Ed.), *Teaching and learning English as a global language. Native and non-native perspectives* (pp. 247-258). Tübingen: Stauffenburg.

Lado, R. (1957). *Linguistics across cultures.* Ann Arbor: University of Michigan.

Meißner, F.-J., & Reinfried, M. (Eds.). (1998). *Mehrsprachigkeitsdidaktik. Konzepte, Analysen, Lehrerfahrungen mit romanischen Fremdsprachen.* Tübingen: Narr.

Meißner, F.-J., & Burk, H. (2001). Hörverstehen in einer unbekannten romanischen Fremdsprache und methodische Implikationen für den Tertiärsprachenerwerb. *Zeitschrift für Fremdsprachenforschung, 12*(1), 63-102.

Odlin, T. (1989). *Language transfer. Cross-linguistic influence in language learning.* Cambridge: Cambridge University Press.

Posner, R. (1991). Society, civilization, mentality: Prolegomena to a language policy for Europe. In F. Coulmas (Ed.), *A language policy for the European Community* (pp. 121-137). Berlin: Mouton de Gruyter.

Rampillon, U., & Zimmermann, G. (Eds.). (1997). *Strategien und Techniken beim Erwerb fremder Sprachen.* Ismaning: Hueber.

Reber, A. (Ed.). (1985). *Dictionary of psychology.* Harmondsworth: Penguin.

Reinfried, M. (1998). Transfer beim Erwerb einer weiteren romanischen Fremdsprache. Prinzipielle Relevanz und methodische Integration in den Fremdsprachenunterricht. In F.-J. Meißner & M. Reinfried (Eds.), *Mehrsprachigkeitsdidaktik. Konzepte, Analysen, Lehrerfahrungen mit romanischen Fremdsprachen* (pp. 23-43). Tübingen: Narr.

Riccò, A., & Sandfuchs, U. (Eds.). (1996). *Insieme.* Bad Heilbrunn: Klinkhardt.

Rieder, K. (2001). *Intercomprehension. Fremdsprachige Texte entschlüsseln.* Wien: öbv & htp.

Ryle, G. (1949). *The concept of mind.* London: Hutchinson.

Thorndike, E. L. (1913). *Educational psychology.* New York: Lemcke & Buechner.

Wolff, D. (1998). Lernerstrategien beim Fremdsprachenlernen. In J.-P. Timm (Ed.), *Englisch lernen und lehren* (pp. 70-77). Berlin: Cornelsen.

Wholeheartedly English
right from the beginning

Foreign language acquisition at the primary school starting in grade one

The new Baden-Württemberg curriculum

Werner Bleyhl

Der neue baden-württembergische Lehrplan „Fremdsprachen in der Grundschule" ist in verschiedener Hinsicht innovativ: er gilt für *alle* Kinder im Primarschulalter; er sieht die Einführung einer Fremdsprache ab Klasse 1 vor, die in Klasse 5 fortgeführt werden soll; er basiert auf allen erreichbaren und relevanten Forschungsergebnissen zum Sprachenlernen und zielt so auf ein nichtlineares Fremdsprachenlernen, das zunächst großen Nachdruck auf die Sicherstellung des Verstehens legt.

The new Baden-Württemberg curriculum "Foreign languages at primary schools" is innovative in various respects: It is the first in Germany to cater for *all* primary school children. It establishes that one foreign language is to be taught starting in year 1 and that the same language will be continued in secondary school; it aims to take into consideration all available and relevant research findings with regard to language learning establishing a framework for nonlinear language learning with major emphasis on comprehension in the beginning years.

In der Entwicklung [des Kindes] geht es nicht darum, was, sondern mindestens so sehr, wie das Kind lernt. Wenn wir uns Gedanken zur Entwicklung eines Kindes machen, sollten wir uns immer wieder fragen: Kann es Lern- und Problemlösungsstrategien entwickeln? Wie wirken sich die Lernerfahrungen auf sein zukünftiges Selbstwertgefühl aus? Sinnvolles Lernen besteht in selbstbestimmtem Handeln, in dem sich das Kind bewähren kann.
Remo H. Largo[1] *(1999, p. 227)*

---

1 Largo is professor of pediatry and head of the department of child development at the University of Zurich children's hospital.

1. Setting

At the start of the 21st century foreign language instruction at state schools in Germany is challenged on at least two levels, on a practical level and on a theoretical/psychological level.

The problems at the *practical level* have become conspicuous because the modern world of globalisation requires that foreign languages learned at school lead to a certain level of practical, functional linguistic competence of the learners, which – alas – is not felt to be generally achieved in a satisfactory way by traditional foreign language instruction. The *theoretical/psychological level* concerns the concept of (foreign) language learning, i.e. language learning theory, since the old concepts have evidently failed.

The present obvious need for improvement is being met, primarily by the schools themselves. The interesting fact is that the established authorities, whose professional task should be to find practical responses to help optimise foreign language teaching at school, have so far left schools to their own devices with the task of finding practical responses themselves.

2. A paradigm shift

Traditional foreign language instruction – in spite of all the high-sounding, but in fact only cosmetic changes and refinements since the end of the 19th century (Freudenstein, 2000) – is firmly grounded in a learning concept that emerged from the teaching of classical languages like Latin or Greek. The language to be learned is seen as being based on a set of classical texts from which certain rules may be distilled. These (grammatical) rules had the function of an aiding device to decode – or reconstruct – similar classical texts. It is only now, when language competence has to stand its test of functionality in actual practical use, that it becomes obvious how ineffective such an approach is when dealing with a living language.[2] It remains Johannes-

---

2 Corpus-based linguistics, using the computer as a means of handling mass data, shows us among other things that there is no one grammar of English (Biber et al., 1999) but that there are "important linguistic differences among registers" which

Peter Timm's merit to have helped open the door for a paradigm change with his publications (Bach & Timm, 1989; Timm, 1995; Timm, 1998).

Research at the end of the 20th century, particularly in the field of first language (Bruner, 1997; Moerk, 1992; Szagun, 1993) and second language acquisition (Wode, 1988, 1995; Ellis, 1994, 1997), foreign language instruction research (Ellis, 1997; VanPatten, 1992a, 1992b; Bleyhl, 2001c), in child development (Largo 1999, 2001), in the cognitive sciences (Gardner, 1991; Gopnik et al., 1999) especially in cognitive neurobiology (e.g. Changeux, 1983; Roth, 1997; Singer, 1997, 1998) all contributed to a better understanding of language learning. To put the findings in a nutshell:

(1) Language(s) is/are learned/acquired most effectively if the focus of attention is primarily on meaning, on content and not on form.

(2) Language(s) is/are learned/acquired most effectively if language can be experienced functionally in interpersonal interaction and in rich environments. (Incidentally, the latest research undertaken on bilingual subject matter teaching clearly underlines this result [Curtain & Pesola, 1988; Wode, 1995; Melenk & Dörfel, 1999; Le Pape Racine, 2000; Zydatiß, 2000]. Form-focused instruction may help later when the learner has already accumulated a "critical mass" of language experience and asks for particular clarifications.)

(3) In spite of language development being systematic and rather universal, the speed at which individuals develop language varies considerably.

(4) The basic learning strategies (as developed by evolution and the individual brain) are: (a) firstly readiness for *experience* and *reception* to develop relevant hypotheses, (b) then *experimentation* in private, later in social interaction (note the importance of atmosphere, particularly in the phases of uncertainty), and (c) finally *reflection* and *recognition* (the flexible application of appropriate, then also metacognitive, strategies based on previous rich personal experience of problem-solving).

---

are "overlooked in the teaching and study of English grammar" (p. 11), or that "the 'sentence' is a notion that is not applicable to spoken language" (p. 10).

A change in the climate of opinion in the natural sciences, notably in biology (and even more so in physics; see Haken, 1981) support these findings. Broadly speaking, in order to come to terms with complex phenomena there must be a move away from the linear, Newtonian cause-and-effect way of thinking towards an understanding of complex systems and of life in general along evolutionary lines. Key terms are: *complexity*, *self-organisation*, *dynamics*, *non-linearity*, (Prigogine, 1979; Krohn & Küppers, 1992), concepts that help explain surprisingly well the phenomena observed in the development of cognition (Roth, 1997; Singer, 1998), but also in first and second language acquisition (Bleyhl, 1989, 2000, 2001c; Brinkmann et al., 1997; Karpf, 1990; Larsen-Freeman, 1997; Peltzer-Karpf & Zangl, 1998).

3. Foreign languages at the primary school in Germany

Foreign language instruction at the primary school level in Germany looks back on a fairly long tradition. The Waldorf Schools (Rudolf Steiner schools) have been teaching foreign languages (mainly English *and* French or Russian) since 1919 and have developed a most respectable, rich, and powerful methodology (Jaffke, 1996). First research results of a wave of new attempts in the seventies to teach foreign languages at the primary school level showed as early as 1977 that such an endeavour is worthwhile (Doyé & Lüttge, 1977). In 1980 the so-called Homburg Recommendations (*Homburger Empfehlungen*) were published advocating strongly the learning of at least two foreign languages. This appeal enhanced a number of projects which had introduced foreign language teaching at primary school, mainly starting in grade three, that is, with eight-year-olds.

By the nineties there was a new wave of interest in teaching foreign languages at the primary level. However, a certain amount of energy was absorbed by the controversy whether the "encounter approach" (for example, *Lerne die Sprache des Nachbarn*, practised along the German-French border since 1984; see Pelz, 1989) or the "systematic foreign language teaching" approach should serve as a model (Doyé, 1993). Neither approach really won the day. The liberal "encounter model" (any foreign language or several languages can be chosen), often adopted because it is financially less demanding and politically easily saleable stressing "intercultural" qualities, proved unconvincing because of its uneven effectiveness. The "systematic approach" requires basically a rather homogeneous learner group, which the comprehensive primary school with its wide ability range does not provide. Severe doubts as to whether or not such an approach (which basically tries to follow a grammatical progression) is learner-appropriate for children aged eight to ten years – or younger – can no longer be disregarded. These doubts are all the more substantial if one takes into account that learners are unable to cope effectively with such theoretical categories as word classes beyond verb or noun, or with theoretical grammatical rules till much later, in grade seven or eight. This is a problem which also faces the teaching of grammar in the mother tongue (Ingendahl, 1999).

Moreover, neither model is founded on a solid theory of language learning, didactics, or methodology. The "systematic approach" is based on a rather "mechanistic", linear concept of language learning (*present-practise-produce*), where brick is to be laid on brick till the (language) wall stands. The "encounter model" with play here and a game there pleads for intercultural understanding, an objective gently floating on the milk of human kindness.

Meanwhile parent pressure and the demand for linguistically more competent school leavers have increased steadily with the globalisation of Europe and the introduction of the Euro. Private schools have responded faster with bilingual teaching starting often in grade one (see Zydatiß, 2000). The public state school system has had to move and to react as well.

4. The Baden-Württemberg curriculum 2001: "Foreign languages at primary schools"

So, with the research findings of the various linguistic and cognitive science disciplines on the one hand and the political pressure for more linguistically proficient school leavers on the other, time is ripe for a radical re-thinking of language instruction in schools.

As a first step towards a more comprehensive language teaching concept – badly needed at all levels – a commission was set up. It comprised teachers of all types of schools, from grammar school to diverse schools for handicapped pupils, as well as school administrators, parents, members of the parents' association of dyslexic pupils, and representatives of universities of education (*Pädagogische Hochschulen*). The task consisted of establishing and putting in writing a foreign language teaching curriculum for the primary school, that is for the initiation period when the young learners should be given opportunities to experience the use of the foreign language in social interaction. The committee had to decide the standards and describe this first stage.

4.1 Political cornerstones

Several political cornerstones had been set in advance:

- Instruction is to *start in grade one.*
- *All the children*, from every ability range, are to be given the chance to learn a foreign language at primary school.
- *Two additional lessons a week* (i.e. 90 minutes) in every primary school year are to be allotted to the foreign language (which meant that for the whole state of Baden-Württemberg 1,600 new teacher jobs will have to be financed – quite a task for the Ministry of Finance!).
- No grades will be given in the first two years, but *in grade 3 and 4* there have to be *school marks/grades* to demonstrate to everybody that foreign language teaching is not an irrelevant pastime but to be taken seriously. (These marks, however, are not to be taken into account when, after grade four, the children are streamed into the various types of secondary school.)
- Since the language that started at primary school is to be continued in secondary school, a *free choice of language is ruled out* for organisational reasons (see Bleyhl, 1999). French will be offered in certain areas along the German-French border, along the Rhine, whereas in central and eastern Baden-Württemberg English will be taught.

- A more organisational aspect is that a pilot phase should start with grade one in about 450 of the schools at the beginning of the school year 2001/02. The rest of all the 2,500 primary schools are to follow in 2003/04.
- A further organisational consequence is that the secondary foreign language teaching curricula for all school types will have to be adjusted. A major problem for secondary schools will be where exactly to "pick up" their pupils and how to carry on from there. This is already a major point of concern and worry to many secondary school foreign language teachers.

The outcome of the many long debates in the committee is the present, so-called "preliminary", curriculum. It aimed at (and achieved) a synthesis between the demands of what primary school didactics requires and what language acquisition research demands. (It was actually almost a surprise to everybody involved to discover that – once the focus of attention moves to the young language learner – the interests and concepts of the foreign language representatives and the primary school teachers overlap to a surprising degree.[3])

4.2 The major features of the new curriculum

The outcome was a curriculum whose major features are as follows:

- The language has to relate to the world of the young pupils.
- The approach has to be *holistic*, that is
  - *action*-oriented,

[3] Since on the one hand primary school is truly comprehensive and primary school education aims at developing the skills of all the children by meeting the various needs of the children and not just by streaming them into ability groups and, on the other hand, foreign language teaching methodology over the centuries has acquired the reputation of being the touchstone for streaming school children, the two camps had each lived at opposite ends of the educational spectrum. And where age-long neglect, mutual distrust, if not contempt, were the rule, now with a new understanding of the learning processes themselves, it was discovered that there is no conflict between the camps.

  - *learner-oriented* taking the age and learning styles into account (this means that schools must refrain from the traditional "marching in step" foreign language instruction)
  - *process-oriented*,
  - *experiential* for the learners and
  - has to contain an amount of *play*fulness, and
  - prepare for *social interaction* between expert and learners, and among learners.
- The approach has to be *content-based*, which means that other school subjects such as elementary science, sport, music, arts and crafts and others may – perhaps even should – be taught in the foreign language to be acquired. So there will be an approach supporting bilingual teaching (or *integrative teaching*) which may also be labelled a *partial immersion approach*.
- Accepting that "L2 acquisition is systematic and, to a large extent, universal, reflecting ways in which internal cognitive mechanisms control acquisition, irrespective of the personal background of learners or the setting in which they learn" (Ellis, 1997, pp. 24-25) a *grammatical syllabus indicating a sequence of grammatical structures to be instructed becomes superfluous*.
- Instead, a *list of topics to be treated* (largely identical with the curriculum content established in the other subjects) has been drawn up, and a few examples of linguistic means which can be used to deal with them have been given.
- Stress should be laid more on *lexis* (see Bleyhl & Timm, 1998), since syntax requires a "critical mass" of lexis before it can develop (Marchman & Bates, 1994).
- *The non-linearity of the learning process has to be taken into account.*[4] This concept is derived from the holistic approach, pro-

---

4 In a few years the next generation will have difficulty understanding how traditional foreign language teaching before the 21st century could have believed in its – counterproductive – way of procedure: the first tense/aspect to be taught has most recently been the *present progressive* (e.g. "he is running"). When after about six months most pupils seem to have coped with it and produce sentences respecting the formal rules, the *simple present tense* is introduced, and so on.

viding learners with the possibility of acquiring the foreign language using the same strategies with which they "naturally" acquire their first (or second) language. The consequences (put forward by all recent – and older – research on language development of various kinds; see the literature mentioned earlier) are that

- learning a foreign language at school also has to take into account that *understanding is a prerequisite for subsequent competent language productivity* ("the trick of evolution"; see Bleyhl, 2000). The stage of understanding cannot be bypassed as is all too frequently the case in traditional foreign language teaching. That is *comprehension has to be stressed and assessed first*[5],
- the oral form of language acquisition has to precede the introduction of the spelling system of the foreign language because of two reasons: First, the sound system with the establishment of the phonemic categories must come prior to the spelling system.[6] This is particularly crucial for English

---

Never are the learners given the chance to establish – internally – the respective time and tense relationships. (English and German differ in rather subtle ways; see von Stutterheim, 1997). Result: Learners usually never achieve native-speaker-like security with tense and aspect and continue to make their errors. Primary school, by contrast, has long given up the belief in the effectiveness of a linear approach to spelling; the times of "The cat sat on the mat", the systematic sequential teaching of the alphabet, are over.

5 This is a point where those teachers who still measure language learning by linguistic yardsticks will have problems. Yet perhaps a quote from Ellis (1994, p. 343) can help to reset their out-dated parameters. Talking about the U-shape of language development, Ellis refers to the difficulty of competence assessment and of "how to determine which stage of development each learner ... has reached. Given that learners can produce the same correct feature at both an early and a late stage of development, this is obviously not an easy task." Not wanting to encourage, for the time being, seemingly objective testing (e.g. by making learners write a dictation), the only diplomatic and least counterproductive way out of the dilemma is: testing comprehension. Those who can produce *may*, but none should be forced to.

6 Those who advocate the use of spelling for beginning language learners are either computer freaks or old-fashioned (i.e. Latin learning shaped) hardliners who have never observed true beginners of living languages closely nor made a careful analysis of the trickiness of the English (or French) spelling system with its hundreds of phoneme-grapheme correspondence rules for the most basic voca-

and French. It has been established that due to the higher degree of complexity of the English phoneme-grapheme relationships American primary school children need about double the time of German primary school children to reach about the same level of certainty in their respective mother tongues, that is, four years for English and two years for German (Bleyhl, 2000). Second, the spelling system of the first language has to have reached a certain degree of stability before the spelling system of the second language is introduced. This is the only safe way to avoid confusion and a further load of teaching-induced problems (Kielhöfer & Jonekeit, 1998). So spelling is generally introduced only in grade three due to the complexity of language (each phenomenon gains its importance within the system only in contrast with the other phenomena of the same level; see Bleyhl, 2000) there cannot be a one-to-one relationship between teaching and learning. Furthermore the language learner requires (both evolution and the biology of the brain necessitate this) *a period of incubation*, as Palmer & Palmer (1925) or Billows (1961) and others have postulated (recently the term "silent period" has been also used to describe this stage). The didactic consequence is that the learners must not be put under pressure to produce language, but are only invited and challenged to do so, a procedure mothers also apply when rearing their children.

The findings of the long-term Austrian project at a bilingual school in Vienna should perhaps be mentioned here – a project where pupils also started foreign language learning in grade one: This was carefully re-

---

bulary (see Smith, 1978). They are recommended to read Elke Heidenreich's mini-drama *Mother learns English* where the teenage daughter teaches her mother how to read English, and where the mother, after being corrected about the proper pronunciation of "doing" runs into problems with "going" and decides to give up learning English altogether. Cultural evolution has arranged it well that the sound form precedes spelling; the learner must have *bound* the concept of "star" or "war" to a sound pattern before he/she learns the written form. He/She will then classify "star" and "war" into different categories, correspondingly "no" and "know" and spelling-sound interferences will rarely occur. The key to learning is meaning and functional use – not form.

searched by Annemarie Peltzer-Karpf and her team (Peltzer-Karpf & Zangl, 1998; Zangl & Peltzer-Karpf, 1998). The results support the solidity of the approach adopted, both with regard to theory and practice.

The fact that the curriculum contains lists of words or phrases is an example of the remnants of the traditional shape of a curriculum. They may serve as a help for the production of teaching material. The danger, however, is that they will be taken as the core and as a must by those who refuse to realise that there has been a shift of the overall paradigm and who want to keep living in the familiar spirit of the old mechanistic tradition.

4.3 The standards

With the introduction of the European Framework of Reference for Languages (Council of Europe, 2001) it is becoming a general requirement that demands of quality and excellence in education have to be met, that standards defining a cumulative body of knowledge and a set of competences are set up. Even if the traditional categories of listening, speaking, reading and writing are used, it is obvious that the limited amount of time given (a maximum of 90 minutes a week for partial immersion) can only lead to a limited initial competence.

The educational objectives have to be realistically attainable. A teaching goal which expected pupils to be able to fly would be nonsensical. To ask for sequential operational goals to be attainable by *all the pupils* along the whole range of the ability scales would be equally unrealistic since the faster learners – not being allowed to carry on learning according to their pace – would become frustrated. What is needed, therefore, is the provision of possibilities to differentiate in class so that the faster pupils can "run ahead" while the slower pupils can still be kept actively engaged in the language learning process and come to experience success, come to realise that their effort is also worthwhile. In other words, what foreign language learning at school has to face is a situation that is not basically unlike that of the family, in which, although of different ages, all the family members nevertheless engage in the family conversation. If English is the language taught at primary school it is all the more important that no learner is "turned off" and adopts the fox's role (as many learners do at secondary school) by declaring that the grapes are too sour.

It has nevertheless been made clear that the curriculum assumes that a classroom is a place where the foreign language can be taught in the foreign language and that the learners can achieve the ability to interact socially at a functional level. Strong emphasis is laid on the foundations of social interaction, i.e. that *all* the learners can understand and react appropriately when addressed in the foreign language. This implies that the beginners are given the benefit of being beginners, they are not expected to react without error (not even native speakers do that at that age), that their risk-taking is not penalised. Teachers are expected to react the way parents react – by expansion, repetition and particularly by being focused on the content, not the form of the utterance. The aim is that the learners can make themselves understood (or can express their "not-understanding") and show, verbally and/or nonverbally, the social skill of keeping up a communicative engagement. This is what pupils in immersion programmes, unlike the traditionally taught pupils, are capable of doing, it is this attitude that keeps them actively learning by asking "for more". Marks are only to be given for comprehension skills.

5. Problems

5.1 The teachers

The introduction of a foreign language as a school subject in primary school is indeed an almost revolutionary event in Germany. It is in fact a break with the tradition ever since the introduction of schooling for all in Württemberg way back in 1559, which became compulsory in 1648, way ahead of other territories. Although the prime minister of Baden-Württemberg had already announced the plan in 1996, it obviously needed a long period of internal negotiations and calculations before the Ministry of Finance finally consented. Early in 2001 the irreversible decision was taken – unopposed, since all political parties complied; the strongest opposition party even promising to introduce foreign languages in all primary schools in 2001/02 straight away if they won the elections.

The administrative preparations have started partly with the brakes on. The problems of how well the teachers are prepared for their task must not indeed be minimised. Hardly any primary school teacher has studied a foreign language and is professionally prepared for foreign language teaching.

Late in the nineties teacher education regulations were changed, and at least a third of the teacher training students now studying to take up teaching at a primary school are being prepared for their task as foreign language teachers. Other in-service programmes for teachers-in-preparation have been set up and are in high demand since the successful participation increases a teacher's chances of becoming enrolled at once.

The most intensive teacher in-service training programme in the state's history has been set up by the ministry advised by another special task force. It should be noted that the introduction of foreign languages at primary schools is not the only reform that is being implemented at primary school. There is also the programme "reliable school" (*Verlässliche Schule*; parents should be guaranteed that their children are taught what is on the timetable, regardless of whether a teacher has fallen ill or is away, say on an in-service training course.) Another programme is "The Open School" (*Schulanfang auf neuen Wegen*), specifying that when a child is ready to start school he or she may do so; so now at least two dates are offered to school starters. This requires a certain amount of flexibility on the part of the school administration as well as on the part of the respective teachers. It is no exaggeration to say that these programmes alone would have sufficed to cause unrest in most schools and therefore for the large majority of teachers "Foreign languages in primary school" is a real extra burden.

To cut a long story short: Teachers have now to be prepared in two new areas:

(1) in their personal foreign language competence and

(2) in their methodological language teaching skills, in other words – since this is the kernel of the matter – in their understanding of foreign language acquisition processes.

Both tasks are gigantic.

The personal foreign language competence of the teachers. Most doubts about the project are fed from the disbelief in the teachers' foreign language competence. Funnily enough, these doubts are cast by a number of (grammar school) teachers who think that only their way of teaching is truly justifiable. Without realizing it, these critics denigrate their own teaching concepts, or at least teaching practice. If the primary school teachers who have experienced foreign language instruction at school for nine years are not capable of handling communicative everyday situations at school, the setting of their schooling, then there is no better proof of the inefficiency of the traditional school approach.

Since diversity of language competence is the rule, each teacher has to be made individually responsible for attending the various courses – of varying quality – offered by different organisations, usually paid for by the state, and to take on personal responsibility for acquiring adequate language competence, difficult as that may be. Of course, specific TV programmes for language learning, special audio-cassettes issued by publishing houses are also offered for sale.

It goes without saying that in spite of the increasing general improvement and surprisingly intensive personal interest and commitment on the part of the teachers, for years to come it would be unrealistic to have too high expectations. There will always be room for improvement. Life is not perfect. And what native speaker is perfect in his or her mother tongue?

The methodological in-service programme. The above-mentioned task force, the in-service commission *Fremdsprachen Lernen in der Grundschule (FLiG)*, has set up a programme of six half-week courses, which are to be held in the various teacher academies in Baden-Württemberg, for those teachers whose task it will subsequently be to run the in-service programmes for their local teachers in their respective school districts.

The courses try to dovetail theory and practice by engaging different experts in the various fields from language acquisition, media, games to assessment. Here, too, the openness and eagerness of those – usually already heavily burdened – teachers really deserves unqualified praise.

One further aspect is worth mentioning. There is a relatively basic difference among those "multiplicators" (as is their official name tag). Some are professional secondary school language teachers. The majority, however, are experienced primary school teachers. The professional foreign language teachers were generally educated in the tradition of behaviouristic or later cognitivistic language learning theories and methodologies. These professional language teachers therefore have difficulty understanding what was referred to above as the "non-linearity" of the language acquisition process. They secretly long for the old "brick-on-brick" concept of language teaching. Some seem to have difficulty in recognizing the great similarity between natural language learning out of school and what modern acquisition research teaches us and what is to be implemented now at school according to the new curriculum.

The primary school teachers on the other hand, who participated in intensive discussions on how to teach reading and spelling to their young pupils a decade ago, usually understand immediately what this "non-linearity" in the learning processes of complex systems (such as the spelling system in German) means. They know that teachers cannot learn for their pupils, that there is no one-to-one relationship between teaching and learning. They know that they can only challenge their pupils and support their respective processes of interior self-organisation. On top of that, they are familiar with the fact that each pupil is at a different stage in his/her first language development and knows how to cope with the differences, while secondary school teachers (who usually teach previously streamed learners) only feel comfortable in classes with rather homogeneous abilities.

Thus, primary school teachers are a source of high hope with regard to their evident natural understanding of the new (yet basically straightforward) learning concepts, in spite of the unavoidable uncertainties they may experience in the linguistic domain. Their clearer understanding of language learning processes will help them to master the really gigantic task ahead. Language cassettes recording the voices of native speakers may prove to be a useful aid in ensuring proper pronunciation models to the highly sensitive young learners. Still, the temptation to fall back on old learning concepts is lurking. There are plentiful stocks of material geared to the old (and latent) concepts of immediate production according to the old "present-practice-produce" paradigm offered by major publishing houses. Pseudo-dialogues where learners are to repeat a certain role remain pseudo-communication and are not content-oriented. Expecting the correct repetition of chunks of language to lead to the internalisation of the linguistic system is bound to create disappointment and frustration. So the old naive reductionist learning concepts are kept alive by "false friends" and risk jeopardizing the endeavour to really adjust foreign language instruction in state schools to the needs of the learners and to the needs of society badly in need of competent school leavers. Should the old concept survive in spite of the guidelines offered by the new curriculum then this would be further proof for those who fear that written curricula are hardly worth the paper they are printed on and only serve to support the good conscience of school administrators and politicians.

5.2 The choice of language

Globalisation favours the big ones; St Matthew's principle "For whoever hath, to him shall be given, and he shall have more abundance" applies also to languages on the intercultural level. English is about to become the "killer language" (helped on by Microsoft and its global dominance; see Purdy, 2001). Yet Europe's strength in the past, her rich diverse thinking, is based on the plurality of languages. It is not the moment to discuss this issue here, but the parallel with the Roman Empire and its consequences for the language developments in Europe cannot, however, be overlooked (see Bleyhl, 1985). Yet it must remain clear that it is the task of all European educators to do all they can to preserve the richness of Europe. (This is all the more vital knowing what we do about how languages affect and shape our thoughts; see Bleyhl, 2001b).

It is extremely difficult to stand up against the almost suffocating power of English. The principle which the European Union advocates is that after learning one's mother tongue one should first learn the language of one's neighbour and only after that the world language – English (see the Homburg Recommendation; Bleyhl, 1995, 1999, 2001a). The struggle to adhere to this principle can be studied – almost as a model case – in the attempts to establish French as the neighbour language along the Rhine here in Baden-Württemberg. "English is the most useful worldwide language, so start with English. We will wait and see about the other languages later." This is roughly the parents' attitude. It remains to be seen whether the political will of the Baden-Württemberg government leads to success, whether French will be accepted as the first foreign language beyond the opening years even in the relatively restricted areas in Baden where it is now being introduced as a compulsory subject, not just as a voluntary supplement, as *Lerne die Sprache des Nachbarn* has been so far.

6. Tasks ahead

Whenever relatively new territory is entered, unforeseen problems arise. It is therefore all the more important that those who are heading for those territories have competence and confidence which in turn are founded on knowledge about the essential principles, in our case, of learning languages and of cognitive development. Recent findings, published in works such as Gopnik et al. (1999) may be found helpful.

The following steps may prove useful for a satisfactory implementation of the new curriculum:

(1) Teacher in-service training, plus teacher round-table meetings where oncoming problems may be discussed among colleagues. The discovery that colleagues, too, have their questions may reveal itself more as a relief than a personal flaw, so that the spirit of cooperation, traditionally lacking among teachers, may lead to a more relaxed and trustful atmosphere in schools.

(2) A comprehensive programme of evaluation of the curriculum and its implementation, in which a number of schools and educators of various institutions will be involved, is being set up. It is under the tutorage of Erika Werlen, formerly from Karlsruhe, now at the University of Berne, Switzerland.

Broadly speaking, it has been found that – just as life requires the richness of experience – teaching a foreign language cannot be done by using a particular coursebook. This is also the outcome of four reports and a number of interviews about the use of *Dinocroc*, a multi-media, musical, rhythmic, narrative and multi-sensory programme, which nevertheless relies too much on repetition. (The programme – interspersed with remnants of behaviouristic imitation learning concepts – requires each format to be repeated 15 times, which risks becoming boring and quickly asks for variation; see Schnaitmann, this volume). Yet the teachers engaged in its first application have come to realise that the six- or seven-year-olds really can understand unknown words and phrases quite easily *if* the situation, the context, the intonation, the gestures, the mimics and the body language of the speaker are comprehensively adequate. So even rough means can help one forward and serve as a "tin-opener" to the enterprise by giving the teachers involved confidence and success, and eventually the learners, too.

All those teachers who have put their heart into implementing the curriculum, as it has been set up in their pilot schools, report of highly positive experiences, for teacher and pupils alike, far beyond their expectations. Yet to foretell whether the pupils will successfully learn or acquire a foreign language at school – essentially a process of a second enculturation – is difficult. It should be kept in mind that such a success is the result of the interdependence and mutual cooperation of

(1) the inborn language learning faculty,

(2) the motivation of the individual learner, i.e. their sense of necessity,

(3) the quantity and

(4) the quality of their language experience, that is, of their rich social environment, which means: of the quantity and quality of instruction.

The curriculum presented for the initiation period of learning a foreign language is designed to lead learners into the domains of social interaction by means of the foreign language and into the beginning of finding access to and making use of the various linguistically accessible sources of information. It cannot set up and describe standards of final achievement, which a comprehensive language curriculum will later have to do, but it can help pave the way toward later success.

References

Bach, G., & Timm, J.-P. (Eds.). (1989). *Englischunterricht. Grundlagen und Methoden einer handlungsorientierten Unterrichtspraxis.* Tübingen: Francke.

Biber, D., Johansson, S., Leech, G., Conrad, S., & Finegan, E. (1999). *Grammar of spoken and written English.* Harlow: Longman.

Billows, F. L. (1961). *The techniques of language teaching.* London: Longman.

Bleyhl, W. (1985). Quo vadit? Wohin führt letztendlich unser Englischunterricht? Eines Englisch- und Französischlehrers geheime Zweifel. *Neusprachliche Mitteilungen, 38*(2), 74-78.

Bleyhl, W. (1989). Psycholinguistische und pragmadidaktische Überlegungen zum handlungsorientierten Fremdsprachenunterricht. In G. Bach & J.-P. Timm (Eds.), *Englischunterricht. Grundlagen und Methoden einer handlungsorientierten Unterrichtspraxis* (pp. 22-41). Tübingen: Francke

Bleyhl, W. (1995). Fremdsprachen an Grundschulen? Ja – aber! In J.-P. Timm (Ed.), *Ganzheitlicher Fremdsprachenunterricht* (pp. 216-229). Weinheim: Deutscher Studien Verlag.

Bleyhl, W., & Timm, J.-P. (1998). Wortschatz und Grammatik im Kontext. In J.-P. Timm (Ed.), *Englisch lehren und lernen. Didaktik des Englischunterrichts* (pp. 259-271). Berlin: Cornelsen.

Bleyhl, W. (1999). Fremdsprachen an Grundschulen – Eine Herausforderung für uns alle. *Bildung & Wissenschaft,* 53(6), 14-17.

Bleyhl, W. (Ed.). (2000). *Fremdsprachen in der Grundschule. Grundlagen und Praxisbeispiele.* Hannover: Schroedel.

Bleyhl, W. (2001a). Fremdsprachen in der Grundschule: eine Herausforderung für die Grundschule, die Fremdsprachendidaktik und das Schulsystem. In D. Abendroth-Timmer & G. Bach (Eds.), *Mehrsprachiges Europa. Festschrift für Michael Wendt zum 60. Geburtstag* (pp. 191-206). Tübingen: Narr.

Bleyhl, W. (2001b). Die schulische Sprachenwahl oder: Ist es gleichgültig, in welcher Sprache man denkt? Anmerkungen zur Mehrsprachigkeit in einer Welt der Globalisierung. *Frühbeginn Fremdsprachen, 2*, 5-10, & *Frühbeginn Fremdsprachen, 3*, 5-9 .

Bleyhl, W. (2001c). Projekt 'Implizite und explizite Lernstrategien im fremdsprachlichen Anfangsunterricht'. In A. Bonnet & P. W. Kahl (Eds.), *Innovation und Tradition im Englischunterricht* (pp. 58-77). Stuttgart: Klett.

Brinkmann, E., Brügelmann, H., Otto, M., Rickelt, K., & Sommer, J. (1997). Rechtschreibmuster organisieren sich. Rechtschreibschwierigkeiten und orthographische Richtigkeit von Lisas ersten 1.800 Wörtern. In R. Voß (Ed.), *Die Schule neu erfinden* (pp. 209-215). Neuwied: Luchterhand.

Bruner, J. (1997). *Wie das Kind sprechen lernt.* Bern: Huber.

Changeux, J.-P. (1983). *L'homme neuronal.* Paris: Fayard.

Council of Europe (Ed.). (2001). *A common European framework of reference for languages: Learning, teaching, assessment.* Cambridge: Cambridge University Press.

Curtain, H. A., & Pesola, C. A. (1988). *Languages and children – making the match.* Reading, Mass.: Addison-Wesley.

Doyé, P., & Lüttge, D. (1977). *Untersuchungen zum Englischunterricht in der Grundschule.* Braunschweig: Westermann.

Doyé, P. (1993). Fremdsprachenerziehung in der Grundschule. *Zeitschrift für Fremdsprachenforschung, 4*(1), 48-90.

Ellis, R. (1994). *The study of second language acquisition.* Oxford: Oxford University Press.

Ellis, R. (1997). *Second language acquisition.* Oxford: Oxford University Press.

Freudenstein, R. (2000, April). *Ziel des Spracherwerbs in einem modernen Europa*. Paper presented at the *Forum Realschule*, Akademie Calw.

Gardner, H. (1991). *The unschooled mind. How children think and how schools should teach.* New York: Basic Books.

Gopnik, A., Kuhl, P., & Meltzoff, A. (1999). *The scientist in the crib. Minds, brains, and how children learn.* New York: Morrow.

Haken, H. (1981). *Erfolgsgeheimnisse der Natur. Synergetik: Die Lehre vom Zusammenwirken.* Stuttgart: DVA.

Ingendahl, W. (1999). *Sprachreflexion statt Grammatik – ein didaktisches Konzept für alle Schulstufen.* Tübingen: Niemeyer.

Jaffke, C. (1996). *Fremdsprachenunterricht auf der Primarstufe. Seine Begründung und Praxis in der Waldorfpädagogik* (2nd ed.). Weinheim: Deutscher Studien Verlag.

Karpf, A. (1990). *Selbstorganisationsprozesse in der sprachlichen Ontogenese: Erst- und Fremdsprache(n).* Tübingen: Narr.

Kielhöfer, B., & Jonekeit, S. (1998). *Zweisprachige Kindererziehung* (10th ed.). Tübingen: Stauffenberg.

Krohn, W., & Küppers, G. (Eds.). (1992). *Emergenz: Die Entstehung von Ordnung, Organisation und Bedeutung.* Frankfurt/M.: Suhrkamp.

Largo, R. H. (1999). *Kinderjahre. Die Individualität des Kindes als erzieherische Herausforderung.* München: Piper.

Largo, R. H. (2001). *Babyjahre. Die frühkindliche Entwicklung aus biologischer Sicht.* München: Piper.

Larsen-Freeman, D. (1997). Chaos/complexity science and second language acquisition. *Applied Linguistics, 18*(2), 141-165.

Le Pape Racine, C. (2000). *Immersion – Starthilfe für mehrsprachige Projekte. Einführung in eine Didaktik des Zweitsprachunterrichts.* Zürich: Pestalozzianum Verlag.

Marchman, V. A., & Bates, E. (1994). Continuity in lexical and morphological development: a test of the critical mass hypothesis. *Journal of Child Language, 21*, 339-366.

Melenk, H., & Dörfel, H. (Eds.). (1998). *Fremdsprachenunterricht in der Grundschule: das amerikanische Immersionsmodell.* Baltmannsweiler: Schneider-Verlag Hohengehren.

Moerk, E. L. (1992). *First language taught and learned.* Baltimore: Brookes.

Palmer, H. E., & Palmer, D. (1925). *English through actions.* London: Longman.

Peltzer-Karpf, A., & Zangl, R. (1998). *Die Dynamik des frühen Fremdsprachenerwerbs.* Tübingen: Narr.

Pelz, M. (Ed.). (1989). *Lerne die Sprache des Nachbarn – Grenzüberschreitende Spracharbeit zwischen Deutschland und Frankreich.* Frankfurt/M.: Diesterweg.

Prigogine, I. (1979). *Vom Sein zum Werden. Zeit und Komplexität in den Naturwissenschaften.* München: Piper.

Purdy, J. (2001, August 23). Wir und die andern. Warum die Amerikaner nicht begreifen, dass der Rest der Welt sie als Imperialmacht fürchtet. *Die Zeit,* p. 3.

Roth, G. (1997). *Das Gehirn und seine Wirklichkeit. Kognitive Neurobiologie und ihre philosophischen Konsequenzen.* Frankfurt/M.: Suhrkamp.

Singer, W. (1997). Der Beobachter im Gehirn. In H. Meier & D. Ploog (Eds.), *Der Mensch und sein Gehirn. Die Folgen der Evolution* (pp. 35-65). München: Piper.

Singer, W. (1998). Zur Selbstorganisation kognitiver Strukturen. In E. Pöppel (Ed.), *Gehirn und Bewusstsein* (pp. 45-59). Weinheim: VCH.

Smith, F. (1978). *Reading.* Cambridge: Cambridge University Press.

Stutterheim, C. v. (1997). Zum Ausdruck von Zeit- und Raumkonzeptionen in deutschen und englischen Texten. *Zeitschrift für germanistische Linguistik, 25*(2), 147-166.

Szagun, G. (1993). *Sprachentwicklung beim Kind. Eine Einführung* (5th ed.). Weinheim: Psychologie-Verlags-Union.

Timm, J.-P. (Ed.). (1995). *Ganzheitlicher Fremdsprachenunterricht.* Weinheim: Deutscher Studien Verlag.

Timm, J.-P. (Ed.). (1998). *Englisch lehren und lernen. Didaktik des Englischunterrichts.* Berlin: Cornelsen.

VanPatten, B. (1992a). Second-language-acquisition research and foreign language teaching. Part 1. *ADFL Bulletin, 23*(2), 52-56.

VanPatten, B. (1992b). Second-language-acquisition research and foreign language teaching. Part 2. *ADFL Bulletin, 23*(3), 23-27.

Wode, H. (1988). *Psycholinguistik. Eine Einführung in die Lehr- und Lernbarkeit von Sprachen.* Ismaning: Hueber.

Wode, H. (1995). *Lernen in der Fremdsprache. Grundzüge von Immersion und bilingualem Unterricht.* Ismaning: Hueber.

Zangl, R. (1998). *Dynamische Muster in der sprachlichen Ontogenese. Bilingualismus, Erst- und Fremdsprachenerwerb.* Tübingen: Narr.

Zydatiß, W. (2000). *Bilingualer Unterricht in der Grundschule. Entwurf eines Spracherwerbskonzepts für zweisprachige Immersionsprogramme.* Ismaning: Hueber.

Early foreign language learning in first grade elementary school

Results from a school experiment in Baden-Württemberg with the European project DINOCROC

Gerhard W. Schnaitmann

Im Bundesland Baden-Württemberg gab es bis zum Jahr 2000 keine systematische Planung für frühes Fremdsprachenlernen weder in der Lehrersausbildung an den Pädagogischen Hochschulen noch an den Grundschulen selbst. Dieses Faktum hing damit zusammen, dass das Erlernen von Fremdsprachen an Grundschulen bislang nicht Bestandteil des Bildungsplanes für Grundschulen war. Die ersten Entwicklungen für Englisch- und Französischunterricht gab es in Grundschulen bereits 1965 und 1976 und in den frühen 90er Jahren. Dies gab die Grundlage für weitere Versuche und für das Fremdsprachenprojekt DINOCROC, das durch die Europäische Union gefördert wurde. In dem Schulversuch wurden in den ersten und zweiten Klassen die Methode und die Materialien des EU-Projekts unter den schulischen Bedingungen, die durch das Kultusministerium bzw. die geltenden Bildungspläne für Grundschulen vorlagen, getestet. Es geht dabei darum, dass die Kinder der Grundschule in einer kindgemäßen Art, wie beim Erwerb der Muttersprache, eine Fremdsprache erlernen. Bei dieser Methode werden kurze kommunikative Phasen in der Fremdsprache in den regulären Unterricht integriert. Im Vordergrund der Methode DINOCROC steht die Förderung der Phantasie, des Vorstellungsvermögens, der Kreativität und der Ausdrucksfähigkeit in der Fremdsprache. Diese Fähigkeiten konnten bei den Schülerinnen und Schülern in den empirischen Untersuchungen des Schulversuchs nachgewiesen werden.

In the federal state of Baden-Württemberg there has been a lack of systematic planning in the training for elementary school foreign language teaching given at teachers' colleges, as well as in elementary school foreign language teaching itself up until now. This results from the fact that elementary school foreign language learning has not been an element laid out either in the school curriculum or in the study and examination guidelines of teachers' colleges.

The first approaches to teaching French and English in elementary schools in 1965 and 1976 and in the early 1990s form the basis of the trial phase and systematic planning of a new approach to foreign language teaching and learning, as is laid out in a project supported by the European Union.

At the beginning, the elementary-school children are supposed to learn the foreign language, English, in a child-friendly manner, likened to the learning of their mother tongue with the mother. In this process, the short communicative phases of the foreign language take place within the regular school hours. It is shown from experiences made with this project that a child's degree of withdrawal, the degree of disruptive behavior, and the ability in "let's pretend play" (degree of imagination / creativity / initiative / expressiveness) are crucial to successful learning while working according to the psycholinguistic approach.

1. The pilot study DINOCROC – a European project for early foreign language learning

Originally, the DINOCROC project was a European Sokrates-Lingua-A-Project for early foreign language learning with 12 partners from 8 European countries. Prior to the project, the DINOCROC method was used exclusively in kindergartens in Italy and pre-school classes in the Netherlands. From 1998 to 2000, DINOCROC was tested for the first time in the first and second grades of elementary school in all of the European countries that participated. Baden-Württemberg was the only participating partner in Germany.

The word DINOCROC is created by blending the two English words "DINOsaur" and "CROCodile". Two dinocrocs, called Hocus and Lotus, are the main characters of the DINOCROC method and textbook.

The DINOCROC project was introduced in Baden-Württemberg in the context of a school experiment in the school year 1998/99 with 20 elementary schools, 60 classes and over 1300 children, mainly in the cities and the surrounding areas of Göppingen, Heilbronn, Ludwigsburg and Stuttgart. 30 schools with approximately 90 classes were then involved in the school year 1999/2000. In all cases the introduction and application of the DINOCROC method was based solely on the voluntary decision of each school and each class teacher to teach foreign languages in the first and second grades. Additional teaching hours or reductions of the participating teachers' normal teaching load could not be provided. This school experiment, which was guided by the State Institute for Education and Teaching in Stuttgart (*Landesinstitut für Erziehung und Unterricht Stuttgart*), was related to the plans to introduce foreign language learning beginning in the first grades of Baden-Württemberg's elementary schools.

2. The textbook *Dinocroc – The Adventures of Hocus and Lotus*

The textbooks *Dinocroc – The Adventures of Hocus and Lotus* contain a series of short stories designed for early foreign language learning (Taeschner, 1997, 1999a). It currently consists of three teaching units, six exercise books, audio tapes, vocabulary cards, a teacher's handbook and a T-shirt. It was developed by Taeschner, a psycholinguist, at the University La Sapienza in Rome (Taeschner, 1991) and is based on the principles of holistic learning oriented towards L1 acquisition. Major concepts are action-orientation, affective motivation, music and imagination, a narrative approach, identification with the instructor, imitation and role plays.

2.1 Content

The textbooks (Taeschner, 1997, 1999a) pick up situations from the life of children and transfer them to the two main characters Hocus and Pocus in a manner suitable for children (infant scheme, cartoons, adequate gender roles, stimulating imagination). The two dinocroc characters resemble a mixture of a dinosaur and crocodile living together, along with other animals, in a park.

Moreover, each story contains a few easy exercises for children already able to read and write. The stories are first sung on the audio tapes followed by a karaoke version; a game of dominoes with pictures allows children to learn the most important words.

The stories in each format can be dealt with in the order presented, but it is also possible to deal with the stories of each kit in any order, for example by mixing them. However, the latter is only possible after Format 2 in Kit I: "Hocus meets Lotus" (Taeschner et al., 1997)

A "Teacher's Guide" in English (Taeschner et al., 1999b) is available for teachers with a detailed description of the implementation of each format in class. This guide contains ideas for a general introduction, considerations of lexical content as well as grammatical categories and grammar in the texts. A detailed description of each story (very much in the form of a screenplay script) is also included.

Figure 1. Sample script (excerpt taken from Format 1: "Hocus the Dinocroc")

Summary:
Hocus, a dinocroc, hatches from an egg. When he meets a bird, he wonders if he is a bird. When he meets a duck, he wonders if he is a duck. When he meets a frog, he wonders if he is a frog. But he isn't any of these. Then he finds a mirror and decides he is Hocus the dinocroc.

Act I

Actions	Language
The pupils are in a circle. The teacher is one step outside the circle. The teacher indicates the centre of the circle. Here lies the imaginary egg.	
The teacher as narrator:	*Once upon a time there was an egg.*
The teacher makes an egg form with her hands. Then she says:	*The egg of a dinocroc. And inside the egg was Hocus!*
The teacher goes back into the middle of the circle and crouches small as if she were inside an egg:	Croc croc croc!
The teacher as narrator outside the circle, cups her ear and whispers:	*Ssss.... Ssssss listen!* *Ssss.... Ssssss listen!*
The pupils cup their ears and listen. They say:	Ssss.... Ssssss listen!
The teacher returns to the position of the curled up Hocus and knocks against the inside of the eggshell with her fists:	Croc croc croc!
The teacher beckons the children to imitate her:	Croc croc croc!
The teacher as narrator:	*Hey, what's that?*

Since Hocus represents the male role and Lotus the female role in the stories, both boys and girls are able to identify with the characters. Vocabulary and grammar are not presented in a linear progression but are adapted to the specific context. Redundancy and/or difficult grammatical structures are accepted within the context of the natural approach to foreign language learning. On this matter, reports from practice have not mentioned any difficulty in the children's learning process.

2.2 Method

The DINOCROC method is based on a narrative technique, gestures, mimicry and music. The teacher and the children's identification with the teacher play a central role (Blondin et al., 1998).

Studies by Taeschner on the quality of the lessons (Spadola & Taeschner, 1991; Taeschner, 1993) proved the teacher's narrative technique to be a decisive factor. An analysis of the instructor's teaching behavior showed the difference between individual teachers: While some were able to create the "magic moment" in story-telling, others, despite following the textbook guidelines, lacked this entrancing ability.

The basic element in the DINOCROC method is the so-called format. It is based on J. S. Bruner's "format approach" (see Taeschner, 1991) in which a format describes regular and recurring daily events (for example eating, drinking, sleeping). Due to the repetitiveness of these events it is possible to predict others' actions. This is a common trait in human nature: Expectations about the behavior of others are determined by shared and repeated actions, i.e. the format. The necessity of communication is a result of these expectations. Shared habits and actions are the basis for an understanding of children's and adults' needs to communicate.

The formats provide for a good relationship between the teacher and the children. The adult actively picks up the child's intentions and is involved in a permanent effort of interpreting, commenting, expanding, repeating and perhaps even misunderstanding to finally result in understanding or a new task. This is defined as a "shared action" by Bruner.

The adult's behavior within this shared action must exhibit certain characteristics in order for a successful exchange and interpretation of experiences to take place. His behavior should be consistent and systematic, thus offering clues leading to an increase in predictability. Therefore, the need for communication grows with these shared actions or formats.

Additionally, the "meaning" of words is also "developed". Initially a word presents a meaningless cluster of sounds. It is then gradually connected with the context in which it is used by the adult. The child observes, rearranges objects and shares experiences. In this way the word is experienced in concrete terms, it is manipulated and connected with specific situations, objects and actions. After many repetitions the word is eventually separated from its original context and becomes the symbol for an object. The child has now understood the meaning of the word and learns to use it actively himself.

A language is not learned without a suitable context. Preparing such a context for foreign language learning requires specific organization, as for example in the game "Hocus and Lotus at home and at school" and the enthusiasm to play it over and over again. For this game it makes sense to take up a new role in which the child is no longer allowed and able to speak German. Ideally, this role switch can be made clear by using a symbolic object, for example by wearing the "magic T-shirt" or working with the puppets Hocus or Lotus. The instructor should stick to the rules during the game so as not to disappoint the child or disparage the game.

Unambiguous gestures, mimicry and a consistent narrative structure also make the story or format comprehensible without the use of words. This makes it easy to include words of the foreign language in acting. The more the children repeat the stories, the better they understand them. Whatever remains unclear while acting becomes clear with the help of the textbook pictures or transparencies.

Furthermore, a "mini-musical" was composed for each story in which song, dialogue and sounds express the course of events. This enables the child to learn vocabulary and sentence structures by heart in a pleasant and emotionally appealing way. A song version of each story can be found on side one of each tape. The child listens to these songs until he/she has learned the text. It is then able to sing the songs along with the instrumental version on side two of the tape.

The "magic relationship" between the narrator and the fictitious characters stands in the center of the entire introductory phase and the entrance into the foreign language world of Hocus and Locus by symbolic means such as wearing the magic T-shirt, by imitative speech while acting, by movement and by music. This gives the children the chance to enter a world of imagination and practice the new language. Even shy children, children with motor problems, and children from different cultural backgrounds with difficulties in using the German language have the opportunity to express themselves. In the role of a fictitious character these children are able to act without being hindered by the obstacles they encounter in daily life.

As in all lessons, the teacher's personality as a "magic teacher" plays a decisive role. The successful instructor is positively and completely involved in the story. She tells, lives and experiences the story. Gestures, mimicry and personal involvement in the story are crucial factors for success. The "audience", as addressees of the story, must be borne in mind. The instructor's role is to present the subject matter in an interesting and entertaining manner. Enforcing discipline or exercising strict control over the pupils is inappropriate in this phase and would destroy the magic of the story. The children would be agitated and further disciplinary measures would have to be taken. Hence, it is important that the teacher can let go of his "normal" striving for order and control.

The positive approach of this narrative, creative, musical, and reinforcing method, which allows for student identification with a model, is appropriate for children and converges with holistic and action-oriented methods for elementary school teaching.

3. Feedback from practice and analysis of first empirical studies

The above mentioned features of the DINOCROC method have been acknowledged by a first questioning of the participating instructors (Rattay-Förstl & Schnaitmann, 2000; Schnaitmann, 1999, 2000, 2001) reporting overall great successes in both first and second grades of elementary school. Especially the music and the fantasy world have been widely accepted. The repetitive patterns, to which some variety can be introduced with the supplementary material, rapidly allow children to use the foreign language independently at a very early point in the learning process. They are able to transfer and apply this knowledge in other situations, for example in other lessons such as math, sports and music as well as in everyday situations, for example at home when trying to teach interested siblings or friends elements of the foreign language. Despite a lack of performance pressure, achievements are high (in some cases, two volumes of the textbook were covered and played in the first year and were partly read by the children themselves). This is appreciated by both children and instructors.

The experience of the majority of parents and students, teachers and school boards in this study with the DINOCROC method has been good. They support this method as a suitable approach for the early introduction of foreign language learning into the school system.

Already the first questioning of teachers in the school year 1998/99 yielded the following positive feedback:

- All participants were very interested in foreign language lessons beginning in the first grade.
- The material is very popular with children and parents.
- The material allows a varied and flexible implementation and can be expanded in the form of songs, action-orientedness and the communicative approach (drama, mime, role play, visual instruction).
- The instructor plays a central role in motivation and the implementation of the material.
- The material is suitable for student-centered and topic-centered teaching and enhances open and autonomous forms of learning (teachers have reported discussions amongst pupils in the corridor about the meaning of individual words).
- The songs, song texts and musical accompaniment are fun, much enjoyed and grasped quickly. Reports state that pupils in a poorly sound-proofed school building sang along when hearing the songs coming out of another classroom. Up to six different classes joined in singing, even in a math lesson. This was seen as cheering up rather than disrupting.

- The visual presentation of the materials is adequate for children (cartoons, infant scheme, adequate gender roles, stimulating, imaginative, suitable for daily situations, according to pupils "hip" and "cool").
- The material prompts individual work and role plays. It is passed on to younger siblings and kindergarten children. Participants from other classes are "instructed" by the "English children" and the songs are sung by pupils who are not part of the study.
- Transfer to everyday situations is possible (see above).
- An integrative approach is possible. Currently, 15-20 minute sequences are taught rather than the intended 30 minutes. The integration of English into other subjects such as math and local history, geography, and natural history is guaranteed by the flexible use of complementary material (numbers, colors, etc.).
- Both the material and the method are suitable for children and their abilities. The level of performance is high in most classes and the material of the subsequent formats is needed.
- There is no pressure on performance and children have positive learning experiences.
- The vocabulary is well-structured and well-sequenced allowing transfers to new situations even at an early stage of foreign language learning.
- "Storytelling" satisfies the child's need for listening to (and reading) coherent stories. This corresponds to the recommended storytelling practice in elementary school pedagogy.
- Instructors are able to expand and further develop their own methods as well as the material.
- Participating teachers have initiated successful groups for the exchange of information and experience.

When questioning the participating instructors, it was striking that everyone was informed about the DINOCROC method prior to having worked with it. Foreign language learning concepts for elementary school were unknown to only 10% of the questioned teachers. However, 24% claimed to be unfamiliar with publishers' student materials for elementary school foreign language learning.

The evaluation of students' performance is generally considered problematic at this beginning level due to the lack of written performance. However, only 14% of the teachers stated that they had not evaluated their students' performance. The majority (53%) of the teachers worked with observation profiles (also individual observation), 5% wrote a school report, and 21% "evaluated" the students' learning progress and performance through reading, oral checks and playing the formats.

With respect to the methodological approach in early foreign language learning, 34% of the teachers claimed to have worked exclusively according to the DINOCROC concept while 23% used additional material (games, pictures, transparencies, English songs). Other methodological means were used by 31%. Many used fewer repetitions than suggested in the handbook.

80% of the questioned teachers were able to confirm the students' learning progress ("The students understand a lot of English even outside the format", "Students' pronunciation improved continuously as did sentence structure. Students used English phrases and sentence structures when playing", "Some children even talked to each other like Hocus and Lotus", "The children understand the stories more and more and, in some cases, continue them on their own").

With respect to learning difficulties, only 15% claimed that students had problems, 42% did not encounter any difficulty and 31% observed occasional learning difficulties. The teachers' concerns included the following:

- "Some boys felt awkward when acting and were inhibited to gesticulate" (from the beginning, a number of colleagues were confronted with and still face this problem; some of them left the study after having been introduced to the DINOCROC method).
- "Acting and mime were impeded by the great number of students in class" (29 students in the first grade).
- "The constant repetitions were tiring. Some students were no longer interested or bored after a number of repetitions."
- "The frequent switching of roles led to comprehension difficulties."

Finally, another teacher's comment:

> The DINOCROC model can be integrated without difficulty and it is fun for children. The characters and stories to identify with are appealing. The children enjoy the catchy songs and rhythms. There is a constant learning process. The children feel prompted to play the stories over and over again - even at home. This approach supports the feeling for and openness towards a foreign language.

Detailed information on the results of the extensive questioning of teachers and students in the second year of the project (1999/2000) can be obtained from the author (gerhard.schnaitmann@t-online.de).

References

Blondin, C., Candelier, M., Edelenbos, P., Johnstone, R., Kubanek-German, A., & Taeschner, T. (1998). *Fremdsprachen für die Kinder Europas. Ergebnisse und Empfehlungen der Forschung*. Berlin: Cornelsen.

Rattay-Förstl, B., & Schnaitmann, G. W. (2000). Aus dem Fenster gesehen: Das europäische Fremdsprachenprojekt I.D.E.A. DINOCROC. *Unterrichten, erziehen. Die Zeitschrift für kreative Lehrerinnen und Lehrer, 19*(1), 4.

Schnaitmann, G. W. (1999). *Zweiter Bericht zum Sokrates-Lingua-A-Projekt I.D.E.A DINOCROC in Baden-Württemberg für den Zeitraum September 1998 bis August 1999*. Stuttgart: Unveröffentlichtes Manuskript und Abschlussbericht für das Kultusministerium Baden-Württemberg.

Schnaitmann, G. W. (2000). Das europäische Fremdsprachenprojekt I.D.E.A. DINOCROC – ein europäischer Schulversuch für frühes Fremdsprachenlernen an Grundschulen in Baden-Württemberg. *Lehren und Lernen, 26*(4), 3-9.

Schnaitmann, G. W. (2001). *Frühes Fremdsprachenlernen in der Eingangsstufe der Grundschule. Konzeption zu und Erfahrungen aus einem pädagogischen Schulversuch in Baden-Württemberg.* Publikation zum 18. DGFF-Kongress in Dortmund, Oktober 1999. Retrieved May 22, 2002, from the World Wide Web: http://www.dgff.de/publ-schnaitmann.html

Spadola, L., & Taeschner, T. (1991). Recitando s'impara in La scuola si aggiorna. *Nuova Eri – Edizione Rai,* 27-31.

Taeschner, T. (1991). *A developmental psycholinguistic approach to second language teaching*. Ablex: Norwood.

Taeschner, T. (1993). *Insegnare con il format*. Roma: Anicia.

Taeschner, T., Plooij, F. X., Etxeberria, F., Arzamendi, J., & O'Halon, C. (1997). *The adventures of Hocus and Lotus. Impariamo L'Inglese con le Favole*. I e II Livello (Format 1 to 12). Milano: FrancoAngeli/Le COMETE.

Taeschner, T., Plooij, F. X., Etxeberria, F., Arzamendi, J., Garagorri, X., & O'Halon, C. (1999a). *The adventures of Hocus and Lotus. Impariamo L'Inglese con le Favole*. I e II Livello (Format 13 to 18). Milano: FrancoAngeli/Le COMETE.

Taeschner, T., Plooij, F. X., Etxeberria, F., Arzamendi, J., Garagorri, X., & O'Halon, C. (1999b). *Teacher's guide: The adventures of Hocus and Lotus*, Scripts 1-6. Rom: DINOCROC International Training Institute.

Language learning
in a cooperative, holistic, task-oriented, student-centred way

Foreign language practice and cooperative learning

Claudia Finkbeiner

Im folgenden Beitrag wird fremdsprachliches Üben in einem kooperativen Lehr-/Lern-arrangement beschrieben. Dazu werden lernpsychologische Grundlagen aufgezeigt, die implizieren, dass Üben für einen Zuwachs an Kompetenz im Allgemeinen sowie für eine Professionalisierung des eigenen Fremdsprachenlernens im Speziellen wichtig ist. Die Affinität, die zwischen Üben und kooperativem Lernen besteht, wird anhand von ganz konkreten Beispielen aus der Unterrichtspraxis belegt.

In this article foreign language practice will be described within the context of cooperative learning and teaching arrangements. Learning psychological principles will be described, which imply that practice is especially important for growth in competence as well as for professionalism in foreign language learning. The affinity which exists between practice and cooperative learning will be demonstrated with reference to concrete classroom examples.

1. Setting the ground

In the most recent PISA (Program of International Student Assessment) study, German students received bad marks in all three domains of literacy defined by the OECD consortium: reading, mathematics and sciences (Organisation for Economic Co-operation and Development, 2001). Despite the bad news, PISA can only be seen as another wake-up call following TIMSS (Third Mathematical and Science Study) which had shocked people in Germany before. A few years later one seems to be a bit more prepared for yet another renaissance of mind-boggling outcomes. These outcomes have triggered a very intense discussion on the question whether German students can still compete with students in other countries on the basis of the learning standards defined by the OECD consortium.

Some of the reasons for the poor performance both in the TIMS and PISA studies are of major interest for foreign language teaching and learning and emphasize the importance of practice activities. Even though reading literacy was tested in the mother tongue only, the PISA results mirror findings from my own foreign language reading study to a certain degree. My reading research was conducted between 1994 and 1998 (Finkbeiner, 1997, 1998, 2000). One of the most important outcomes of that study is that a high percentage of grade-nine students performed on a surface level rather than on a deep level when reading EFL (English as a Foreign Language) texts. The explanation is that the students who participated in my study seemed to have adapted to their particular school system with its specific testing procedures.

This can be explained as follows: Risk taking leads to a higher error quotient, which in turn results in a deduction when students' tests are graded. This implies that risk taking can have a dramatic and negative effect on test results in foreign language learning, whereas word-to-word processing, at a lower risk level, can lead to success. In other words, students unconsciously develop and use certain "strategies" which help them earn a passing grade. These "strategies" differ highly in quality from the learning strategies we actually would like to be taught and learned in schools.

Another important explanation for the German students' low scores in the TIMS and PISA studies is that according to Baumert, head of the Max-Planck-Institute for Educational Research in Berlin, lessons do not provide enough time for reflection and higher thinking. Mere learning phases and phases of performance and testing are mixed too often.[1] Hence, phases with open and autonomous practice, group learning, experimentation, logical problem solving in a team on the basis of challenging tasks, as in riddles or brain teasers, etc., are rare. Such phases, which allow the students to practice together without having to face reprehensive consequences if a failure occurs, must be consciously and willingly planned by the teachers. They must be set in contexts which are basically free of anxiety and pressure.

This means that space and time have to be allotted for phases in which mistakes can be made and questions can be posed with reference to other students' contributions. This is an absolutely necessary pre-

---

1 "Wie klug sind die Deutschen?" In: *Focus, 25*, 1999, pp. 67-78.

condition for higher-order thinking since students can only ask intelligent questions and make intelligent mistakes if they have had the chance to actually grasp and understand the subject matter.

Another explanation for the poor results of German students in TIMSS and PISA lies in the importance of life-long learning. Due to the rapid out-datedness of information and knowledge it becomes essential that learners permanently develop and improve their competences and abilities from infancy to old age. Life-long learning and, thus, life-long practice, are to make a socially acceptable and meaningful form of life possible, enabling survival in the era of mass media and mass information. One factor in this endeavor is to be able to cooperate with others in different learning situations, both in homogenous and heterogeneous groups.

It is also important to prepare our students for the unpredictable and unknown. To use a metaphor: In some school settings, too many questions and tasks seem to orbit around "known" planets in our own "known" solar system. Even though we know that there are so many more galaxies, stars and even planets, we usually ignore this fact and see our own system as the center of the universe. This way, learners are led into a meta-cognitive dead-end street as they are neither challenged by the unknown nor are they prepared to cope with new learning situations in a productive and intelligent way. Instead of underrating students with monotonous exercises we have to challenge them with stimulating and brain-activating scenarios.

2. Learning psychological principles and EFL practice

In order for practice to be successful, it has to follow certain learning psychological principles. This will be clarified within the context of several scientific concepts and controversies which include the following:

- critical period
- comprehensible input
- interaction and cooperation

- autonomous learning
- explicit versus implicit learning
- elaboration
- continuing practice
- motivation and interest
- authenticity
- awareness

Critical period: The so-called critical period is a very important notion to begin with, as it is used as an argument in the debate about what age would be best to start practicing a second or foreign language. The term critical period was coined by the linguist Eric Lenneberg (cf. Lightbown & Spada, 1994, p. 11) and describes the period from an age of two years up to puberty which is characterized by neuronal brain plasticity. This period is marked by an increase in language development and competence on the one hand and lateralization of the brain on the other hand. Accordingly, scientists assume that foreign language practice should start as early as possible (Lightbown & Spada, 1994). The concept of the critical period is therefore a main argument for proponents of early foreign language learning.

However, it should be taken into consideration that the exact nature of the impact of the brain's lateralization on the development of language competence has not yet been proven in neuro-psychological studies, thus leading to controversial discussions (Crystal, 1991, p. 265). Empirical research confirming the existence of a critical period does not exist. Of course, there is evidence that children who do not acquire their first language before puberty (for example, due to social deprivation) will never be able to do so thereafter. Yet this L1 principle cannot simply be applied to L2 learning.

Furthermore, the issue of the so-called lateralization of the brain has been increasingly and critically scrutinized. The left-right model does not seem to explain certain phenomena sufficiently, such as the brain's high compensation capacity. For example, when parts of the brain get injured, other parts, which are located somewhere totally different, can take over specific brain functions.

Despite these restrictions with regard to the application of the critical period hypothesis on foreign language learning, there is a clear consensus that certain abilities, such as pronunciation and listening comprehension, can best be practiced and developed at an early age. In addition, a young child's positive and unbiased approach to a foreign language very much supports early learning of a foreign language.

Comprehensible input: This principle focuses on the questions of quantity and quality in practice. How much foreign language input do we need and how can the quality of that input be characterized? According to Krashen (1996), new structures and words can be learned best if the learner is exposed to as much comprehensible input as possible. Krashen's theory states that rather than offering highly structured practice activities, tasks enabling successful communication should preferably be provided (ibid.). Thus, it would be a fallacy to conclude that we could actually provide such input by media alone. For input to be effective in foreign language practice, it has to be easily understood and communicated.

Interaction and cooperation: According to Vygotsky (1978), social interaction plays a crucial role in the development of cognition: learning occurs through social contact. Vygotsky states that every function in the child's cultural development appears twice: first on the social level and then on the individual level. Thus, comprehension processes can best be mediated by social interaction with communication partners (teachers, tutors, mediators, mothers, fathers, siblings, peers, etc.). Butzkamm underlines that the phenomenon of "motherese", which describes a mother's or caretaker's talk to a child, follows typical patterns of an ideal instructional practice situation, such as communicative error feedback, distinct and slow speech and repetition (Butzkamm, 1989).

Autonomous learning: Socio-cultural and individual learning are not exclusive of each other (Vygotsky, 1978). Depending on the individual learner type, the material to be practiced is autonomously acquired with the use of different learning techniques and learning strategies (Rampillon & Zimmermann, 1997). This, however, does not imply that teachers do not have any responsibility for the learner's learning process. On the contrary, teachers must create optimal and rich language learning environments that allow their learners to acquire fundamental qualifications, construct a profound general knowledge, and develop a good command of the target language.

Explicit versus implicit learning: Research on explicit and implicit learning has discovered a great discrepancy between knowledge that was acquired implicitly and knowledge acquired explicitly. It cannot be simply deduced that knowledge which was acquired by a learner explicitly can later be applied as implicit knowledge in an ordinary conversation. On the contrary, explicit knowledge is often not applied as implicit knowledge in natural conversations. This question remains most virulent in our discussion, since precise statements on how practice is to be performed best cannot be made (Ellis, 1994; Finkbeiner, 2001; Krashen, 1996).

Elaboration: Within the whole range of strategies, elaboration strategies play an important role in intellectually and academically inspiring practice (Finkbeiner, 1997). The organization of learning activities must link up to the world and to the experiences students make in their daily lives. Only in this way can practice help to develop social competence and offer orientation. We must focus on the question: Do our students have the prior knowledge necessary to link up to a certain subject matter? If this prior-knowledge base is not provided, then the best learning strategies cannot compensate for complete non-knowledge and ignorance.

Continuing practice: Recent findings in learning psychology emphasize the importance of repeating material in certain periods of time in order to internalize and memorize what has been learned. Continuing practice activities are also important to prevent language loss. A new word has to be repeated frequently; for best results, repetition should take place after a minute, after an hour, after a day, after two days, after a week, after a month, after six months. If the word is still known after six months, one can assume that it has been stored in long-term memory (Finkbeiner, 1995).

Motivation and interest: Motivation and interest play a vital role in learning by enhancing a thorough processing of the language being learned (Finkbeiner, 1997, 1998). They contribute to higher and more complex intellectual thinking.

Authenticity: Practice activities should be based on an authentic background that bears relevance to and importance for the learner (van Lier, 1996). This means that the content of the subject matter itself as well as the tasks connected to it should be considered as the center point of interest rather than concentrating on structural elements of the foreign language such as grammar, vocabulary, and pronunciation.

This supports the creation of tasks which allow functional and communicative practice.

Awareness: Learning awareness, meta-cognitive awareness, language awareness, and cultural awareness are considered important vehicles in language learning. Language awareness can be described as "a person's sensitivity to and conscious awareness of the nature of language and its role in human life" (Donmall, 1985, p. 7). Cultural awareness, by analogy, can be understood as a person's sensitivity to and conscious awareness of the nature of culture, its role in human life and its reflection in language. Learning awareness comprises metacognitive awareness, that is, the reflection upon how to learn. Furthermore, it includes the reflection on the social factor of learning, such as individual versus group learning.

3. Foreign language practice between individualization and socialization

As shown above, practice is a highly individual process which depends on both motivational and cognitive aspects. At the same time, the demands posed in a modern society can only be dealt with in forms of cooperative management and mutual support. This dichotomous relationship between individualization on the one hand and socialization on the other conforms to the concept of "cooperative practice".

The following description of practice activities applies Huber's concept of cooperative learning to foreign language teaching (Huber, 2001). Additionally, van Lier's principles for foreign language learning – authenticity, awareness, and autonomy – will be taken into consideration (van Lier, 1996). These two approaches will, in the following, be exemplified for the teaching of English as a foreign language in cooperative learning arrangements for the primary school level (age 6 to 10) and the secondary school level I (age 10 to 16).

3.1 Models for the organization of cooperative learning

Three conditions are necessary in order to initiate and carry out cooperative learning processes: (1) room for making decisions, (2) mutual responsibility for the learning process of all participants involved, and

(3) individual responsibility for the group performance (Finkbeiner, 2001; Huber, 2001). These conditions logically follow the principles outlined before, such as interaction and cooperation, autonomous learning, explicit versus implicit learning, elaboration, motivation and interest, authenticity, and awareness. This type of practice includes a change in the role and function of teacher and learner since both of them have responsibility. It requires the assessment of each individual's performance as well as an evaluation of the group's performance.

Different models for organizing cooperative practice are: the partner model, the jigsaw model, the problem-solving model, the project model and the fractal model (Huber, 2001). No matter which model one chooses, one has to carefully consider the following criteria: (a) goal, (b) time frame, (c) learners, (d) learning situation, (e) authentic tasks, (f) form of cooperation, (g) complexity, and (h) organization. Examples and explanations for the partner model and the jigsaw model will be given below. All of these models have been tested in learning arrangements for different groups, and the sequence of the models has to be seen as a progression as it ranges from easy to more complex ones.

The fractal model of cooperative learning is the most elaborate model. It has the aim of supporting topic- and subject-specific knowledge as well as social competence over a long period of time (for example, for a whole school year, in a cross-disciplinary manner). This model was developed for students aged 16-19 (Herold, Landherr, & Huber, 1997). It requires a completely new organization of traditional structures, such as abandoning 45-minute lessons and the division of learning processes into single subjects.

In the following I will focus on the partner model and the jigsaw model. I will describe the models and demonstrate how to implement them in the EFL classroom. In addition, I will give a description of the materials and procedures required as well as of the accompanying evaluation and assessment.

3.2 Learning vocabulary through the partner model: Primary school level

Model description: The partner model follows the principles of peer tutoring in which both learners take turns in teaching and controlling functions (Huber, 2001). Usually two partners A and B cooperate with each other. The students are in charge of the correctness of their partner's productions and answers. The tasks have to be formulated clearly and narrowly so that control is possible. This form of cooperation is the least complex model and can therefore easily be implemented in the classroom. It is very suitable for all kinds of practicing and strictly focuses on the learning content (Huber & Roth, 1999, p. 141).

Implementation in the EFL classroom: Working in pairs is a frequently-used method in the EFL classroom. Tutoring is an appropriate means to practice vocabulary, grammatical structures, and irregular verbs. It combines the individual aspect of practicing foreign languages and the demand for a promotion of social competences in the classroom. The controlling function may prove to be difficult to fulfill by learners at the primary school level since their language competence still needs to be developed. Therefore two pairs of learners may take the place of partner A and two may take the place of partner B so that there are altogether four students playfully involved instead of originally two. Further regulations are necessary to guarantee an active and correct control of the practice activity (for example, regarding the time frame).

Looking at an example of vocabulary practice, the procedure may be as follows: Partners A pick up one card and show it to partners B. Partners B exchange their ideas and finally decide on the word for the object and/or the color represented on the card. Should partners B have difficulty in naming the object, partners A may give hints in the form of suggesting letters or syllables, or by means of gestures and mime. If partners B finally succeed in naming the object, both partners A and B will be rewarded: partners A for their effective support and teaching and partners B for finding the right solution. Partners B then practice in the same manner with partners A.

Materials: Since the teaching of written language is subordinate in teaching English as a foreign language at the primary school level, the following exercise makes use of visual and acoustic materials. The students have produced different cards with drawings of objects they have just learned to name in the foreign language. These objects may be taken from fields such as clothing, toys and colors. To enable a controlling function, partners A have to make a choice out of five different arrangements of the cards. The cards must be arranged according to the chosen sequence. The five different sequences are given on a worksheet.

A Walkman and a tape, which has to be chosen from a range of five different tapes in order to correspond with the five different sequences, are used for control. The tapes with the recordings of the different possible sequences have been prepared in advance by the teacher and the students. This form of controlling requires time-consuming preparation. However, it is of great importance for an effective form of tutoring and controlling in the early foreign language classroom.

Evaluation and assessment: Finally, the sum of all the cards (stack Partners A, stack Partners B, stack both Partners) is added for both pairs of partners A and B. There is an individual winner A or B. Additionally, AB's common and final score is compared to the results of the other pairs (CD, etc.) in class. There is one group winner in the class. Furthermore, the score for the whole class is listed. This practice activity is repeated over a period of two or three weeks.

The progress in learning (scores, percentage of hints given) is recorded over this period. Partners A and B as well as the whole class should gain increasingly higher scores with a decreasing number of hints needed.

Variation: This practice activity can be varied (a) by depositing the five possible sequences of cards in different corners of the classroom so as to create a vocabulary circuit training, (b) by including jokers to increase competition and motivation, (c) by using empty cards on which the pupils can include words they may have picked up in everyday language use or from the media (e.g. jeans, kids, T-shirt, sweatshirt, time-out, etc.), and (d) by combining the cards (e.g. object and color, or object and other adjectives) in order to increase the difficulty level of the activity.

3.3 Literary text learning through the jigsaw model: Secondary school level I

Model description: A jigsaw is a form of cooperative learning which is used for complex topics as well as for the application of complex knowledge. As a precondition, one has to divide a given topic into several specified subtopics. In general, a jigsaw consists of four main stages (see Figure 1). First of all, the students are grouped into so-called core groups. The core groups are heterogeneous groups with regard to performance, prior knowledge, sex and cultural background. Every member of a group is assigned a different part of the overall topic. His or her task is to study this part in detail to become an expert in the specific field. All groups of the class are involved in the same tasks and subtasks. As a consequence, the class has more than one expert per subtopic.

In a second phase, the experts meet in the so-called expert groups. As far as the subject-specific knowledge is considered, these groups are quite homogenous as each member has worked on the same specific task. The experts cooperate on their specific task.

In a third step, all core groups meet again. All the experts in the core group present the results of their specific fields, while the others listen and ask questions.

At the end, all members of the core groups will have been informed of every part of the topic and will, thus, have gained a complete overview of the initial topic's complexity. In a fourth step, there is a reflection on and an evaluation of the cooperation, the learning process, and the degree of success.

Material: For literary text learning, a wide range of 46 different texts can be found in *The House on Mango Street* by Sandra Cisneros (1991). The class may select the texts they would like to work with.

Implementation in the EFL classroom: The aim of the following exercise is to implement the study of "multi-ethnic literature" in coop-

Figure 1. The jigsaw model

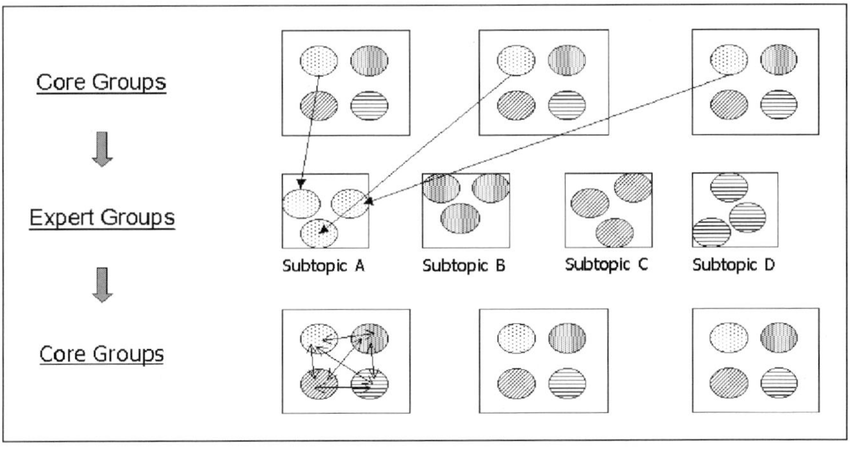

erative learning arrangements in grades 9 and 10. Heterogeneous learner groups (ABCD, etc.) are formed including 4-6 students (Aa, Ab, Ac, Ad; Ba, Bb, Bc, Bd, etc.). Each member of a group is in charge of fulfilling the following tasks: (a) reading the assigned texts, (b) writing a short summary of the assigned texts, and (c) commenting on and interpreting the assigned texts on the basis of given criteria. This means that in the case of the book *The House on Mango Street*, for example, each member of the group has to read at least one text but not more than seven texts (considering a group of six learners). The group has to produce a report on all texts assigned to the group.

The students of the different groups who have read the same texts (experts) get together to form expert groups in which they discuss their texts and find evaluation criteria in order to be able to present their texts. Each expert finally returns to his or her own group presenting the results obtained. In this phase, every individual member of the group alternately holds the role of the teacher explaining and presenting the material while the other students have the chance to ask questions.

Evaluation and assessment: In order to evaluate and assess the learning process, reports and text reviews have to be written and put together into a portfolio by each group. The group has to reflect on their cooperation as well as on the learning process and the learning products on the basis of criteria the class has agreed upon. It is very important for the teacher to suggest clear and precise criteria, particularly for classes that have not used the jigsaw before.

Variation: (a) Creative tasks connected to the texts can follow. The final aim would be to produce one's own literary texts and/or drawings; (b) elaborations can be made by relating Cisneros' texts to other texts from the field of multi-ethnic literature by authors such as Amy Tan, Julia Alvarez, Toni Morrison, and others; (c) Cisneros' texts can be examined with reference to their relevance for gender or youth issues; (d) the texts can be compared to those of male authors.

4. Prospects

Practice activities in cooperative learning arrangements in the foreign language class do not only require a good command of the target language but also organizational as well as social competences in both teacher and learner. Not all teachers and learners can be expected to learn and practice in such settings right from the beginning and without any training. As a consequence, cooperative learning must be taught and learned just as the subject matter itself (Finkbeiner, 2001). Teachers as well as students must recognize the individual and mutual responsibility for the learning and practice process. They must be able to deal with criticism and criticize constructively.

Additionally, they must have the ability to reflect, assess, and evaluate their own behavior and actions. Learners with high ambiguity tolerance are open for different results, methods and aims (Huber, 2001). As a consequence, they are not inhibited by cooperative learning arrangements and are therefore able to work effectively and successfully. Learners with low ambiguity tolerance, however, need a clear structure, a set of rules, and a defined target. As a consequence, they tend to be confronted with difficulties in cooperative learning settings.

This problem may be solved by organizing settings in a way that allows both learner types to work efficiently and profit from the practice activity. The partner model as well as the jigsaw model are facilitative in this respect, as they support the individual's effort as well as the group effort.

One fact remains clear: The future of our culturally globalizing world is uncertain. It is only through culture and language education that we can prepare ourselves and our students for this new world. The cooperative approach discussed above, if implemented in schools, at universities as well as in teacher training, will provide the basic tools for this cultural and linguistic learning process.

References

Butzkamm, W. (1989). *Psycholinguistik des Fremdsprachenunterrichts.* Tübingen: Francke.

Cisneros, S. (1991). *The house on Mango Street.* New York: Vintage Books.

Crystal, D. (1991). *The Cambridge encyclopedia of language.* Cambridge: Cambridge University Press.

Donmall, B. G. (Ed.). (1985). *Language awareness.* NCLE Reports and Papers. London: CILT.

Ellis, N. C. (Ed.). (1994). *Implicit and explicit learning of languages.* San Diego, CA: Academic Press.

Finkbeiner, C. (1995). *Englischunterricht in europäischer Dimension. Zwischen Qualifikationserwartungen der Gesellschaft und Schülereinstellungen und Schülerinteressen.* Bochum: Dr. Brockmeyer.

Finkbeiner, C. (1997). Zum Einfluß von Interessen auf das Verarbeiten von Texten. Bericht von einer empirischen Studie. In L. Bredella, H. Christ, & M. Legutke (Eds.), *Thema Fremdverstehen* (pp. 313-332). Tübingen: Narr.

Finkbeiner, C. (1998). Neue Lern- und Arbeitsmethoden im Englischunterricht: Exemplarische Analyse einer Umsetzung des Bildungsplans Baden-Württembergs am Beispiel eines Englischlehrwerks. *Lehren und Lernen, 24*(6), 3-18.

Finkbeiner, C. (2000). Zur Förderung expliziter *und* impliziter Lernstrategien im Englischunterricht: ein notwendiges Desiderat? In E. Klein, K. Knapp, F.-W. Neumann, & W. Schaller (Eds.), *Anglistik in der Remediatisierung der Informationsgesellschaft* (pp. 189-222). Trier: Wissenschaftlicher Verlag.

Finkbeiner, C. (2001). One and all in CALL? Learner – moderator – researcher. *Computer Assisted Language Learning, 14*(3-4), 339-361.

Herold, M., Landherr, B., & Huber, G. L. (1997). *Fraktale Lernorganisation in der gymnasialen Oberstufe: Ergebnisse eines Schulversuchs.* Paper presented at the *6. Tagung der Fachgruppe Pädagogische Psychologie in der Deutschen Gesellschaft für Psychologie*, Frankfurt am Main.

Huber, G. L. (2001). Kooperatives Lernen im Kontext der Lehr-/Lernformen. In C. Finkbeiner & G. Schnaitmann (Eds.), *Lehren und Lernen im Kontext empirischer Forschung und Fachdidaktik* (pp. 222-245). Donauwörth: Auer.

Huber, G. L., & Roth, J. H. W. (1999). *Finden oder suchen? Lehren und Lernen in Zeiten der Ungewissheit.* Schwangau: Ingeborg Huber Verlag.

Krashen, S. (1996). *Speaking of English* [Interviewee: Dr. Stephen Krashen, Interviewer: Andy Tighe, Producer: Sean Keegan]. BBC English.

Lier, L. v. (1996). *Interaction in the language curriculum. Awareness, autonomy and authenticity.* Harlow, Essex, UK: Longman.

Lightbown, P. M., & Spada, N. (1994). *How languages are learned.* Oxford: Oxford University Press.

Organisation for Economic Co-operation and Development. (2001*). Knowledge and skills for life. First results from PISA 2000.* Retrieved June 25, 2002, from the World Wide Web: http://www.pisa.oecd.org/Docs/Download/PISAExeSummary.pdf

Rampillon, U., & Zimmermann, G. (1997). *Lernstrategien.* Hueber: Ismaning.

Vygotsky, L. S. (1978). *Mind in society.* Cambridge, MA: Harvard University Press.

"Brainlinking": Holistic learning and learner orientation

Renate Löffler

In diesem Beitrag wird der Begriff des ganzheitlichen Lernens als einer sinnvollen pädagogisch-didaktischen Forderung neu betrachtet und von zwei Seiten her theoretisch untermauert und in Verbindung gesetzt zur Vorstellung der Lernerorientierung. Auf der Basis der humanistischen Psychologie und Pädagogik bedeutet ganzheitliches Lernen die Einbeziehung von Körper, Seele und Geist der Lernenden, d.h. seiner kognitiven und affektiven Fähigkeiten und Ressourcen in den Entwicklungs- und Lernprozess. Von der zeitgenössischen Neuropsychologie und Hirnforschung her bedeutet ganzheitliches Lernen die Verbindung der linken und rechten Hemisphäre des Neocortex, bei vorliegender Linksdominanz die Förderung der Kooperation der beiden Hemisphären. So verstärkt ganzheitliches Lernen die Fähigkeit zum Einsatz der individuellen Möglichkeiten in den Lehr- und Lernprozess.

Es geht nicht um die Einführung einer neuen Methode sondern um die Zusammenstellung von didaktischen Prinzipien und von methodischen „Bausteinen" für die Förderung ganzheitlichen Lehrens und Lernens.

This article discusses the educationally important concept of holistic learning (*ganzheitliches Lernen*) within the field of foreign language learning and teaching. On the one hand holistic learning can be defined on the basis of holistic psychology and education. In this context it stands for the integration of the physical, the psychic and the intellectual faculties of the learner. On the other hand, seen from the position of current neuropsychology and brain research, the idea of holistic learning implies the cooperation of the left and the right hemisphere of the neocortex: The left hemisphere, tending towards the rational faculties, and the right hemisphere, tending towards the affective and imaginative functions, can be coordinated and mutually invigorated by an enhanced integration. A list of didactic elements will be compiled that can activate the cooperation of the two hemispheres and thus help to develop and unfold the learner's full potential.

1. Why do we need holistic learning?

Many books and essays on holistic learning have already been published. Is holistic learning still relevant in the face of new educational ideas and developments, is it still up to date in a rapidly uniting Europe, in a world where new media and communication technologies offer an ever increasing range of chances and opportunities on the road to globalization? Does holistic learning still make sense under the growing pressure of achievement and efficiency, especially in the field of foreign language learning and with regard to the early stages of foreign language learning in elementary schools?

In view of these many questions it would seem advisable to review the concept of holistic learning and in so doing combine the concept with educational aspects of learner orientation.

2. Holistic learning – a clarification of the concept

As a starting point I will use the concept introduced in *Brainlinks* (Löffler & Schweitzer, 1988), where "holistic" is defined as follows:

> the learners – not counting age, preconditions and learning situation – should be enabled and encouraged to use all their resources of body, soul and mind within the learning process. . . [T]his means that the teacher too will have to enter into this process with all his own faculties, in teaching as well as in the process of planning any learning process. (ibid., p. 8)

Holistic in this sense means the use of all intellectual, emotional, social and creative abilities as well as the physical resources within the educational situation and in the learning process. The teacher will in the process function simultaneously as a model for his pupils and will thus encourage them to apply their own faculties.

This "appeal for wholeness" is supported and corroborated by two different fields of scientific research:

1. In the domain of the arts, it was the idea of "humanistic education", developed above all in the USA as a branch of humanistic psychology and psychotherapy during and after World War II, that began to comment on and criticize the educational principles of the time. A catalogue of principles and new values regarding the needs of any learner was put together, emphasizing the necessity of positive conditions for his/her development (Moskowitz, 1978, p. 18). For a full and unhampered development of a person's capacities, the "learning environ-

ment" was regarded as being of utmost importance – a demand, which of course implied heavy social and political criticism. A suitable environment should enable children to display and use all their cognitive-intellectual as well as affective-emotional faculties. In the course of this development "togetherness" was to play an active role: Teamwork and group activities were regarded as important conditions of the individual's development.

On the whole the idea of humanistic education is based on the belief in the intrinsic good in every child that should be given a chance to come to light. Nowadays we are probably more realistic. But it is also based on the realization that only increasing self-regard through self-awareness will strengthen the zest for recognizing and developing new ideas of one's own.

The humanistic psychologist Carl Rogers introduced ideas of general humanistic education into learning theory. In an essay on "Bringing together Ideas and Feeling" (Rogers, 1975) he accuses the learning situation of his time as being "education from the neck up" which neglects the emotional and physical energies that could enable children to discover ideas by themselves, at their own speed and according to their own needs.

In her book *Caring and Sharing in the Foreign Language Class* (Moskowitz, 1978), the content of which is as valid today as when it was published, Gertrude Moskowitz introduced the principles of humanistic education into foreign language teaching. In a collection of games and self-awareness exercises for different stages and levels of learning she gives practical advice for teachers on how to stimulate their pupils in many different ways, including their zest for physical movement, for laughter and joy. The benefits of perceiving the learner as a "whole" being and initiating learner-oriented processes in teaching have been widely recognized. Many of those approaches have shown visible success, and continue to do so, regarding motivation as well as the learning processes and the results of learning.

2. The concept of holistic learning is also corroborated by science and medicine, as we can see from research into the modes of cerebral functioning in brain psychology and neuropsychology. The special branch of neuropsychology which deals with the development of language and social behavior has, in many studies, proven the importance of physical motion, as well as the use of the senses in the development

of the faculties of listening, understanding and speaking in the child's mother tongue. The lateralization of the brain for speech and non-speech stimuli is decisive for children's later use of their mother tongue (Löffler & Schweitzer, 1988, pp. 10-15). It would seem logical that research regarding "natural language acquisition" should be taken into consideration also in the field of second or foreign language learning. Therefore a brief discussion of the present state of neuropsychological research and of the structure of the human brain will precede the application of those results within the concept of holistic learning in the area of foreign language teaching:

The human brain is approximately the shape of a mushroom (see Figure 1): Rising from the spinal cord into the skull is the brain stem, also called reptile brain due to its shape being similar to a reptile's brain. It is responsible for basic functions such as breathing, heartbeat and bowel function. Above the reptile brain, in a double bow, there is the diencephalon: As the limbic system it is the center of feeling; it allows us to view the world through emotions. Memory and emotions converge here and "without the faculty of remembering what we experienced as pleasant or unpleasant there will not exist anything like happiness, anxiety, sadness or being in love. One could say: A living per-

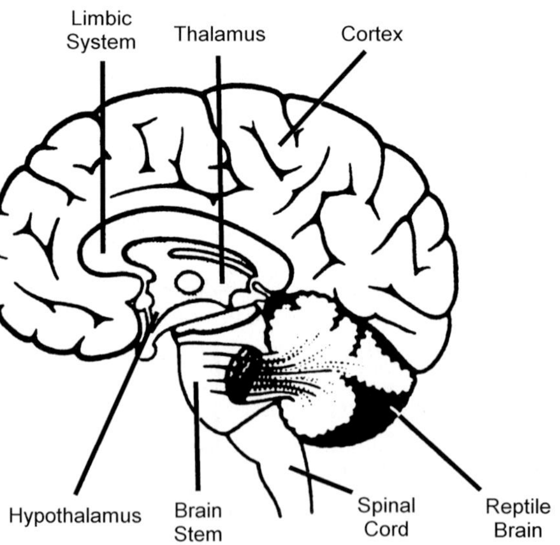

Figure 1. Main regions of the brain (adapted from: Russell, 1982, p. 64).

son is a memory in action" (Laborit, as cited in Fischer, 1985, p. 25).

On top of the diencephalon is the cortex, the "crust" of which, the neocortex, is the evolutionarily youngest part of the brain in higher mammals as well as in man. This is where the special human faculties are situated. Next to it is the cerebellum, responsible for movement and equilibrity and connected with all the larger bundles of nerves.

A phenomenon most striking for the concept of holistic learning is the manifold connection between the limbic system and the neocortex; there is, for instance, a relation between olfactory perception and the functioning of the memory. This connection between rational faculties and sensual-emotional impressions is most intense in younger children, but remains so in a similar way in adults.

In the following we will deal exclusively with the cortex, which comprises about ¼ of the complete brain volume, but contains 75% of the 10 billion neurons. The cortex is a paired organ; its two halves, the hemispheres, are connected by the corpus callosum, which consists of nerve bundles and functions as a bridge between the hemispheres. The two hemispheres are symmetrically organized, so that each controls the opposite side of the body and receives information from there in a contralateral organization (see Figure 2).

In the course of the development of the human child, both hemispheres acquire different additional tasks, which gradually leads to a cerebral asymmetry on top of the still existing basic symmetry. These differences become more comprehensive with age and development.

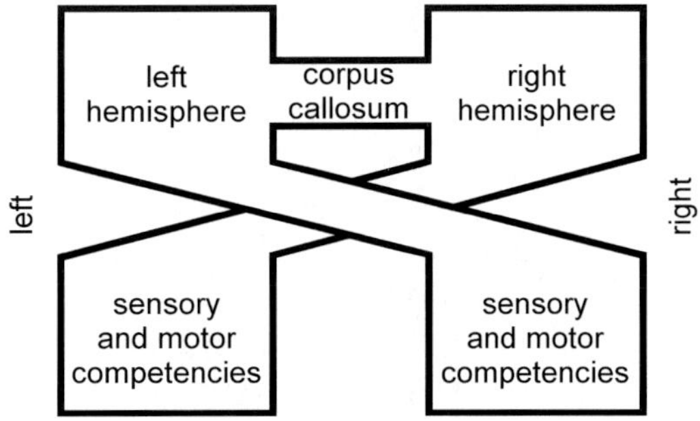

Figure 2. The bilateral organization of the nervous system (adapted from: Bindel, 1979, p. 8)

They were discovered and studied in split-brain patients, when following an artificial therapeutic intersection of the corpus callosum the two hemispheres could not communicate anymore and therefore worked independently, each in its acquired special way. Research has especially shown the different functioning of the right and the left hemispheres regarding speech and language. It has been observed and later proved that one obvious characteristic of the left hemisphere (in genetic right-handers!) is its dominance with regard to the production of words or names, whereas the right hemisphere, working separately, can identify pictures of objects or subjects, but is unable to produce their names without the help of the left side.

In connection with research on right/left-handedness and other apparent preferences in paired organs (like feet, eyes, ears), the two now well-known centers of verbal production within the left hemisphere were found by Paul Broca in 1864 ("motor-center") and by Karl Wernicke in 1876 (the "sensorial center"). In connection with this one-sided position of the language centers, the faculties of listening, comprehension and speech have concentrated slightly more on that side. However, special capabilities such as quick visual perception, gaining an overall view of an area or a locality and the orientation thereof have developed more intensively within the right hemisphere.

Thus according to their different accentuation of faculties, the cerebral asymmetry of the neocortex has, by a number of neuropsychologists, been referred to as the situation of two personalities with two different styles of thinking and working whenever they function individually and independently. However, "when the two hemispheres interchange their experiences and combine their perspectives and their approaches there comes about a synthesis that opens up an infinite variety of problem-solving possibilities" (Rothenberg, 1979).

The differences between the hemispheres are shown below in Figure 3, which – although it does not show "brain-reality" – is still didactically useful to describe brain functions.

The cerebral asymmetry, the differences of the logical-rational and the intuitive-creative dimension of the neocortex have been proved in numerous clinical studies: The left hemisphere, specified in analytical processes, mainly determines the linguistic and mathematical capacities of an individual; the right hemisphere, on the other hand, as the specialist for nonverbal and emotional comprehension and intuitive recognition shapes the sensual perception and the imaginative handling of symbols, signs and images.

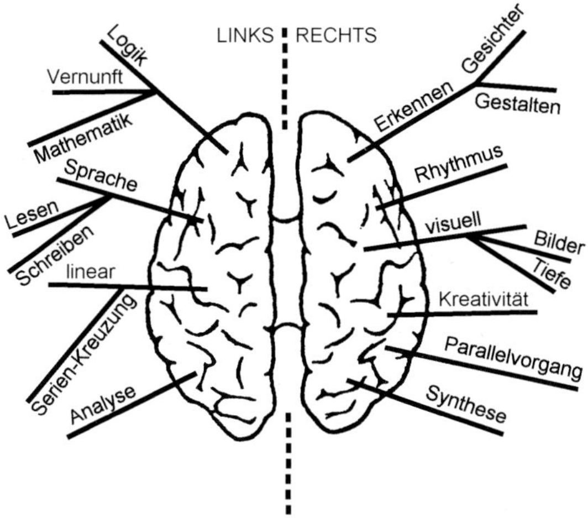

Figure 3. Left- and right-brain functioning (from: Ornstein, 1976, p. 218)

We have seen that the two hemispheres do not function independently, but are both specialists for certain dimensions. Therefore it is important to make them cooperate. More recent studies have shown that each hemisphere is capable of solving many kinds of problems, but each performing in its own way; they differ in the evaluation of the goal. In a situation of "left-dominance" this interchange will be hampered or even impossible. Our aims therefore must be

- to strengthen the functions and skills of the right hemisphere, encouraging its development
- to activate the corpus callosum in its function as a "bridge" between the two halves of the neocortex.

In society as well as in industry and scientific research, this principle of cooperation and fruitful interchange of hemispheric faculties has already begun to be recognized as being of great benefit to creative processes or other complicated tasks. Why should it not be applied equally in schools?

3. Double-brain learning

Holistic learning has been defined as a form of learning in which the balance of the two hemispheres is set for the best possible cooperation. What external conditions in the learning environment and what kind of didactic support can best assist that integrative functioning of the hemispheres as well as the activation of the corpus callosum in its connecting task? A number of recognized didactic possibilities are as follows:

- Suitable structuring of the learning process
- Limitation and clear arrangement of materials
- Beginning from the learner's point of view
- Starting with material already familiar to the learner
- An overall learner-oriented selection of materials
- A sensible sequence of materials
- Taking into consideration the mental capacity of the learner
- Taking into consideration his time-span of attentiveness
- Appropriate alternation of learning activities.

These didactic principles are not new and have already been taken into consideration for some time. They will certainly stimulate left-hemispheric activities and, in some cases, also support right-hemispheric functions. But are there any didactic elements that particularly help to activate the functioning of the corpus callosum and to stimulate especially right-hemispheric faculties, and by doing so support and increase the integration of both sides? In the following we will discuss some didactic principles that may lead to some helpful methods for integrative learning.

4. Motion

Motion is important in its widest definition. Physical movement (such as walking, standing up, sitting, even lying down, or simply moving parts of the body to act, using gestures and mimics of all kinds) as well as the perception of the movement of others not only lessens tension but also increases the controlling and perceiving activities within both sides of the neocortex in a more or less equally intense way. Through this parallel stimulation of both hemispheres the wavelength in both halves will be approximately the same, allowing the connecting activity of the corpus callosum to reach its full range. Here are some proposals:

- Short phases of well defined motor activities, walking a certain distance, walking or running or hopping on the spot, etc., then stretching and expanding, taking a deep breath before finishing the phase.
- Games that include motion, where the rules of the game may regulate or define the movements (Löffler & Schweitzer, 1988).
- The so-called "right-left-activities"; here is one example of many possibilities: The left hand touches the right knee; then the learner watches and consciously perceives first the hand, then the knee. This is a playful exercise in body perception that may stimulate the interchange between the hemispheres, which at the same time makes constant use of the connecting "bridge". Exercises of this kind take some time to get used to, and they should always remain playful; ritualized repetition may prove helpful here.

By the way: All activities of this kind, when incorporated into the language lesson, can easily be handled in the target language.

5. Relaxation

Empirical studies have shown that under a condition of continuous stress (e.g. an exam), the activity of the left hemisphere increases, whereas the right hemisphere simultaneously lowers its activity. The consequence is an enormous contrast of brainwave activity between the hemispheres, measured through an EEG (electroencephalogram). The person feels tense and nervous and gradually the condition of well-being decreases. It has been shown in experiments that after a time of relaxation the brainwave-frequencies of both hemispheres become approximately the same again: Beta-waves have a frequency of

15–35 Hertz and show that a person is awake and active, unless involved in a one-sided activity where it would mean he/she was nervous and hectic; alpha waves have a frequency of 7–14 Hertz and reveal a relaxed state of mental and muscular concentration. This alpha state can be reached through combined right-left-exercises (see above) or through meditative concentration. A higher state of brainwave activity than beta-frequency indicates stress plus exaggerated and hectic (brain) action, whereas lower frequencies than alpha waves appear in sleep and in states of unconsciousness or coma.

The state of concentrated relaxation can also be reached through music of about 60 beats per minute (adagio, andante, largo), a phenomenon well-known in music therapy. When relaxation sets in, the attention of a person moves slowly from the outside to the inside, regeneration begins, and anxiety diminishes. These experiences can be utilized in some didactic elements:

- Short phases of silence (up to one minute)
- Closing one's eyes
- Listening to any noise outside and recognizing what is being heard
- Putting one's head on one's hands and resting there for one minute, breathing in and out
- Guided physical relaxation with conscious perception of parts of the body such as feet, hands, back, etc.
- Holding an object like a stone in one's hand
- Playing soft music to accompany all of these exercises.

Relaxation exercises increase the balance and interaction of the hemispheres and therefore strengthen the learning power, but they also help the learner to feel refreshed and free of anxiety. When using activities like those listed above it is important to build up rituals that create a feeling of familiarity and at the same time offer an opportunity for individual implementation.

6. Images, imagination, fantasy

Pictures have always been an important didactic medium for vivid illustration of subject matter and also for teaching ideas and concepts. The right-hemispheric capacity of thinking in images even before verbal thinking sets in can be exploited through visualizing new ideas or structures before finding their verbal equivalent: Words are "left", pictures are "right"; thus "picturing" the meaning of a thing can become a major support for memorizing not only vocabulary but also concepts and processes or chains of events and dates, etc.; symbols and icons can help to memorize messages or names. The method of picturing was discovered and used in memory training, but it is also helpful for the comprehension and memorization of written texts.

Figure 4 shows a practical application of mind-mapping as a basis for planning and writing.

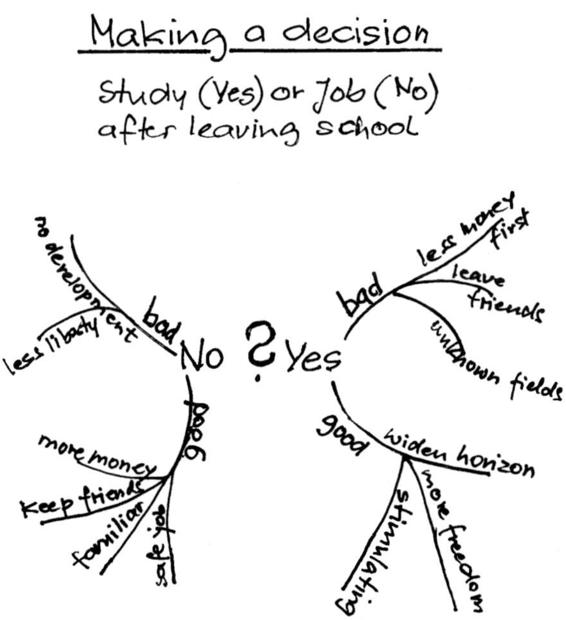

Figure 4. Mind-mapping as a basis for planning and writing (adapted from: Buzan & North, 1997, p. 75)

7. Networking

Networking is a method applied in many fields. It uses associations and images in a way similar to mind-mapping. The term is familiar to us in an electronic context, but it can be used intentionally in learning situations. Following ideas through association, connected with fantasy and images, is a typical right-hemispheric activity: Such a process is marked by the absence of logical connection and of self-criticism; it follows its own course. In a second step the ideas can be elaborated upon and finally transferred into sentences and passages that will be verbally and logically structured.

Association (see Figure 5) is the initiation of new ideas, even far from reality, and can thus pass the barriers of logical control and run free, uncovering never-thought-of ideas which may open up new horizons: an excellent method for brainstorming and for problem-solving.

Clustering breaks the dominance of the systematic working of the left hemisphere and opens up the apparently accidental associations put on paper in a playful and non-linear way. Syntax and logical connection are not important at first, while images enable the flow of ideas. The created pattern will later function as a basis of an intricate combination of images and linguistic faculties in the production of an essay or any other piece of writing, prose or poetry. (For many useful examples see Rico, 1984.)

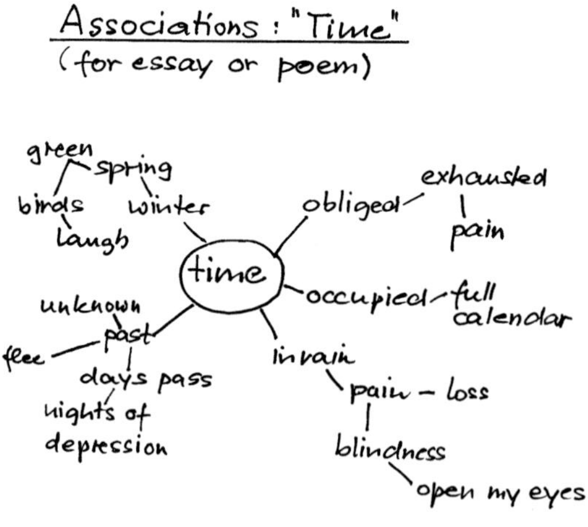

Figure 5. Association (adapted from: Rico, 1984)

8. Conclusion

This survey shows that in many "alternative" approaches physical, motor faculties as well as the senses, fantasy and imagination play an important role. But it is significant that holistic learning and learner-orientation are above all dependent on the teacher, on his willingness to open up and enter into social and learning processes with the pupils, which ultimately does not depend on the one special method he/she uses.

Therefore I do not intend to rely on one specific method or add a new one to those existing already. It seems important, however, to define a number of elements that should be present in teaching that encourage and stimulate right-hemispheric activity and the integration and cooperation of both hemispheres

These elements, a few of which have been listed above, can be used as modules or "building-blocks" to be integrated into teaching. This requires the willingness and attention of the teacher, the school and the educational system.

> The best teachers are those who establish rapport, and enter into the world of the learner, and so make it easier for the learner to enter into a greater understanding of their subject or skill. (O'Connor & Seymour, 1993, p. 21)

References

Bindel, R. W. (1979). *Lateralität, Geschlecht und Intelligenzstruktur.* Frankfurt: Fischer.

Buzan, T., & North, V. (1997). *Mind Mapping – der Schlüssel für deinen Lernerfolg.* Wien: Hölder-Pichler.

Fischer, E. P. (1985). *Die Welt im Kopf.* Faude: Libelle.

Löffler, R., & Schweitzer, K. (1988). *Brainlinks – Bausteine für einen ganzheitlichen Englischunterricht.* Weinheim: Beltz.

Moskowitz, G. (1978). *Caring and sharing in the foreign language class. A sourcebook on humanistic techniques.* Rowley, MA.: Newbury House Publishers.

Ornstein, R. E. (1976). *Die Psychologie des Bewußtseins.* Frankfurt: Fischer.

O'Connor, J., & Seymour, J. (1993). *Introducing neuro-linguistic programming.* San Francisco: The Aquarian Press.

Rico, G. L. (1984). *Garantiert schreiben lernen: Sprachliche Kreativität methodisch entwickeln.* Hamburg: Rowohlt.

Rogers, C. R. (1975). Bringing together ideas and feelings in learning. In D. A. Read & S. B. Simon (Eds.), *Humanistic education sourcebook*. Englewood Cliffs, NJ: Prentice Hall.

Rothenberg, A. (1979). *The emerging goddess. The creative process in art, science, and other fields*. Chicago: University of Chicago Press.

Russell, P. (1982). *Der menschliche Computer*. München: Heyne.

“Do they love each other?”

Learner autonomy in university literature courses

Liesel Hermes

Der Beitrag ist ein Plädoyer für wachsende Lernerautonomie auf Universitätsebene und zeigt Wege zu ihrer Realisierung durch Gruppenarbeit auf.

This paper makes a plea for the development of learner autonomy at the university level and aims at showing ways and means how to achieve it through group work.

1. Introduction

“Do they love each other?” was a question students frequently asked in an advanced literature course on Australian short stories, stories which were admittedly more often than not centred on human beings and the vicissitudes of their relationships in the view of hard living conditions, for example, in the Australian outback. Not infrequently the students were stuck, so to speak, with this question, unable to get out of the impasse in their discourse because they were too much concerned with the contents of the text alone and failed to observe the interrelatedness of contents and style and/or structure. The question in the title can thus be interpreted as a metaphor for the students’ willingness to cope with a literary text, but also as a metaphor for their limited methodological competence, limited literary experience and, above all, for their limited ability to reach a moderate level of abstraction and metacognition.

This situation may give rise to the question of what the instructor can do to ensure that she does not have to take the students by the hand and guide them towards a more abstract and more demanding level of literary interpretation, but also how the students themselves can aspire to these aims. It is common knowledge that the traditional lecture on literature confronts the students with their academic teacher’s view of literature, and little is known about what they actually take home from such a lecture, which works on the principle of transmission of knowledge only. There seems to be hardly any empirical data to confirm or refute the view that fairly little is being learned in a learning environment of purely teacher-fronted instruction or that the notes the students take are of high or low value for them, should they later refer back to them at all.

By the same token, even if one does not know the individual student's learning style or preferences, one is fairly safe to assume that their ability to reflect, think abstractly, formulate complex thoughts, let alone be critical of themselves and evaluate their own achievement is far from perfect when they come to university, and needs constant training and encouragement throughout the course. It would therefore seem to be of paramount importance that university courses be used as stepping stones towards learner autonomy, guiding the students on their way to becoming autonomous and lifelong learners.

This paper will deal with the question of how this goal can be achieved in whole-class instruction work and in group work in literature seminars, in other words, how the transmission process can be replaced by experiential learning processes that involve the students.

2. Autonomy

Autonomy has come to be a buzzword in Germany (see Pemberton, 1996, p. 2). Theories of learner autonomy, construction of knowledge and group-centred learning abound. Students are showered with progressive theories, but in their university courses are mostly confronted with very traditional teaching methods like lecturing or a succession of student papers, in short with methods which make a mockery of the theories conveyed, namely student-centred learning and learner autonomy. What is sadly lacking in undergraduate programmes is experiential learning, that is, the actual experiencing of what is being preached, such as group work and the development of learner autonomy.

David Little provides the following description of autonomy: "[T]he basis of learner autonomy is acceptance of responsibility for one's own learning" (Little, 1997, p. 227). He envisages the development of learner autonomy as a "never-ending effort to understand what one is learning, why one is learning, how one is learning, and with what degree of success" (ibid.). Autonomy is directly linked with constructivism, which is seen as its theoretical foundation: "Der Konstruktivismus *ist* die theoretische Grundlage des autonomen Lernens..." (Wolff, 1999, p. 162, author's emphasis). Learning according to Wolff involves the subjective construction of knowledge. Human beings learn by constructing their own reality on the basis of what they perceive and recognise as relevant or valuable for themselves.

Teaching in this context does not imply transmission of knowledge any longer, but a learner-centred concept in which the instructor provides a learning environment which is favourable to students' independent activities. They are themselves responsible for what they choose to do, how they do it and what aims they achieve. The role of the teacher is modified and reduced to that of a mentor, mediator or facilitator, words that have come to be so fashionable that one hesitates to use the old-fashioned word "teacher" at all, which has assumed something of a taboo quality, because it seems to be invariably connected with an authoritative role.

Arnold and Schüßler, among others, criticise old "learning cultures", by which they understand the following: "… die toten Lernkulturen einer frontalunterrichtlich verkopften Lehre" (1998, p. 17), *frontal* and *verkopft* being used ideologically as something utterly wicked. Later they make the following claim: "Für einen grundlegenden Wandel der Lernkultur, der an die Stelle einer verkopften Wissensmast ein lebendiges, kooperatives und selbstorganisiertes Lernen setzt, ... ist der Gedanke der Freiheit konstitutiv" (ibid., p. 173). Here they identify *Wissen* with *verkopft*, with the word *Wissensmast* constituting the climax of their abhorrence. They construct an irreconcilable contrast between knowledge, which is cognitive and therefore "dead", and cooperative learning, which is alive. Why, one has to ask, is knowledge so bad? And why is cooperative learning the only way out of the supposed misery? Unfortunately the two authors never come up with an answer.

This seems to be a good example of an elaborate theory that does without empirical validation. These authors and others, who can be regarded as ardent proponents of autonomous learning and make elaborate demands on teachers and students alike (see, e.g., Wolff, 1994, p. 422; Wolff, 1999, p. 157), are hardly ever concerned with the formal teaching and learning environments of school or university and their respective constraints (Hermes, 2000, pp. 337-340). Except for

Little (1994, p. 439) and Dubs (1995), hardly anyone mentions vital factors such as the age of the learners, the size of the learning group, the level of proficiency in the target language, not to mention the time required to promote or impede learner autonomy (Hermes, 1999b).

Proponents of autonomy never quite make clear what kind of human being they intend to guide along the arduous trail towards autonomy. The whole concept, if taken seriously, presupposes an immensely optimistic vision of humans as ever-learning beings. For autonomy to develop, they have to be mature, intellectually advanced and self-confident. Apart from having ample pre-knowledge, including world-knowledge in general, they have to have a clear view of the objectives to be achieved. They have to be highly motivated with a natural and sustained drive to learn. They have to be highly critical of the whole process of learning and critical of themselves when it comes to the stage of self-evaluation.

Paradoxically enough, autonomy does not come by itself but has to be introduced and practically "taught" by the teacher, which means living with the paradox that autonomy can only be reached after having been denied it in the process of instruction (Benson & Voller, 1997, p. 9; see Williams & Burden, 1997, p. 71). In other words, the autonomous learner is not born, but taught. For the instructor it does not suffice to make materials available, to provide favourable conditions of learning, to create motivating learning environments, to set stimulating assignments, to guide the students with appropriate stimuli. Construction of knowledge will only take place if the students actually agree to shoulder their own burden of joint responsibility for the outcome of learning. In other words, development of autonomy means rigorous demands on the students' work ethics, reliable preparation of the assignments set, sustained willingness to voice their own opinions, to decide on objectives, to negotiate methods and, lastly, to evaluate honestly and critically the aims achieved.

3. Autonomy and whole-class instruction

Dubs (1995) is one of the few authors who has empirically examined the lofty assumptions of theories of learner autonomy. Not surprisingly, he emphasises the time constraints in any formal learning environment. Any child who learns autonomously learns without being concerned about the time taken. But the formal learning environment of the university demands that the students conform to a rigorous time frame of one session per week. It is understandable therefore that Dubs draws the conclusion that autonomy cannot be a top priority objective in the first semesters. As long as the acquisition of basic knowledge and fundamental concepts of a subject are priorities, he makes a plea for teacher-fronted instruction (see also Reinfried, 1999, p. 176). This makes sense for two reasons: without the basics of, for example, concepts of literary criticism and a critical terminology, students do not have the tools to work with literary texts at an academic level; and since they come to university with highly diverging experiences in literature, the instructor has to ensure through her teaching that a common base level of knowledge is achieved, from which the road to autonomy can be followed. In view of constant time pressure, time economy should be carefully observed, which means that it would be irresponsible to let each learning group invent the wheel anew. Moreover, it would be highly unfair to the weaker students, who need guidance at all stages. Therefore, the instructor would do well to proceed at first through instruction rather than self-determined learning, and when it comes to actually transferring knowledge at a more advanced level, she will then have the opportunity to show ways to autonomous learning.

Not only is time limited, but university courses also tend to be large. Individualisation in courses of 50 to 80 students or more is obviously an illusion. Therefore a certain amount of input has to be given and, not surprisingly, students demand just that. It is of course open to speculation why, be it that they are used to it in most university courses, be it that they know their own apathy when it comes to reading beyond the minimum required, be it that they hope to get everything from the instructor herself, which spares them the bother of doing research themselves.

However, a certain amount of autonomy can be achieved even in large courses, the prerequisites being that the procedure is well-structured and the students are well-prepared, motivated and sufficiently self-assured to conduct a discussion largely without the instructor. Structuring can be done on the basis of a brainstorming phase, in which the students volunteer all the questions that have occurred to them when preparing the text as well as all the topics they would like to discuss. This paves the way for future autonomy. The students themselves can structure the results of their brainstorming and thus lay the foundation for a joint discussion. The discussion can then be conducted mainly without the interference of the teacher, the advantage being that the students do not direct their comments to the teacher, but rather to their fellow students. A discussion in which the teacher consistently refrains from providing guidance means ideally that the students really communicate with each other, keeping eye contact, supporting or refuting each other's comments.

At first glance, this may sound promising in view of the time constraints mentioned. The drawbacks, on the other hand, are obvious (see Hermes, 1998, pp. 154-155; Hermes, 1999a, p. 201): the students very often do not refer back to the brainstorming results, but get caught up all too easily in matters of content and, without a guiding hand, remain pretty much on the surface of a text ("do they love each other?"). They may neglect or altogether overlook aspects of structure and style, which may be immediately related to content. Thus their discussion remains fairly superficial because of lack of guidance. Or, worse, they may go round in circles without noticing (Hermes, 1998, p. 159). Autonomy in plenary discussions is therefore a fairly modest proposal; however, it can be achieved to a certain extent if one is prepared to accept a certain lack of depth and thoroughness in the discussion. A better way to learner autonomy, however, is through group work.

4. Group work

A consistent theory of group work does not yet exist (Gohla, 1977). If one differentiates between formal and informal groups, a class of students is a formal group, which is characterised, for example, by a sort of membership for one semester. If within this class of students spontaneous group work is done, the students will work in informal groups, which only form for one session to work on a specific task.

Groups can be formed arbitrarily on the basis of the accidental seating arrangement. This is often the worst possible scenario, since the students are forced to work in an accidental social framework they may not actually favour, which will, of course, have consequences for the quality of their work. Group formation can also be planned, for instance, on the basis of familiarity with each other. Spontaneous group formation can also occur on the basis of special interests. Once the tasks are set, groups form spontaneously according to which task they would like to work on.

Of equal importance is group dynamics. Groups of even numbers may be at a disadvantage, because they can form sub-groups (Gutte, 1976, p. 67), whereas groups of odd numbers cannot subdivide so easily. It is uniformly agreed in theories of group work that each member in a group assumes a certain role (Gohla, 1977, p. 93). The larger the group, the easier it apparently is for the group members to play their specific roles such as, for example, leader. Leadership suggests a hierarchy which often evolves even in small groups. The leader normally has the longest speaking time, gets the others' attention by making eye-contact, takes the initiative, steers the discussion, and often structures the whole process. Other roles may be those of supporters, the "clown" or the quiet ones who just sit back and relax.

Assuming that group dynamics work satisfactorily, group work can give any group of students a kind of protection, i.e. they experience a learning arrangement where their own contributions are evaluated by just three or four fellow students. *Communication* is intensive and made easier especially for the introverted ones. Shy students can overcome their fear of contributing, for it is a lot easier than in a large plenary to make personal comments, for example, express their feelings or be emotional. Thus group work has important *psychological functions*, especially for the otherwise quiet students.

Group work creates a social framework in which interaction occurs very directly. Thus group work also means *social learning.* In groups, students have to find their own objectives, or if the tasks have been set, their own ways of reaching the objectives. They have to negotiate the tasks as well as choose the methods. This entails a high degree of *self-determination.* They also experience themselves in new roles. The objectives of group work therefore address students' communicative and social abilities and their personal development.

Group work offers a much more communicative framework than any plenary. It is a highly dynamic process with a lot of interaction and turn-taking. The social framework of group work means cooperation and responsibility that is informed by mutual respect for each other. If the group members see their work as a self-determined joint effort, the outcome will consequently be seen as their joint achievement. This can often result in a feeling of group solidarity.

For the sake of objectivity, some possible objections should perhaps also be mentioned. The learning process in group work is considerably more time-consuming than in a lockstep class. However, who knows what students take home from a lecture and what, by the same token, they take home from a group work session? Group work is bound to fail if there is a general lack of commitment or if the instructor does not supervise the students. It may fail, too, if group dynamics intimidate one member or a leader takes over and entirely controls the whole process, if a group splits into subgroups that disengage themselves from the activities agreed upon, or if the members of the group are incompatible or refuse to cooperate (Vielau, 1997, pp. 291-292).

If autonomy is to be achieved by group work, the students have to show good social as well as communicative competences on top of the ones mentioned above. Group work should take into account the individual learner's "needs, purposes, capacities" (Little, 1994, p. 431), which he/she brings into the group and which are addressed in the process of the interaction of the group members. This strategy takes account of the individuals and at the same time of the communicative processes within the group, the negotiation of objectives and working methods and reflection on the process of learning.

Even if these prerequisites are given, it takes a lot of time and effort on the part of the learners. The first steps towards autonomy have again to be taken by the teacher, who introduces her students to the concepts and objectives of autonomy. She has to create a learning environment which is favourable to learner autonomy, and has to encourage constant reflection and foster self-awareness. Students have to be highly motivated for their work and have to be prepared to assume responsibility for their individual learning as well as for the activities in their groups. In this respect learner autonomy is not isolated work, but eminently joint discourse.

5. A case study in group work

In an advanced literature course, in which the students were introduced to the principles and objectives of learner autonomy, group work was conducted throughout the semester with one group being filmed in each session, normally four or five students for about 25-30 minutes. An analysis of the videos yielded varying results. Interestingly enough, within the first five minutes roles were assumed that were "played" consistently throughout. The films showed that autonomy is jeopardised if one student takes over the role of the teacher and dominates or steers the discussion, but it can be achieved to a certain degree if the members of the group are fairly homogeneous, well-prepared and cooperative.

In one group a leader emerged right from the start who directed and dominated the discussion. She suggested methods to choose, details to attend to and steered the discussion throughout, challenging anyone who was not concentrating. The film clearly showed that the others directed their comments mainly to her and maintained eye contact with her. Her role as a leader was unchallenged throughout. Not surprisingly, she had the longest speaking time by far. The procedure was highly effective, but bore resemblance to a teacher-fronted classroom.

The fact that length of speaking time does not automatically coincide with the leader's role became apparent in another group, where a female student obviously had difficulty in expressing herself. Very early on she took the floor and sometimes monopolised it rambling along, but only because she had a hard time making herself clear to the other group members. They listened politely, asked for clarification, which provoked more rambling monologues. What the students certainly learned in this process was the negotiation of meaning. However, the results with regard to the discussion of the text in hand were fairly poor.

Another group, a very quiet and deliberate one, started with a period of prolonged silence, in which they reread parts of the text, made annotations and only then negotiated the points to discuss. In this group no leader emerged, and the speaking time was fairly evenly distributed among all the members. This quiet group made the best effort at clarifying and negotiating meaning at a much more abstract level than the previous one. They came up with highly original ideas including intertextual references.

A fourth group had a "clown" right from the start, who loved entertaining the others by making silly comments which aroused laughter. This group plunged head over heels into the text and found out after a couple of minutes that it might be advisable to restrict the number of topics to discuss. Only then did they decide on a silent period of rereading parts of the text before plunging into another discussion which, however, moved along somewhat erratically and without any observable coherence.

In a fifth group, five somewhat older students had come together, all between 35 and 50. They did not have a leader, but rather an expert, since one woman was Australian and the Australian short story under discussion dealt with aboriginal topics. The other members looked to her for help when a term needed clarifying, and she provided linguistic explanations of terms dealing with aboriginal culture. On the whole they emerged as a very egalitarian group, which was also reflected in the roughly equal amounts of speaking time by each member.

Strikingly, in a group of four, the members sitting opposite each other talked to each other right from the start, so that at times two dialogues emerged. It appeared that the two sub-groups were not actually listening to each other. Right up until the end of the group-work phase they did not manage to develop a discussion in which all four of them were involved with each other. This may be a point in favour of groups with an odd number of members. However, in one group of five, one student practically dropped out. She had by far the shortest speaking time.

6. Conclusion

Group work is a path to, but does not guarantee, autonomy. The degree to which autonomy can be achieved is dependent on various factors: the quality and stimulation of the learning environment, the quality of the individual student's preparation of the group work, the maturity and self-confidence of the individual student, the role in the group he/she assumes, individual language proficiency and rhetoric, communicative ability, general cooperativeness and ability to work in a team, the stability of the group, sincerity in the evaluation of the group work and in self-evaluation.

Autonomy is a lofty goal which can be seen as an ideal always to be aspired to, but never fully attained, for – to be honest – one all too easily lapses back into the role of the passive learner who is happy to be spoon-fed, to be taken by the hand. It will therefore require the continual effort on the part of the instructor to provide motivating learning environments that encourage self-determined learning, and on the part of the students to face up to the challenges posed and to shoulder responsibility.

References

Arnold, R., & Schüßler, I. (1998). *Wandel der Lernkulturen.* Darmstadt: Wiss. Buchgesellschaft.

Benson, P., & Voller, P. (Eds.). (1997). *Autonomy and independence in language learning.* London: Longman.

Dubs, R. (1995). Konstruktivismus: Einige Überlegungen aus der Sicht der Unterrichtsgestaltung. *Zeitschrift für Pädagogik, 6*, 889-903.

Gohla, G. (1977). *Theorie und Praxis der Gruppenarbeit.* Heidelberg: Quelle & Meyer.

Gutte, R. (1976). *Gruppenarbeit. Theorie und Praxis des sozialen Lernens.* Frankfurt a.M.: Diesterweg.

Hermes, L. (1998). Reden über Literatur. Selbsterfahrung in Seminarveranstaltungen. *Fremdsprachen Lehren und Lernen, 27*, 146-162.

Hermes, L. (1999a). Learner assessment through subjective theories and action research. *Assessment & Evaluation in Higher Education, 24*(2), 197-204.

Hermes, L. (1999b). What do students learn in groups? Development of learner autonomy in higher education. *Fremdsprachen und Hochschule, 54*, 34-46.

Hermes, L. (2000). Überlegungen zur Theorie und Praxis von Lernerautonomie. In K. Aguado & A. Hu (Eds.), *Mehrsprachigkeit und Mehrkulturalität. Dokumentation des 18. Kongresses für Fremdsprachendidaktik* (pp. 335-341). Berlin: Päd. Zeitschriftenverlag.

Little, D. (1994). Learner autonomy: A theoretical construct and its practical applications. *Die Neueren Sprachen, 93*(3), 430-442.

Little, D. (1997). Learner autonomy in the foreign language classroom: Theoretical foundations and some essentials of pedagogical practice. *Zeitschrift für Fremdsprachenforschung, 8*(2), 227-244.

Pemberton, R., Li, E. S. L., Or, W. W. F., & Pierson, H. D. (Eds.). (1996). *Taking control. Autonomy in language learning.* Hong Kong: Hong Kong University Press.

Reinfried, M. (1999). Der radikale Konstruktivismus – eine sinnvolle Basistheorie für die Fremdsprachendidaktik? *Fremdsprachen Lehren und Lernen, 28*, 162-180.

Vielau, A. (1997). *Methodik des kommunikativen Fremdsprachenunterrichts.* Berlin: Cornelsen.

Williams, M., & Burden, R. L. (1997). *Psychology for language teachers. A social constructivist approach.* Cambridge: Cambridge University Press.

Wolff, D. (1994). Der Konstruktivismus: Ein neues Paradigma in der Fremdsprachendidaktik? *Die Neueren Sprachen, 93*(5), 407-429.

Wolff, D. (1999). Autonomes Lernen – ein Weg zur Mehrsprachigkeit. In H.-L. Krechel, D. Marx, & F. J. Meißner (Eds.), *Kognition und neue Praxis im Französischunterricht* (pp. 151-164). Tübingen: Narr.

Student-centred approaches and teachers' experiential knowledge

Joachim Appel

Lernerzentrierter Unterricht und insbesondere Lernerautonomie sind seit geraumer Zeit zentrale Begriffe in der pädagogischen und fremdsprachendidaktischen Diskussion. Unter anderem hat sich das Konzept der Freiarbeit als einflussreich für die Schulpraxis erwiesen. Bisher ist jedoch wenig darüber bekannt, wie solche Konzepte im Schulkontext wahrgenommen werden und insbesondere wie sie sich zu den Notwendigkeiten alltäglichen Unterrichts verhalten.

Auf der Datengrundlage einer qualitativen Studie über das Erfahrungswissen von Fremdsprachenlehrer/innen versucht der folgende Artikel, eine Reihe von Aspekten zu untersuchen, die für die Verwirklichung von Lernerzentriertheit und Lernerautonomie in der Schule wichtig sind. Dies sind u.a. situative Bestimmungsgrößen, die durch den Schulkontext gegeben sind, sowie die Entwicklung persönlicher Unterrichtskonzepte im Laufe einer Berufsbiographie.

Student-centred teaching and learner autonomy have become important ideas in education and language teaching. It is especially through self-access work (*Freiarbeit*) that they have proved influential in the classroom. Comparatively little is known, however, about how these ideas work in a school context and how they relate to the constraints of day-to-day teaching.

Based on data from a qualitative study on language teachers' experiential knowledge, the following article will look at a number of aspects affecting the realisation of learner-centredness and learner autonomy in the school classroom. These are: situational constraints given by the school context as well as the development of a personal teaching philosophy in the course of a professional career. [1]

A story

A school teacher attends an in-service seminar given by two English as a Foreign Language (EFL) experts. During the seminar she is introduced to some of the principles of student-centred language teaching

1 I would like to thank Jim Martin and Andrea Wagner for their advice and help.

and to a repertoire of techniques for giving learners more autonomy. She returns to the school classroom keen on putting what she has learnt into practice. However, when trying to implement the new ideas in her advanced class, she is confronted with considerable resistance from her pupils, who are not prepared to speak the foreign language during group work and would prefer teacher-centred classes in order to get immediate feedback on the accuracy of their utterances. One reason that emerges for this resistance is that the class had previously been taught by a teacher who was perceived as highly effective because of his brisk and well-structured way of teaching. In the face of pupil expectations shaped by this style of teaching, our teacher finds it hard to maintain the principles she has learnt.

The following article tries to address some of the questions raised by this story: How do classroom teachers perceive and implement principles like learner autonomy in their daily work? What constraints are they confronted with? What are their solutions? What conditions are required if student-centred teaching is to stand the test of classroom reality?

1. Student-centred teaching

Student-centred teaching has become one of the most influential movements in present-day education. Drawing on a wide range of educational philosophies the core values of student-centred teaching encompass

- learner autonomy and independence,
- student activation and involvement,
- personally relevant content,
- self-awareness,
- partnership between students and teacher,
- holistic integration of cognition, emotion and body.

The above principles have served as a theoretical foundation for a number of grassroots movements in education. These have to a certain extent been culture-specific. Two important traditions can be distinguished. Within an Anglo-Saxon context humanistic education, which makes personal development and self-awareness its prime concern, has had a profound influence on language teaching. One important reason for using humanistic approaches in language teaching is the assumption that they bring about conditions considered to be conducive to quasi-natural second language acquisition. Such conditions include individualisation, motivation and a positive emotional climate.

In continental Europe student-centred principles formed the core of the Reform Movement (see, for example, Scheibe, 1977; Jürgens, 1998) early in the 20th century. Some ideas from this movement have recently experienced an astonishing renaissance in Germany. This applies especially to the so-called self-access work (*Freiarbeit*). Student-centred teaching in this tradition focuses on choice, independence and self-determination. Basing itself, among other things, on the ideas of Montessori (1968) self-access work relies on a stimulating physical learning environment and on aesthetically appealing, task-based materials. Self-access is a method that can be applied in most subjects. It is also used in foreign language teaching (Gnass-Franke, 1993).

The relevant literature has tended to present student-centred approaches in the form of practical suggestions. A vast repertoire of learner-centred exercises designed around the principles mentioned above has been made accessible through resource books. However, little has to date been said about what actually happens when student-centred principles and techniques meet classroom reality. The same seems true for self-access work, which has only recently been looked at empirically (Henning, 1996).

If we consider it necessary to take a look at student-centred teaching in the context of classroom reality, then teachers' knowledge and beliefs are important factors, because ultimately it is the teachers who decide whether and in what form student-centred teaching is used in the classroom.

2. Teachers' knowledge and beliefs

Teachers' cognitions have been studied since the seventies. First based on studies of teachers' decision making, theory in the field has since shifted its focus several times, widening its scope to embrace teachers' knowledge and beliefs. In a turn against a cognitive bias, studies in the eighties and nineties have shown an increasing interest in personal, moral and biographical aspects of teachers' knowledge. More recently, the social and linguistic aspects of such knowledge have attracted research attention.

Research into language teaching has been slow to take up the concept of teachers' knowledge. It was not until the mid-nineties that work in this area gathered momentum. Studies on language teachers' knowledge have since focussed on both cognitions (Woods, 1996) and personal knowledge (Bailey & Nunan, 1996). German research has gone in a slightly different direction, working on the role of *subjective theories* in language teaching and learning (Kallenbach, 1996).

The field as a whole has been noted for its heterogeneity. Tentatively pulling together the strings, one could say that teachers' knowledge has been conceptualised in the following ways:

(1) as teachers' *cognitions*, focussing on decisions made during the planning of lessons and interactive teaching (Shavelson & Stern, 1981; Calderhead, 1984, 1987; Clark & Peterson, 1986; Borko & Livingston, 1989);

(2) as teachers' *personal knowledge*, highlighting the importance of the person, biography and values in teaching (Elbaz, 1983; Clandinin, 1986);

(3) as teachers' *subject knowledge*, pinpointing teachers' personal conceptions of their subject matter (Freeman, 1993);

(4) as teachers' *cultural knowledge*, drawing attention to the fact that teachers' beliefs are not just personal but also shaped by institutional and professional cultures (Breen, 1985; Feiman-Nemser & Floden, 1986; Hargreaves, 1994; Appel, 2000).

Each of these aspects marks an extension in the development of the field. A task yet to be completed is the integration of the various component parts of teachers' knowledge. One concept which lends itself to this task is that of experience or experiential knowledge. Experiential knowledge embraces the four aspects mentioned above. It refers to both personal views and beliefs but also relates these to the shared values of the professional community, which are shaped by and are a response to institutional constraints.

One important way of investigating experiential knowledge is using interpretive methods to uncover – on the basis of verbal data – the underlying shared assumptions of the cultures of language teaching. The following discussion tries to confront some principles of student-centred teaching with these assumptions, that is, with teachers' culturally determined solutions for dealing with the demands of the classroom situation (section 3). As a second step it analyses student-centred teaching as a biographical and personal concept (section 4).

The data for the analysis come from a corpus of 20 semi-structured, in-depth interviews with secondary school teachers of English in Germany. Typically these teachers had 15 or more years of professional experience and came from different types of schools (*Gymnasium*, *Realschule*, *Waldorfschule*, *Gesamtschule*).[2]

As part of the interview teachers were asked about their views on learner autonomy in school education. In answering, several of them referred to either recent innovations like self-access work or to concepts from EFL which they had learnt about during in-service training. These answers will be analysed in the following sections.

3. Situational constraints

In analysing the school situation two contexts have to be considered. The first is a wider institutional one embracing persons, factors and constraints beyond the classroom. The second is classroom interaction itself.

3.1 Wider context and cooperation

It is commonly assumed that teachers work on their own. Classroom autonomy is indeed one of the central values of the professional culture. Once teachers have closed the classroom door, they can work more or less free from outside interference. However, research into teachers' work experience has shown that there are limits to classroom autonomy. Psychologically, teachers are, as Hargreaves (1994) points

---

2 The interviews formed the database of a more extensive study of language teachers' experiential knowledge (Appel, 2000).

out, never alone. The story told at the beginning of this chapter showed, for instance, that the teacher's lack of success with the methods she had learnt during the seminar was, in the final analysis, caused by another teacher.

Influences between this wider context and the classroom need not, however, be unidirectional. In the case of the teachers interviewed, at least one of them had experienced that deciding on self-access as a classroom technique did make a difference in terms of the wider work context. This teacher pointed out that the large number of high-quality materials required for self-access work made it imperative to share work in a group of teachers. The self-access project became an occasion for these teachers to cooperate with each other producing materials, furnishing rooms, re-adjusting timetable slots, etc.

3.2 Classroom situation

Teaching in a school classroom makes at least two important demands on teachers (Lortie, 1975; Connell, 1985; Feiman-Nemser & Floden, 1986). They have to cope with:

(a) a *low degree of voluntary participation*, that is, they are faced with a situation in which they cannot automatically assume that students will participate in classroom activities;

(b) the *grouped nature* of the teaching situation, that is, they always have to balance the needs of the individual student with those of the whole group.

Teachers respond to these demands with a repertoire of institutional solutions and classroom techniques. Both demands and solutions affect the way a concept like learner autonomy is understood and the way a method such as self-access is implemented.

3.2.1 Low degree of voluntary participation

Self-access works on the principle that students are given materials and tasks from which they choose. Being autonomous learners they are then left to do or not to do these tasks. However, given the low voluntarism characterising the school situation, teachers can never be quite sure whether their students will actually use classroom time to do these tasks.

Teachers therefore resort to strategies designed to ensure students' cooperation. Students have, for instance, to do a set number of core tasks before they can choose others. Or they have to achieve a minimum number of credits by ticking off on a list the tasks they have done. For this very reason one teacher criticises self-access work as offering a kind of "pseudo-freedom".

3.2.2 Grouped nature of the teaching situation

A school lesson consists of countless exchanges with different individuals and classroom interaction is renowned for its inherent complexity and simultaneity. Interactive teaching therefore relies on cognitive reductions, making the whole class and not the individual student the primary focus of perception.

On the other hand, learner autonomy or self-access work means letting students proceed through tasks at their own pace. However, if the grouped nature of classroom work calls for synchronisation of student work, then, no matter how individualised self-access work might be, there remains some necessity to have students proceed at approximately the same speed and arrive at approximately the same level.

One teacher described how he let the children of his beginners' class work through the tasks of the workbook at their own pace. At one point a student asked him for a grammatical explanation which would have allowed her to move well ahead of the rest of the class. The teacher refused to give her this explanation because he was sceptical about this student's ability to master the next step. He was worried that it would be difficult to "harmonise" pupils' different levels of knowledge at a later stage.

4. Student-centred teaching as a personal and biographical concept

When looking at teachers who embraced the principles of student-centred teaching as a central belief one notices that this change of personal teaching philosophy and its implementation was probably aided by two factors: previous experience and the availability of concepts.

4.1 The role of previous experience

Innovations in the classroom are part of a longer process of professional development (Goodson, 1980). One teacher had, rather late in her career, decided to make self-access work a regular feature of her classes. She did so of her own free will and well before this type of instruction had become part of mainstream teaching. Before she started to use self-access work in a systematic fashion, she had already done work along similar lines.

She had, for instance, been using worksheets which included both tasks and solutions. She had left it to her students to decide if and how they used the solutions. Quite early on, this had introduced an element of autonomy in her students' work because it was up to students whether they actually solved the tasks or just copied solutions. The decision to use self-access in her classes was taken later, on the basis of a set of beliefs already in place.

4.2 Availability of concepts

The same teacher had previously experienced her students' inability to make original and independent contributions in advanced classes. One reason students gave for this was that they had never been taught to think for themselves. This observation was to be the point of departure for this teacher's personal teaching philosophy, which put independence and autonomy at the centre of becoming an adult person. Only if students were educated for autonomy early was there any chance of improving their contributions to advanced classes. Self-access work appeared to be a way of working towards this aim and learner autonomy served as a focus of conceptualisation and reflection when using it as an instructional technique.

For another teacher learner autonomy never became a guiding principle and consequently never went any further than individual classroom episodes. During one of his lessons this teacher asked pupils to describe their room. Students went to the front of the classroom and were interviewed by the rest of the class. After a lively question-and-answer session students had to write a description of their room. The teacher was surprised by the high amount of student involvement and the quality of work triggered by this task. However, this kind of work remained an isolated incident and was apparently not taken any further. One potential reason for this is that the interview data do not show any conceptual framework (containing notions like, for instance, information-gap or personal relevance) to which classroom experience might have been related.

These two examples point to the importance of concepts in changing practice. It is mainly because the teacher using self-access work had such concepts available that she was able to see the potential of her existing practice and develop it in a principled way.

5. Conditions for change

What conditions are necessary for student-centred teaching to succeed in everyday practice? The analysis of teachers' experiential knowledge suggests the following:

5.1 External factors

Teachers do not work in splendid isolation. The organisational culture of a school can affect teaching decisions in the classroom (Kleinsasser, 1993). When the teachers mentioned earlier introduced self-access work in their classes, favourable external conditions including active support by the principal and genuine cooperation among colleagues led – despite setbacks – to longer-term changes. However, the majority of the teachers interviewed made changes that did not go beyond their own classrooms. These changes seemed to work best when they were the teachers' own decisions and had not been imposed on them from outside.

5.2 Classroom conditions

A second set of factors includes the constraints of school classrooms. Innovative approaches based on principles of student-centred teaching will, so it seems, have a greater chance of acceptance if they are seen as helpful in addressing these constraints rather than making extra demands on teachers. Such help might consist of stimulating tasks for students and the opportunity for teachers to attend to individual students.

5.3 Subject-specific considerations

A third set of factors is related to the characteristics of foreign language teaching. Self-access is in itself a method applicable to all subjects. One vital question is, however, whether or to what extent it works in language teaching.

Henning (1996) points out that children prefer to use self-access for practice and revision rather than for discovering new ideas and insights. These findings are in line with some of the teacher statements in this study. One teacher, for instance, complained that students did not tackle any creative tasks during self-access.

The introduction of new language is a complex matter, definitely requiring more than just the print media self-access is usually based on. Even if audio-visual media are available for individual students, the question remains as to what the language input for each student might consist of. According to the evidence from second language acquisition research, language acquisition will take place only if individually tuned input is available (Pienemann, 1984, 1989). The data from the present study showed, however, that even during self-access work, teachers showed a strong concern for synchronising the learning progress their classes made.

It is significant that a lot of teachers put principles of student-centred teaching into practice when they teach extensive reading. Reading in the foreign language seems to be a skill that, by virtue of being individualised, is compatible with student-centred methods and at the same time remains an authentic, communicative activity in the foreign language.

5.4 Experience and concepts

A fourth factor is the way teachers' experience is related to concepts. Teachers interviewed for this study had considerable teaching experience. However, such experience only seemed to crystallise into a more comprehensive teaching approach when they had concepts to relate this experience to. Self-access, for instance, worked well for one teacher who had discovered its principles in her own previous work. Without such a conceptual framework experience with student-centred approaches was limited to isolated incidents.

5.5 Theory and practice

The findings reported here shed some light on the perennial practice vs. theory debate in language teaching (Clarke, 1994). On the one hand, there is a need for language teaching theories to address the constraints of practice. On the other hand, theory matters. The data suggest that theory allowed experience to fall into place. This would strengthen the case for a reflective approach to teacher education – both pre-service and in-service – allowing student teachers and experienced teachers to derive more general teaching principles from mere techniques. The many learner-centred activities suggested in the resource book literature will have better and more lasting effects if the teachers using them are able to see the principles behind them and use the activities suggested within the framework of their own personal teaching philosophy.

References

Appel, J. (2000). *Erfahrungswissen und Fremdsprachendidaktik.* München: Langenscheidt-Longman.

Bailey, K. M., & Nunan, D. (Eds.). (1996). *Voices from the language classroom.* Cambridge: Cambridge University Press.

Borko, H., & Livingston, C. (1989). Cognition and improvisation: Differences in mathematics instruction by expert and novice teachers. *American Educational Research Journal, 26*, 473-498.

Breen, M. P. (1985). The social context for language learning – a neglected situation? *Studies in Second Language Acquisition, 7*, 135-158.

Calderhead, J. (1984). *Teacher's classroom decision making.* London: Holt, Rinehart und Winston.

Calderhead, J. (Ed.). (1987). *Exploring teachers' thinking.* London: Cassell.

Clandinin, D. J. (1986). *Classroom practice.* London: The Falmer Press.

Clark, C. M., & Peterson, P. L. M. (1986). Teachers' thought processes. In M. C. Wittrock (Ed.), *Handbook of research on teaching* (pp. 255-296). New York: Macmillan.

Clarke, M. A. (1994). The dysfunctions of the theory/practice discourse. *TESOL Quarterly, 28*, 9-26.

Connell, R. W. (1985). *Teachers' work.* Sydney: George Allen & Unwin.

Elbaz, F. (1983). *Teacher thinking: A study of practical knowledge.* Beckenham: Croom Helm.

Feiman-Nemser, S., & Floden, R. E. (1986). The cultures of teaching. In M. C. Wittrock (Ed.), *Handbook of research on teaching* (pp. 505-526). New York: Macmillan.

Freeman, D. (1993). Renaming experience/reconstructing practice: Developing new understandings of teaching. *Teaching and Teacher Education, 9*, 485-497.

Gnass-Franke, T. (1993). Freiarbeit im Englischunterricht – Möglichkeiten eines partnerschaftlichen Lernens. Ein Erfahrungsbericht. *Die Neueren Sprachen, 92*(4), 358-380.

Goodson, I. J. (1980). Life histories and the study of schooling. *Interchange, 11*(4), 62-76.

Hargreaves, A. (1994). *Changing teachers, changing times. Teachers' work and culture in the postmodern age.* London: Cassell.

Henning, G. (1996). *Kritik des offenen Unterrichts.* Bielefeld: Hundt.

Jürgens, E. (1998) *Die ‚neue' Reformpädagogik und die Bewegung Offener Unterricht.* Sankt Augustin: Academia.

Kallenbach, C. (1996). *Subjektive Theorien.* Tübingen: Narr.

Kleinsasser, R. C. (1993). A tale of two technical cultures: Foreign language teaching. *Teaching and Teacher Education, 9*, 373-383.

Lortie, D. C. (1975). *School-teacher.* Chicago: University Press.

Montessori, M. (1968) *Grundlagen meiner Pädagogik* (5th ed.). Heidelberg: Quelle und Meyer.

Pienemann, M. (1984). Psychological constraints on the teachability of languages. *Studies in Second Language Acquisition, 6,* 186-214.

Pienemann, M. (1989). Is language teachable? Psycholinguistic experiments and hypotheses. *Applied Linguistics, 10,* 83-113.

Scheibe, W. (1977). *Die Reformpädagogische Bewegung: 1900-1932.* Weinheim: Beltz.

Shavelson, R. J., & Stern, P. (1981). Research on teachers' pedagogical thoughts, judgements, decisions, and behavior. *Review of Educational Research, 51*, 455-498.

Woods, D. (1996). *Teacher cognition in language teaching.* Cambridge: Cambridge University Press.

Grammar and spoken discourse

Grammar in action – The case for bilingual pattern drills

Wolfgang Butzkamm

Sprache ist nicht nur Kommunikationsmittel, sondern auch Denkorgan. Sie leistet beide Aufgaben, weil sie ihrem Wesen nach *energeia*, produktive Potenz ist. (1) Sie macht von endlichen Mitteln unendlichen Gebrauch. (2) Sie ist Gedanken- und Spracheerzeugende Kraft. Die hier beschriebenen bilingualen Strukturübungen basieren auf diesem generativen Prinzip und haben demnach zwei Aufgaben zu erfüllen: Geläufigkeit zu erzielen und das Inhaltsspektrum einer Struktur und somit auch den kommunikativen Gebrauchswert vorzuführen. Die Schüler sollen nicht nur das grammatische Muster, sondern zugleich die abgewandelten Inhalte im Sinn haben. Satzvariationen müssten also zugleich Sinnvariationen, Strukturübungen zugleich Denkspiele sein und zur Selbsttätigkeit anregen. Daraus ergibt sich ein bestimmter Übungsverlauf, der im Detail vorgestellt wird.

The theoretical basis for pattern drills is the generative principle, i.e. the human capacity to generate an infinite number of utterances from a finite grammatical competence (W. v. Humboldt). Words can be recombined again and again to produce innumerable novel sentences. Teachers have intuitively sensed the importance of the generative principle and have tried to teach in ways which will turn sentences into syntactical germ cells, i.e. into models for many more sentences. However, pattern drills often turned out to be mechanical and monotonous. This has raised the question whether successful practice on sentences can really further communicative competence. To transfer or not to transfer – that was the problem. Bilingual pattern drills as discussed here have a dual focus, on fluency and on content. Sentence variations must be seen as sense or thought variations.

1. The generative principle, or: playing on analogies

Natural languages – as Greek grammarians knew – tend to move between analogy and anomaly, rule and exception, law and chaos. Learners have to identify and memorise the anomalies and irregularities one by one; and the same holds true for every single word stem. How else would we know that bread means bread, or *Brot*, *panis*, *pain*? There's no way out: Somebody must tell us, and we must keep these forms in mind.

By contrast, analogies and rules are our big chance of getting away from mere learning by heart. Whenever there is something like order we are freed from learning individual items of language. We intuit or discover the organizing principle instead.

Take the German plural and the memory load is high; foreigners are well advised to learn the gender assignment as well as the plural form along with the noun stem: *Haus – das Haus – die Häuser*. At the other end of the spectrum is the formation of diminutives:

Steffi – das Steffichen
Elisabeth – das Elisabethchen.

Once you have learnt to distinguish the name from the inflection and have grasped its meaning, there is no need to listen to more examples. Everything works just the same as with Steffi and Elisabeth (apart from the umlaut-rules). You can take risks and start on your own:

Helmut – das Helmütchen.

This creation of new forms according to known forms is captured by the didactic term generative principle, and applies to both word-formation and sentence-formation. To Prendergast, a 19th-century English methodologist, this was the fundamental feature of language:

> Sentences have within them a principle of vitality, an inherent power of expressing many different ideas by giving birth to new sentences." (Prendergast, 1864, p. 19)

The great Danish linguist Jespersen spoke in a similar vein. According to him, words have the power to generate new expressions from known ones. If one uses a particular kind of word or sentence construction often enough, it will turn into something new and become part of a mental mechanism:

> . . . just as the English boy who has often heard superlatives like hardest, cleanest, highest, etc., does not need any rule to be able to construct forms like purest, ugliest, dirtiest, of his own accord, and who, at the moment when he says them, would not be able even by means of the most scrupulous analysis to decide if he has heard the form before and is merely reproducing it, or if he himself is creating it without having previously heard it. . . " (Jespersen, 1904, p. 116)

Harold Palmer coined the term "ergon" (maybe taking his clue from Humboldt's *energeia*). An ergon is a phrase or sentence that presents some sort of syntactic nucleus from which pupils can construct further similar sentences. The learners' task is to acquire these ergons, these familiar parts of speech or "primary material" as a database which will then serve them to generate an infinite number of sentences ("secondary material").

> Were the number of sentences in a given language limited to a few hundreds, or even a few thousands, a student might reasonably be expected to learn them off by heart, and by so doing become a master of the language. The number of sentences, however, being infinite, recourse must be had to the study of their mechanism in order that from a relatively limited number of lesser ergons an infinite number of sentences may be composed at will. (Palmer, 1917, p. 22)

However, something important was overlooked. This is evident when we look at Wilhelm von Humboldt's philosophy of language. For him, the quintessential property of language was energeia, its productive potential or creativity:

> Denn sie [die Sprache] steht ganz eigentlich einem unendlichen und wahrhaft grenzenlosen Gebiet, dem Inbegriff alles Denkbaren gegenüber. Sie muss daher von endlichen Mitteln einen unendlichen Gebrauch machen, und vermag dies durch die Identität der Gedanken- und Spracheerzeugenden Kraft. (Humboldt, 1963, p. 477)

> (For it [language] is confronted with an essentially infinite and truly unbounded territory, the quintessence of everything which can be thought. It must thus make infinite use of finite means, and it achieves this through the identity of the power to produce both thoughts and speech.)

This "identity of the power to produce both thoughts and speech" means that we do not just generate novel sentences, but new ideas at the same time. Sentence variations must be experienced as variations on meaning. The problem seems to be that Humboldt's energeia is usually only familiar in its abbreviated formulation "making infinite use of finite means" and is thus interpreted in structuralist or syntactical terms only.

2. Evidence from natural language acquisition

We know that some children engage in verbal play which is very much reminiscent of pattern drills. This is an important discovery (or re-discovery). Children seem to ask themselves: How can I explore a structure's semantic potential? What has become expressible now? They are interested in content variations. Witness the kind of verbal play that Ruth Weir (1962, pp. 109, 111) overheard and recorded when her son was left alone in the dark before he went to sleep:

> What colour
> What colour blanket
> What colour mop
> What colour glass

Here is an example of a girl of two years eight months, talking to herself (Britton, 1972, p. 83):

> I've been sick every day in the car.
> That's why I've got cold.
> But I don't be sick like this,
> but I don't be sick in bed,
> but I don't be sick on the beach.

This may be sound play and grammatical play, but, to my mind, it is mainly semantic play, even if what the child produces is nonsense. After all, there is sense in nonsense, as Freud reminds us. . . Man is a sense-making animal. We do not accept a semantic vacuum. So we quite naturally find some sort of sense even in what seems to make no sense. The child certainly enjoys playing with words, by repetitions of similar sounds, by his rediscovery of what is familiar to him, by rearranging familiar meanings.

According to Burling (1959, p. 88), who reported on his observations made when his son acquired two languages (English and Garo) simultaneously, the moment when children begin breaking up structures and permutating them, is a milestone in linguistic development:

> My feeling as I observed Stephen's language, and my conclusions now, is that the number of words or morphemes is perhaps the least important criterion of grammatical progress. What from an adult's point of view are multi-morphemic words, or multi-word sentences, were used before their complex nature was recognised by Stephen. The most significant single advance in his ability came when he learned to make substitutions.

3. How to proceed

Frank M. Grittner, school inspector in Chicago, takes stock of pattern drills (Grittner, 1969, p. 203):

> Of all the elements which constitute the new American Method, the pattern drill appears to be most widely misunderstood. In the hands of a knowledgeable teacher, such drills are capable of producing an exhilarating classroom atmosphere with students sitting on the edge of their chairs listening intently for their cues and responding instantly when called upon. However, when used by a teacher who is not aware of the function and purpose of this type of the drill, the results can be as stultifying as the choral chanting of verb conjugations and noun declensions.

Pattern practice should not occur at the expense of communication, but should facilitate it. Ultimately we expect pupils to use the sentence patterns for their own speech intentions and to employ them in free conversation. Therefore, the bilingual pattern drills which I propose in this paper and which I first encountered in a pioneering study by Dodson (1967, p. 72) meet three different needs which are all important:

- The need to notice the pattern in a sentence, to see the slots into which different words may be plugged, in other words to become aware of language as a combinatorial system, as *energeia*.
- The need to achieve fluency, to automatise a given sentence pattern (these two needs have been met by traditional pattern practice)
- The need to probe the communicative radius of a structure and explore its communicative potential. This is mainly achieved by focusing on the meanings of the sentence variations.

Initially, we use simple, easy substitutions. The focus is predominantly on form, i.e. on the first two needs. Any word will do which is easily accessible, fits the sentence pattern and makes sense. Later, we focus more and more on content.

3.1 Example: Contact clause

All sentence frames, working as ergons in the sense of Palmer, should be taken from texts, stories or dialogues and are thus anchored in a situational context. Accordingly, the teacher draws the attention to this at the beginning of the exercise.

Take, for instance, the line "All I want is a room somewhere" from Eliza's song in the musical *My Fair Lady*. Initially, the teacher's idea is simply to practise the formal device of a "contact clause" where the relative pronoun is left out. He explains the structure, which is unknown in German, by giving a literal translation:

All	I	want	is	a	room.
Alles	*was ich*	*will*	*ist*	*ein*	*Zimmer.*

The learner is now aware of the anatomy of the phrase. Then the teacher changes the German sentence to a more idiomatic phrase and starts out with easy substitutions, to achieve fluency:

Ich will ja nur eine Tasse Tee.
All I want is a cup of tea.

Ich will ja nur eine Tasse Kaffee.
All I want is a cup of coffee.

Ich will ja nur ein Glas Milch.
All I want is a glass of milk.

If the teacher thinks the class needs further practice he gives some more cues along the same lines. But then he changes the focus and starts to elicit the following sentence variations from his class, focusing on the things wanted:

Ich will ja nur eine ruhige Klasse.
All I want is a quiet class.

Ich will ja nur brave Schüler.
All I want is well-behaved pupils.

Sie will ja nur einen neuen Freund.
All she wants is a new boyfriend.

In the course of the exercise, we can change the tense and the verb as well:

Ich wollte ja nur einen Kuss.
All I wanted was a kiss.

Ich bekam nur ein freundliches Lächeln.
All I got was a friendly smile.

"Empty" sentences at the beginning, and at the end suggestive sentences powerful enough to conjure up certain situations. In the minds of the pupils, these are no longer grammatical permutations, but variations on the theme of wishes and dreams, rather than a structure drill. Only at the beginning of the exercise is the teacher concerned about how often he has to repeat the structure in order for it to become consolidated. In the second part of the exercise, he asks himself how he can show his pupils through interesting substitution possibilities that this sentence structure is also suitable for their own needs of expression. The exchangeable sentence elements and their meanings become of greatest importance.

This, however, is not yet the end of the exercise. In the third part of the exercise, it is handed over to the pupils. They have now to make up their own sentences, and the exercise becomes monolingual. By now, the pupils are well prepared to produce sentences – and ideas – of their own. Those few who have no ideas of their own are free to select any of the sentences that the teacher had cued before. The teacher might also allow the class a few minutes' silence to jot down any idea that comes to their minds. Most pupils will then produce sentences which are meaningful and relevant to them. This in turn will give the teacher the opportunity to ask the pupil a question and involve him in a brief communicative exchange before resuming the exercise.

3.2 Example: Present continuous

This example is given here to emphasise the difference it makes when mother-tongue cues are used. The exercise is less prone to becoming mechanical, mainly because the teachers can use their voice, their facial expression and gestures to support meaning. Isolated sentences may then not be as isolated as they seem because pupils might spontaneously think of situations that fit the sentences.

1. Teacher: Have you found that sentence "What are you doing?" Could you please underline it? What does it mean here? Could you give us a good German translation? Pupil: *Was machst du denn da?* Teacher: Yes. Now let's practise. I'll give you German sentences, and you give me the English ones.

Teacher: *Was machst du denn da?* (as if accusing someone, frowning)

Was schreibst du denn da?
What are you writing there?

Was liest du denn da?
What are you reading there?

Was isst du denn da?
What are you eating there?

etc.

"Now let's imagine you're preparing a meal in the kitchen." With an inquisitive look, and a voice that indicates that he/she is really curious about what is happening in the kitchen, the teacher may produce the following stimulus-sentences:

Was kochst du denn da?
What are you cooking?

Was schneidest du denn da?
What are you cutting?

Was backst du denn da?
What are you baking?

(Additional explanation to avoid interference and teach an important distinction: *Was machst/tust/treibst du denn da?* = What are you doing? But: *Was machst du denn da?* in the sense of what someone is producing = What are you making?)

2. Another situation, again typical of the continuous form. The teacher's voice carries a hint of indignation, or slightly threatening tone:

Isst du etwa unter deinem Pult?
Are you eating under your desk?

Liest du etwa unter deinem Pult?
Are you reading under your desk?

Liest du etwa wieder Comics?
Are you reading comics again?

etc.

3. In a pleading voice: Schau mal, du störst die ganze Klasse.

   Look, you're disrupting the whole class!
   Look, you're causing a disturbance!
   Look, you're making it difficult for me.
   Look, you're not helping us.

4. Another situation, the teacher again using a pleading voice: *Jenny, bitte, ich versuche mich gerade zu konzentrieren.*

   Jenny, please, I'm trying to concentrate.
   Jenny, please, I'm doing my homework.

3.3 Development and dynamics of the exercise

1. Teacher-directed, mother-tongue cues for ignition. Simple, easy sentences in rapid succession, finally more complex, "loaded" sentences.
2. (optional, written) Short brainstorming to note down ideas. Perhaps meditative background music as used in suggestopedia.
3. Pupils produce sentences of their own. Teacher might intervene and ask questions concerning the idea expressed by the pupils.
4. (optional, written) Pupils write small/short texts of their own, using the new structure at least once.

4. Costs and benefits of bilingual practice

Why is it so important to use mother-tongue cues at the very beginning? Why not do it monolingually all the way through? My answer: The ideas expressed in the sentences are vividly pictured in the mind. Many components contribute to this effect. It is intonation in particular, and the way you use your voice, indicating surprise or indignation, it is body language in general, plus the modal particles that are so typical of German. It makes all the difference.

But what about interference from the mother tongue? Well, it cannot be completely avoided. It is always present especially when we are tired or unconcentrated, even though we haven't heard a single mother-tongue word for quite a while. Won't pupils be tempted to fall for interference?

For instance, pronouns may cause confusion when giving mother-tongue cues:

Teacher:	*Das ist eine wunderbare Idee.*
Pupil:	It's a wonderful idea.
Teacher:	*Sie* [referring to "die Idee"] *ist super.*
Pupil:	She [instead of "it"] is super.

One could of course simply avoid dangerous cognates/false friends or deceptive pronouns. If you have the impression that some of your pupils cannot yet cope with the proper pronouns when cued by the mother-tongue, take care the situation won't arise. At some point, all pupils will be able to deal with this problem successfully. Another possibility of avoiding mistakes is to draw attention to them before they are actually made. You could agree on a special hand signal with your class, meaning "careful, mistakes are likely to occur". Or a more direct hint: "Mind the gender." Or use an anticipatory prompt: "Don't say 'she' now, that's German."

Every solution breeds new problems, so one has to offset the costs of a technique against its benefits. If we are clever, we can end up with an extremely positive cost-benefit ratio. The gains will be mainly achieved through the flexibility of bilingual cues, the smooth transitions from various substitutions to extensions, reductions and transformation, from small and big leaps as you go from one stimulus to the next.

Remember that the teacher has to hand over the exercise to the pupils and these have to build new sentences freely. Producing new sentences on their own is still far away from real conversation; but it is an important step towards it, since the pupils tend to communicate something even through isolated sentences. These sentences can be pegs on which to hang your conversation.

To summarise, the following benefits can be derived from bilingual pattern drills:

- Thought put into language vs mere manipulation of a structure
- Conveyance of sense through intonation, mime and gesture vs loss of meaning through mechanical substitutions
- Emotional involvement vs boredom

- Strictly oral exercise, no written substitution tables
- Flexible change vs fixed transformation pattern (operations: substitution, extension, crossing out, rearranging)
- Communicative dynamics: focus on content vs focus on form
- Development: initially "empty" sentences; then more suggestive sentences, personal, funny, imaginative; and sentences alluding to current events.

Monolingual drills are also welcome, of course, if only for variety's sake, and they can be combined with bilingual cue drills. Our programme is to free method of its dogma, and hence the enrichment of language work and not its impoverishment.

5. Advice for the student teacher: dos and don'ts

Be clear about the grammatical point you want to practise. Have you chosen a productive pattern? Is there a structural contrast between L1 and L2? At the beginning, make absolutely certain that your students fully understand both the meaning of a pattern and its internal structure.

Begin with model sentences from well-practised dialogues. You may write these sentences up on the board.

Don't interrupt the stimulus-response sequence by calling on each student by name.

At first, use only easy substitutions. Centre on one grammatical feature and don't change too many elements when going from one sentence to the next.

Your sentence variations include exchanging elements, adding / leaving out elements, and perhaps structural transformations such as changing tense, negation, interrogation, passivisation. But don't make your sentences too long.

Choose your mother tongue cues carefully. Use only idiomatic German. When in doubt, ask your students for better versions.

Support your mother tongue cues with body language, the proper intonation and the right voice. Can your sentences be easily contextualised?

Insist on fluent delivery and natural intonation. Don't allow students to reflect too long prior to responding. Give a prompt instead, or say the complete sentence yourself and get the student to imitate it.

Make sure your exercise does not degenerate into a tortuous translation puzzle. Don't allow your students to "translate", but keep a lively pace instead.

Watch out for possible sources of interference from the mother tongue and don't trap your students into making those mistakes.

Don't stick to isolated sentences as the drill continues. Try to combine and connect sentences meaningfully.

As the exercise develops, focus more and more on content:

Try to come up with some funny ideas. Stimulate positive emotions.

Try to relate your sentences to topical events and to personal communicative needs in your class.

When you are looking for exciting ideas, don't hesitate to introduce a new word.

Later in the drill, break away from it whenever possible and initiate a brief communicative exchange before you resume the drill.

Don't forget to hand the exercise over to the students so that they can make up their own sentences.

If at the stage where students take over you think your class will need prompts (verbal or visual), put a list of suitable expressions to choose from on the board.

Anyone has the right to pass if they prefer.

Watch out for signs of boredom and fatigue. In general, keep your drills short and rapid.

References

Britton, J. (1972). *Language and learning.* Harmondsworth: Pelican.

Burling, R. (1959). Language development of a Garo and English-speaking child. In C. A. Ferguson & D. I. Slobin (Eds.) (1973), *Studies of child language development.* New York: Holt, Rinehart and Winston.

Dodson, C. J. (1967/1972). *Language teaching and the bilingual method.* London: Pitman.

Grittner, F. M. (1969). *Teaching foreign languages.* New York: Harper & Row.

Humboldt, W. v. (1963). *Werke in fünf Bänden. Band 3: Schriften zur Sprachphilosophie.* Edited by A. Flitner & K. Giel. Stuttgart: Cotta'sche Buchhandlung.

Jespersen, O. (1904). *How to teach a foreign language.* London: Allen and Unwin.

Palmer, H. E. (1917/1968). *The scientific study and teaching of language.* London: Harrap.

Prendergast, T. (1864). *The mastery of languages; or, the art of speaking foreign tongues idiomatically.* London: Richard Bentley, New Burlington Street.

Weir, R. (1962). *Language in the crib.* The Hague: Mouton.

A processing view of teaching English grammar

Uwe Multhaup

Der Fremdsprachenunterricht wird von drei Typen von Ansätzen geprägt. Traditionelle Ansätze sind formorientiert. Sie halten Grammatikunterricht und engführende Übungen für nötig, um Fehler zu verhindern. Eine radikale Alternative bieten Ansätze, die ein angeborenes Sprachwissen annehmen. Sie behaupten, dass formaler Grammatikunterricht nutzlos sei und halten allein *comprehensible input* für nötig. Eine mittlere Position nehmen konstruktivistische und handlungsorientierte Ansätze ein. In diesem Beitrag wird die *Processability Theory* vorgestellt, die einen konstruktivistischen Ansatz vertritt. Ihre Hauptaussage ist, dass Grammatikunterricht nur nützt, wenn gelehrt wird, was Schüler praktisch umsetzen können. Fehler sind unvermeidlich, weil auf dem Wege zum Sprachkönnen alle Lernenden eine Reihe von Sprachlernstufen durchlaufen, auf denen stufentypische Fehler gemacht werden. Die Theorie basiert auf psycholinguistischen und empirischen Zweitspracherwerbsstudien und erklärt, welche Fehler auf welcher Sprachlernstufe gemacht werden. Das ermöglicht eine Prognose der Aspekte von Grammatik, die auf einer erreichten Lernstufe lernbar sind.

Foreign language teaching is dominated by three types of approach. Traditional approaches are form-oriented. They believe that explicit grammar instruction is useful and that exercises must be designed that help prevent errors. Approaches that believe in an inborn Universal Grammar represent a radical alternative. They maintain that all explicit grammar teaching is useless and insist that all learners need is comprehensible input. A middle position is taken by constructivist and task-based approaches. In this essay Processability Theory is discussed, which is a constructivist approach. Its central message is that grammar instruction can only be useful if teachers teach what learners can learn. Errors are to a certain degree inevitable because on their way to language competence all learners pass through a sequence of stages of grammar acquisition and make errors typical of the individual stage. Based on psycholinguistic and empirical studies of second language acquisition, the theory predicts what type of errors learners make at each stage. That allows a prognosis of what parts of grammar are teachable for individual learners at a given stage of their language development.

Everyone knows that learning to speak a second language (a) requires that we learn enough vocabulary to give lexical expression to what we want to say; (b) that we learn to put the words in a morphological form and syntactic order that express what we mean to say and that are "correct" from a native-speaker perspective; (c) that we learn to pronounce the words and phrases more or less correctly. Leaving aside that there are other, pragmatic and cultural aspects to second language acquisition (SLA), the above three components are central to it, and most people consider grammar learning to be the most difficult part. Sophisticated theories of language learning, too, centre on grammar acquisition. Correspondingly, foreign language teaching (FLT) has traditionally based its methods on syllabi that prescribe which forms of grammar must be taught in what sequence. The definition of which forms are easy to learn and which are difficult to learn was based on formal linguistic descriptions of grammar, and on teaching experience. That is why traditional approaches to FLT are all variants of the same type: form-oriented FLT.

In the classroom, form-oriented FLT takes the form of the PPP-Model (Presentation – Practice – Production): First, the grammar forms to be learnt are correctly presented; teachers next provide many opportunities for their practice in "guided exercises" (pattern drills) and aim to stamp out learner errors; finally learners are expected to use the practiced forms creatively and correctly in spontaneous and meaningful communicative interactions. It is well known, though, that the hoped-for learning transfer from the practice to the production phase (communication) mostly does not take place. This is nicely captured by the title of D. Allwright's (1984) essay: "Why don't learners learn what teachers teach?" Many researchers have therefore suggested that a new approach to FLT be developed. But, depending on their views of how grammar is learnt, suggestions for reforms differ. They can be divided into three groups.

1. Three types of approach to FLT

One group of researchers base their suggestions for reforms on pragmalinguistic concepts of language, and on the experience of teachers that learners need plenty of opportunity for using the L2. As a result, communicative and meaning-oriented approaches to FLT were developed. They stress that learners, in class, need to want to say what they say, or else they will not learn to use the target language creatively. At the same time however, communicative approaches, in this country, basically stick to a form-based syllabus that prescribes which grammar forms must be taught when, though underlining that teachers should practice error tolerance and rate fluency higher than accuracy. That however (a) leaves it to the individual teacher to decide how to teach grammar and when to tolerate errors, and (b) brings teachers into a situation that requires them to manoeuvre the learners into a situation which allows them to say what they mean to say while ensuring that the language forms they need for that "happen to be identical" with the ones prescribed by the syllabus.

Quite obviously, that is difficult to achieve. It requires of learners a "willing suspension of disbelief". They must imagine themselves to be in a situation in which the use of the prescribed lexical and grammatical items makes sense. That requires of teachers to find tasks that are both motivating and manageable with the limited linguistic skills that a particular group of learners have. Such tasks, though, provide only a poor substitute for the existential need to learn the L2 in an L2 environment with its many communicatively meaningful situations. Even more importantly, task-based learning does not change the fact that in a FLT context the learners have much less time and opportunity for autonomously figuring out (by trial and error) how the L2 grammar functions. That puts limits to task-based approaches.

A second group of researchers bluntly denies that grammar can be taught. They argue that learners do not need formal instruction nor an explicit knowledge of grammar rules, since they acquire grammar implicitly if they receive enough comprehensible language input (Krashen, 1985). These researchers point, for a support of their hypothesis, to a language acquisition theory which was designed to explain first language acquisition (Chomsky, 1980). It argues that children neither get nor need grammatical instruction; they acquire their first language, even though the language input they get from their parents may be grammatically incomplete or corrupt. That is called "the logical problem of language acquisition". It is speculated that children are able to solve it because they are born with a so-called language acquisition device (later called Universal Grammar [UG]). That theory stimulated SLA researchers to speculate on whether UG-knowledge is available for SLA too or "used-up", so to speak, with first language acquisition, or available for SLA up to a critical age only. Other researchers pointed out that "comprehensible input" is not enough for language acquisition to take place because learners also need to produce comprehensible output (Swain, 1985).

One of the attractions of UG-based theories of SLA is that they offer a seemingly elegant way of explaining "the logical problem of language acquisition", and for the fact that L2 grammars are acquired in universally similar developmental stages (Pienemann, 1984; Long, 1988). If we assume a UG that unfolds following a "biologically built-in syllabus", that would nicely explain these stages. The logical consequence would be, though, to give up syllabus construction, grammar teaching and error correction. We should instead focus on providing learners with plenty of comprehensible language input, leaving it to nature to see to the rest.

There are some serious problems with UG-based acquisition theories, however. They start with the fact that neurobiologists and neuroanatomists say that from an evolutionary and neurophysiological perspective there is no evidence for the existence of a genetically inherited UG (Deacon, 1997); similarly many psychologists object to UG-theories as empirically unwarranted (Hörmann, 1976, p. 320). Apart from that, the evidence for parameter setting processes in SLA is not conclusive, nor has it been shown that better results are achieved in SLA if we stop giving learners support in grammar acquisition by explaining the rules of grammar. Furthermore, the fact that there are universal similarities in SLA processes is not of itself proof of the existence of an inborn UG. They call, though, for a non-nativist explanation. That is provided by the constructivist view of learning (Wolff, 1994). It sees language acquisition as the result of general learning strategies that apply to all domains of knowledge and skills, from learning to swim or ski, for example, to playing chess and solving mathematical problems, and to SLA (Bates & MacWhinney, 1989).

The challenge is, however, to come to a theoretically consistent explanation of such constructive processes in SLA, because only if we do, can we give more precise advice than recommending "awareness raising" as the best strategy to help learners with grammar acquisition. We therefore need a psycholinguistic theory that can explain (a) why there are universally similar developmental stages in SLA, (b) why a late beginning SLA does not lead to native speaker competence, and (c) why explicit rule instruction cannot change the developmental sequence in SLA. The theory should (d) be compatible with what we know from the cognitive sciences about the distributed storage of knowledge and the parallel spreading of activation in the neural network.

The progress made in that direction in recent time is considerable, although we are still some way from a generally accepted theory of how language is mentally represented. I want to show, however, that there is a theory that can explain the universally similar developmental stages in SLA without assuming an inborn UG. The theory is called Processability Theory (Pienemann, 1998); it derives from the well-known teachability hypothesis (Pienemann, 1984), which is famous for the dictum "teach what is teachable". Note, though, that "teachable" must not be confused with "prescribed by the formal syllabus". After presenting Processability Theory, I will discuss its consequences for FLT, focusing in particular on how it relates to task-based and holistic learning (Timm, 1995a).

2. Constructivism and Processability Theory: A psycholinguistic account of SLA

Processability Theory (PT) has an empirical basis in the analysis of several sets of data from studies of SLA in different languages and by different researchers (Pienemann, 1998, pp. 117-230). They are interpreted against the background of (a) a concept of human information-processing which shows that Working Memory (Baddeley, 1986) is the bottle-neck through which all information must go on its way in and out of Long Term Memory, both in learning and doing, and (b) a social-functional model of grammar, Lexical Functional Grammar (Kaplan & Bresnan, 1982; Kempen & Hoenkamp, 1987), and a corresponding model of speech production (Levelt, 1989). The speed with which goal-directed activities like speaking can take place depends on the availability of knowledge patterns that can be fast and incrementally activated (Levelt, 1989, p. 24) to serve the communicative goal. Their processability is a function of the strength of the associative links from conceptual knowledge units to language-specific lexical and grammatical and articulatory processing units that serve to express the concepts. Frequent use of a processing unit (knowledge pattern) enhances the chances of its fast (automatized) processability.

PT shows that in speech production the mind is faced with a number of key grammatical encoding tasks. They are tackled in language acquisition in a developmental sequence that reflects a hierarchy of processing procedures, which is universal (Pienemann, 1998, p. 87). If a learner fails to successfully take a "low down" step in that hierarchy of processing procedures, it has a negative effect on all "higher up" processing procedures. For FLT that would be a point for stepping in with supporting (preventive) measures. That does not mean, though, that there is no individual variation. It is restricted, however, to how fast and well the developmental steps are taken by a specific learner, which is a function of his/her learning motivation and social identity. Before going into details, however, it is useful to first discuss the "mechanisms" that underlie language learning processes.

2.1 From experience and fuzzy concepts to automatized processes

Learning processes transform the flood of incoming sensory data into knowledge patterns, using for their ordering the fact that human beings experience things and events in meaningful contexts which help to structure the data. The contexts prompt learners to remember "things" in terms of their qualities, such as "eatable" or "not eatable", "solid" or "soft", "mobile" or "immobile", "good-for-me" or "bad-for-me", "usually having consequence X", and so on. That indicates how such concepts relate to predicate argument structures and a meaning-based understanding of linguistic categories like "noun", "verb", "adjective", which is essential for grammar acquisition. The point here is, though, that they are not inborn linguistic knowledge but created in learning processes. That is not in conflict with the fact that in the course of the self-organization of knowledge, linguistic units develop a preference for activating other linguistic forms (modular organization). L1 forms generally activate other L1 forms; and L2 forms need to develop equally strong "associative cohesion" before they can be used for the fast expression of meaning.

Memories of the conceptual qualities of "things" are first stored in Episodic Memory. That is a sort of biographical memory that stores information in a distributed but connected form across many parts of the brain. The different parts of a specific concept mutually activate each other if one of them receives activation from outside. Thus, in an animalistic fashion, instinctive reactions to the appearance of certain sensory stimuli can be triggered.

On the basis of its episodic memories the human mind can create, in what is called Semantic Memory, cognitive concepts of things and events. They are the result of processes that abstract away from the qualities of the individual "thing", constructing instead a concept of the type of thing/event they represent. They are "fuzzy concepts" because they comprise, besides their core or defining semantic features, other, possible or likely features, which make them fuzzy on the edge (Timm, 1995b; Multhaup, 1999). Concepts are, over time, subject to a restructuring and re-evaluation of the number and kind of "things" they stand for (mean).

It is the fuzziness of concepts that makes them powerful tools in learning processes. They allow people to adapt to new situations by mental processes which Jean Piaget (1980) calls assimilation and accommodation. From a processing perspective, it means that mental processes are probabilistic calculations, and not based on the "application" of explicit rules and invariable symbols as used by standard computers. From a neurological perspective that means that connectionist models come closest to what goes on in neural networks (Bechtel & Abrahamsen, 1991). With regard to language learning, including SLA, a model of how they work in acquisition processes has been put forward in form of the Competition Model by MacWhinney (1989).

The probabilistic nature of mental processing procedures explains how people come from a conceptual (pre-linguistic) understanding of what "things" are like and can do, to a semantic understanding of their roles in predicate argument structures. In fact children use a whole range of processing strategies to get their grammar acquisition processes started. They range from semantic bootstrapping (Pinker, 1989), that is interfacing semantic structures with syntax, and syntactic bootstrapping, that is guessing the meaning of new language forms from their relationship to known lexical and other items in a syntactic frame, to homing in on the sound quality of utterances (rhymes, stress, intonation). Linked with this is the fact that semantic learning is exemplar-based: Children first learn how a verb like *give* functions before other verbs are (tentatively) fitted into the mould created by it, thus inheriting a preformed syntactic "behaviour pattern". Because of the probabilistic nature of neural processing patterns, they can be modified without a break-down of the old system.

In late beginning SLA learners profit from the knowledge of how language functions which they acquired in L1 learning. But they pay a price for that, which is interference. The semantic mappings from non-linguistic concepts to language forms tend to transfer from L1 forms to seemingly equivalent L2 forms. One of the most difficult things in SLA, therefore, is the un-learning of such automatized mappings. Pronunciation is a typical example; new speech production procedures, which need to establish themselves against the strong competition from deeply ingrained L1 speech habits, are initially at a disadvantage, and it takes plenty of time and practice for them to gain ground. Late beginning L2 learners rarely get rid of their L1 accent. A good description of the nature of the mental processes involved in such language learning processes is provided by the neurolinguist Paradis (1994); it, too, gives a good explanation of the roles of implicit and explicit learning in language learning processes:

> Learners are conscious of the sounds they attempt to produce and they practise until they are satisfied that their performance sufficiently approximates the intended sound. The articulatory (and hence motor) gestures, when often repeated, end up leaving proprioceptive kinaesthetic traces, i.e. automatically available articulatory movement programmes. But even in this borderline case, although the sounds are consciously practised, it is the proprioceptive data (i.e., the cortical record of the position of each organ involved, from the position of the tongue relative to the palate, the teeth and the lips, to the movements of the vocal cords) that are stored in implicit memory. The speaker is not really aware of the simultaneous or sequential position of all the phonatory organs. The speaker is only conscious of the result obtained, not of how it is obtained. The organs' position, of which the speaker is not conscious, is what is stored implicitly and becomes automatic through practice, just as with any other motor skill. What the speaker is conscious of, is the sound that is produced and practised. (Paradis, 1994, p. 401)

This shows that it is futile to debate whether explicit learning always precedes implicit learning or vice versa.

Both lexical learning and grammar acquisition are affected by this competition of old established vs. new forms. With regard to grammar the picture is complicated by the fact that in core areas of grammar there are both universal developmental sequences and language-specific interference effects, with lexical interference being a typical example of the latter. That is of consequence for error analysis in SLA, and for a pedagogical definition of what is teachable at a given stage of a learner's L2 development.

In this context a note on the relation of imitation to cognition seems appropriate, because some language acquisition theories decry imitation. Nobody denies that language learning can take place only if the learners come into "contact" with the target language, that is, have a model on which they can base their acquisition processes. But only if they try to imitate the model will they acquire the target language. It is important therefore to see that imitation and cognition are not two mutually exclusive but complementary learning strategies. They are preceded by reception (a silent period), that is, by processes that try to capture both the physical form and semantic function of the items that are being learnt. That is so because "words" must first be represented in the neural network, as declarative knowledge, before the mind can analyze them. For them to enter the neural net, however, they must first be noticed, and there must be a motivation to further analyze them. That takes us to the crucial role of motivation in learning.

The brain is a biological organ, and its function is to serve the interests of the whole organism. The creation and use of knowledge patterns in the brain is therefore motivated by the interests of the whole organism. That is why new knowledge patterns are created only if a person sees a useful purpose (function) in their construction. With regard to the recall/use of knowledge patterns it must be stated, though, that because in a given situation different knowledge patterns (i.e., options for action, plans or desires) compete, what is needed is a sort of executive committee that decides which of the competing options are realized (Faw, 2000). In the brain (Figure 1), the role of such a central control is reserved to the joint operation of the Prefrontal Cortex and neighbouring parts of the Limbic System. The Prefrontal Cortex is the place where cognitive plans and moral decisions are made; the Limbic System is the emotional brain (Goleman, 1995). It plays a crucial role in the spreading of neurotransmitters, which are essential in the long-term storing of knowledge.

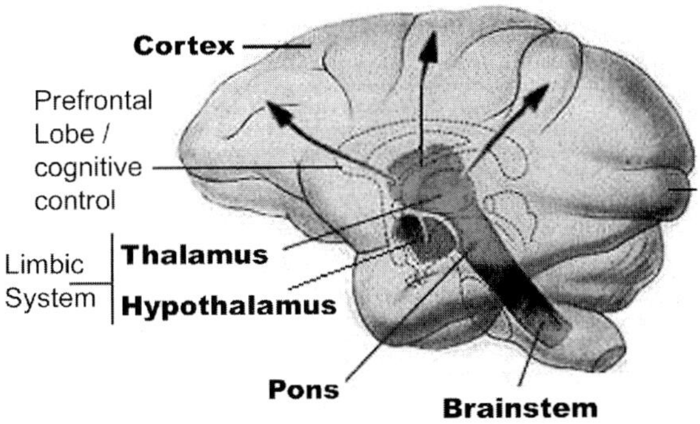

Figure 1. The human brain (from: http://www.biokurs.de/skripten/12/bs12-42.htm)

The Prefrontal Cortex is not itself a seat of knowledge but registers which areas of the cortex are "on", but in competition with other areas "calling for attention". They are "specialists", and together they represent the complete range of actions that could be taken at a given moment. They meet, though, with affective messages from the Limbic System, and it is only by the joint operation of cognition- and affection-based factors that specific processing routines receive "permission to fire". For FLT the message is: No processes without a motivation to reach a specific goal, and no processes without the knowledge patterns (processing routines) that know how to reach that goal. This underlines the need for a functional approach to the study of language and learning, which is in keeping with what teachers who take a pragmatic approach to FLT say on the basis of their classroom experience.

It is essential to remember, however, that the processing capacity of the Prefrontal Cortex is limited. It is identical with the famous 7±2 units Working Memory can handle. It is well-known, too, that the speed and power of mental processes can be enhanced if individual bits of knowledge are compiled in large chunks of knowledge, which are stored in Long Term Memory as processing routines (schemata/skills), which saves processing capacity in Working Memory. The chances of their automatized recall are enhanced through practice. With regard to such processing routines it must be pointed out, though, that their construction is subject to constraints: Some processes presuppose that certain other processing routines have been established prior to them. It is impossible for instance, to learn to jump or dance before learning to walk. What that means for SLA is spelled out by PT, which is discussed in the next section.

2.2 PT and the implicational hierarchy of processing procedures

The goal of general-purpose courses in FLT is to enable learners to use the target language in communication. Considering, however, that oral communication requires a much faster processing of language than writing, what L2 learners say in oral communication is the acme test of their language competence. In other words, although it is possible to train learners to do well in formal grammar tests, they do not provide reliable information on the real stage of their language competence. Speech requires automatized processing routines, or else, with the limited capacities of Working Memory, it would become impossible to construct, within fractions of a second, the morpho-syntactic structures that can translate concepts into linguistic forms appropriate to them.

PT therefore takes the oral productions of L2 learners in (fluent) meaning-oriented oral communication as the measure for assessing their stage of development in SLA. Speech production rests on the fast interaction of several components of the language faculty. Their interplay is described in the well-known model of speech production by Levelt (1989; see Figure 2). It shows that, given that a speaker has decided what he wants to say, which is the work of the conceptualizer, he next has to find in his mental lexicon words (lemmas) that can express that meaning. It is part of the entry of a lemma in a mental dictionary that it contains a set of semantic features with information on the role that it can play in a syntactic frame (predicate argument structure) (Levelt, 1989, p. 191). If we take, for example, the verb "give", its entry in the mental dictionary makes clear that it is a verb that requires three arguments: One argument that provides information on who does the giving (*agent*), a second that says who is the *recipient*, and a third that names the object given (*theme*). The lemma "give" therefore contains information on the morphological form which its arguments must take with regard to the expression of tense, aspect, person, number, etc. Correspondingly, the speaker must find in his mental lexicon the specific morphological forms that can assure that all the words of a sentence agree with the intended message. Seeing to

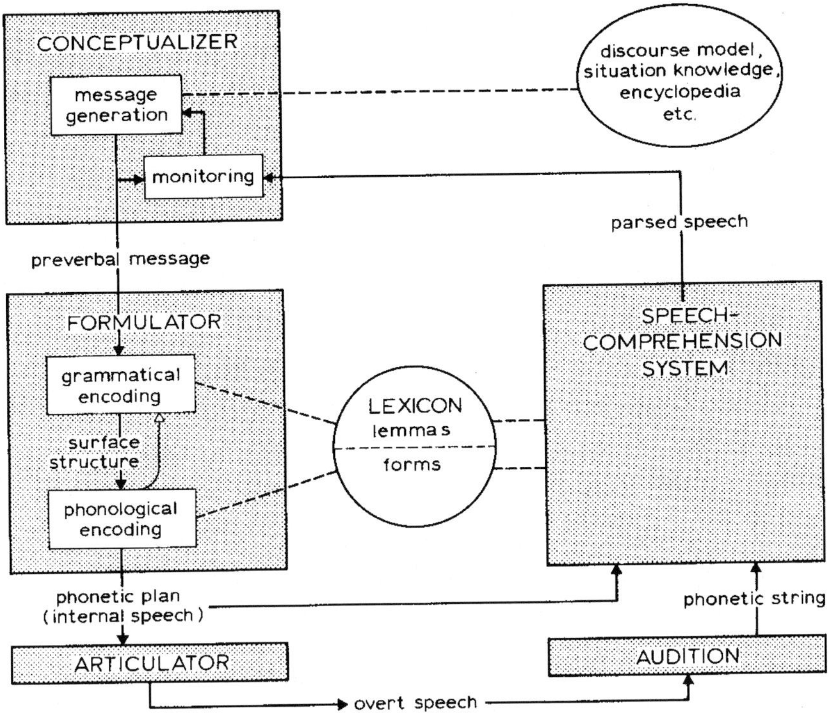

Figure 2. Processes in the generation of fluent speech (from: Levelt, 1989, p. 9)

that is the job of the formulator (grammatical encoder). Finally, the mentally encoded speech plan needs phonological expression.

Traditionally linguists consider the process of sentence generation to be strictly serial in time: First, the conceptual context is specified by the conceptualization process; next the syntactic structure is built for the whole utterance; finally this structure is realized phonetically. But that is, as Kempen and Hoenkamp (1987, pp. 202-203) have shown, a wrong conception of speech production. It really proceeds incrementally, not in a strictly serial order, because otherwise the high speed with which speech is produced could not be explained. In incremental processes a chain of highly automatized processing procedures is set in motion in which "the next processor can start working on the still-incomplete output of the current processor" (Levelt, 1989, p. 24). In other words, speakers mostly start with naming the topic of a sentence before they have a complete plan for how to finish it.

Considering that speakers, in fractions of a second, must (a) find the right words (lemmas) for the different parts of a speech plan, (b) put them in a (syntactic) order that represents their communicative intention (question, statement, negation, etc.), and (c) put the words in a morphological form that agrees with the rest of the utterance, it becomes clear why, in that interlocking chain of processing tasks, the whole procedure can come to a stand-still if one of the processors is not available as a processing routine.

In that context the evidence from SLA studies is that the different processing routines develop in a universally similar sequence that is plausible from a psycholinguistic perspective: At the lowest level, a word must have been entered in the L2 lexicon before a grammatical category can be assigned to it. The latter is needed for the word to find its proper place in a phrase structure with its head and modifiers. Only if such a phrasal procedure has been completed and its value is returned can the function of the phrase (predicate, type of argument) be determined; and only if the function of the phrase has been determined can it find its proper place in a complete sentence. Given that this is the "logic" underlying the development of speech processing routines, the next question is: What happens when an element is missing in this implicational hierarchy? The answer is that the hierarchy will be cut off in the learner grammar at the point of the missing processing procedures, and the rest of the hierarchy will be replaced by a direct mapping of conceptual structures onto surface form, if there are lemmas that match the conceptually instigated searches of the lexicon.

With regard to English, that leads to the implicational hierarchy of processing procedures represented in Table 1. The table shows that language acquisition begins (Level 1) with the use (reproduction) of holistic forms (unanalyzed forms). On Level 2 the learners start with a grammatical analysis of the holistic forms and come to first results, which enable them to distinguish basic word categories and to use semantically motivated word combinations like "many money", or "my house", or "two child". As far as the (syntactic) arrangement of the words is concerned, learners stick to a conceptually instigated sequencing of the words (canonical order).

Table 1. Processing procedures applied to English (Pienemann, 1998, p. 7)

	Processing procedure		L2 process	Morphology/ syntax
6	subordinate clause procedure		main and sub clause	Cancel INV
5	S-procedure/ WO-rules/ -salience	inter-phrasal info-exchange	SV agreement (= 3sg –s)	Do2nd, Aux2nd
4	S-procedure/ WO-rules/ +salience	inter-phrasal info-exchange		Y/N inv, PS inv
3	phrasal procedure	phrasal info-exchange	NP agreement	ADV, Do-Front, Topi, Neg+V
2	category procedure	lexical morph.	Plural possessive pro	canonical order
1	word/ lemma	"words"	invariant forms	single constituent

Once a learner has sufficient experience in the fast production of such strings of words and knows enough words to express his basic communicative intentions without long word searches, the availability of such processing routines frees Working Memory from the task of a consciously controlled and therefore resources-consuming construction of utterances. At this stage the next step in language development can be taken, and that is (Level 3) that learners now add, more or less regularly, a Plural –s to nouns, like in "two dog*s*". But it is typical of this stage that over-generalization of this rule occurs, like in "two woman*s*" or "two children*s*". In psycholinguistic terms: the formulator has now learnt to react to conspicuous (salient) semantic aspects of lexemes like "many" or "two" by automatically adding a plural suffix to the corresponding noun in the same phrase. That is an intra-phrasal information exchange or intra-phrasal unification of forms. Parallel to that, learners begin, on the syntactic level, to modify the overall meaning of an utterance by the fronting of either an Adverb, or a Negation-Particle or a Question-Indicating "Do", while not otherwise changing the canonical word order. This leads to sentences like "Yesterday we to home", and "There children play", and "Do he going home?".

After the formulator has learnt to arrange words in this way, the next step is (Level 4) that processing capacity becomes available for now tackling the task of a unification of the grammatical features of items on an inter-phrasal level, that is across the boundaries of a single Noun-Phrase or Verb-Phrase. Generally learners start with supplying conceptually salient items with formal markers that reflect their agreement; a typical example is that a verb is given a plural (singular) marking in agreement with the corresponding noun in the nominal Noun-Phrase (the Subject). Parallel to such a morphological marking of matching items across phrase boundaries, learners begin, on the syntactic level, to use inversion of constituents as a means of indicating questions. That produces sentences like "Has he seen you?" and "Have you done it?" and "Do he sees it?".

Only after such processing routines have been established in Long Term Memory, which spares Working Memory the task of consciously producing such a formal unification across phrase boundaries each time anew, do learners manage to extend inter-phrasal information exchange to non-salient parts of phrases, like 3rd person singular present –s (Level 5). Parallel to that, but on the syntactic level, the formulator now can do mental operations that lead to the inversions that are typical of *wh*-fronted questions, like "Where has he gone?" or "What is she eating?" (instead of sentence structures like "Where he has gone?" or "What she is eating?" which are typical of Level 3).

And, again, only after sufficiently automatized procedures for the production of such structures have been established, can learners tackle the next task (Level 6), which eventually puts them in the position to reverse, in indirect questions, the inversion they have learned to use in questions. They now learn to produce sentences like "I wonder where he has gone" and "I wonder what she is eating", instead of utterances like "I wonder where has he gone", and "I wonder what is she eating".

The examples illustrate the nature of the implicational hierarchy of processing procedures that is typical of all SLA processes. What needs to be seen is (a) that at each stage of development a learner will make typical – and predictable – (types of) errors; that (b) makes it possible to distinguish errors that a learner should no longer make at that stage – and which teaching should attend to – from errors that are harmless because they are, from a developmental perspective, "inevitable"; it (c) provides teachers with crucial information on "what is teachable". This information is different from the prescriptions of what must be taught when, which are based on formal grammars and structural syllabi; it (d) allows a distinction of serious deficits in core areas of language development, which teachers must attend to, from what is due to individual variation.

What must be stressed is that "universally similar developmental stages" does not mean that there is a biologically pre-programmed guarantee that all learners steer the right course. On the contrary, things can go wrong, and not all learners reach near-native speaker competence sooner or later. The basic thesis of PT is that different outcomes of acquisition processes are, at least partly, due to different developmental dynamics. The basic mechanism behind them is

> the principle that developmentally early decisions bias the further development of the interlanguage system. This percolation of structural properties in developmental processes is known in biology and philosophy and has been termed "*generative entrenchment*"… (Pienemann, 1998, p. 316)

For FLT that means (a) that it is possible, beyond a vague call for "comprehensible input", to define which linguistic forms can be taught at what stage of a learner's language development (either implicitly, by input enhancement, or explicitly by formal instruction), and (b) it means that if a specific learner fails to produce the structures which he should produce at the given stage of development, that is the time for teaching to step in with specific supportive measures.

Another important aspect of PT is that it underlines the need for a meaning-and-form oriented approach, because

> [f]irst of all, there is no reason to assume that learners acquire a structure just because they can process it. A functional need would have to be present for the structure to emerge. Secondly, functional constraints interact with processing constraints. … In other words, even if the basic processing of the grammatical information related to a given structure is in principle possible some of that information may not be available to the learner because of complex form-function relationships. (Pienemann, 1998, pp. 250-251)

That must be put into relation to well-known approaches to FLT which, on the basis of classroom research and the experiential knowledge of teachers, call for a task-based approach to FLT (Long, 1988; Doughty & Williams, 1998).

3. Processability and task-based learning

FLT has always been faced with questions like: Do we need a formal (structural) syllabus? How should it be constructed? Is grammar best learnt and taught implicitly or explicitly? What should we do about learners' errors? Should there be a focus on form, and when should it occur in the overall curriculum? Which forms are amenable to a focus on form? Are some forms resistant to focus on form? Can tasks and techniques be designed during which problematic forms are likely to arise so that an opportunity to focus on form can be provided? Should a focus on form occur only if a learner asks for it? And should it be restricted to awareness raising and the training of learning strategies?

In the introductory chapter of this essay I pointed out that under the three types of approach to FLT different answers are given to such questions. Traditional approaches prescribe which forms must be taught when, and they mostly favour explicit instruction in the rules of grammar. At the opposite end we find radical communicative approaches which trust that grammar can be acquired implicitly and incidentally while the learner's attention is focused on content, with the proviso that SLA may be enhanced by providing comprehensible input. (What makes language input "comprehensible" is a different issue; the options range from structurally and lexically simplified textual input to teacher talk and recasts of learner output in interactions with their teacher.) In comparison, the constructivist approach, with PT as a theoretically consistent example of it, occupies a middle position. What needs to be stressed, though, is that it represents a psycholinguistically well-founded position, not a shady compromise.

PT can predict which forms of grammar a learner can process at what stage of development, but systematically distinguishes individual variation from core developmental aspects of SLA (Pienemann, 1998, pp. 234-249). That includes the option, for syllabus construction, to (a) find tasks and materials that contain a crucial amount of the language forms that a learner can integrate into his learner grammar at a given stage of development ("teach what is teachable"); it (b) makes it possible to help learners notice the targeted forms by, for example, input enhancement, that is highlighting them in print or colour or by making them a point of explicit instruction; it (c) allows to distinguish harmless errors from errors that put learners on the wrong track in all subsequent processes, errors therefore that teachers should not tolerate.

Whether, in this context, the necessary focus on form is best achieved by strategies of implicit or explicit learning must be left to the discretion of the teacher and must be decided on the basis of what is known about the preferred learning style of the individual learner. Both styles of learning are compatible with what was said before about language learning as exemplar-based. The explicit formulation of a rule can cognitively support the compilation of small units of declarative knowledge into processing routines; but rule knowledge cannot replace the development of the relevant processing routines. This position is identical with the one proposed by Paradis (1994) who sums up the case as follows:

> What is automatised is not the explicit knowledge of the rule, … but its application. … What is automatised is the ability to produce the correct sequence of words in their proper inflectional form, whatever the processes have been used to reach this result. These remain in fact for ever opaque to introspection. (Paradis, 1994, pp. 401-402)

That is also what Hecht and Green found out in their empirical study of SLA (Hecht & Green, 1992).

Taking a task-based (function-oriented) approach to FLT is not in opposition to having phases of form-focused learning. Tasks turn the learners' attention to the communicative function (meaning) of the language forms, and – as stated by PT – there is no reason to assume that learners acquire a structure just because they can process it. A functional need would have to be present for the structure to emerge. That however can be provided only by a task-based approach, which has the additional advantage of potentially addressing all the senses of a learner and of tapping motivational resources beyond an intellectual interest in language and grammar (Timm, 1995a). It is a different matter whether to place a task always at the beginning of a learning process, or to have it follow an introductory phase of form-focused activity in a task cycle. Teaching experience speaks for that to be pragmatically decided in the context of specific learning processes and on learner-specific grounds.

References

Allwright, D. (1984). Why don't learners learn what teachers teach? The interaction hypothesis. In D. M. Singleton & D. Little (Eds.), *Language learning in formal and informal contexts* (pp. 3-18). Dublin: Irish Association for Applied Linguistics.

Baddeley, A. (1986). *Working memory.* Oxford: Clarendon Press.

Bates, E., & MacWhinney, B. (1989). Functionalism and the competitive model. In B. MacWhinney & E. Bates (Eds.), *The crosslinguistic study of sentence processing* (pp. 3-73). Cambridge: Cambridge University Press.

Bechtel, W., & Abrahamsen, A. (1991). *Connectionism and the mind. An introduction to parallel processing in networks.* Cambridge: Blackwell.

Chomsky, N. (1980). On cognitive structures and their development: A reply to Piaget. In M. Piattelli-Palmarini (Ed.), *Language and learning. The debate between Jean Piaget and Noam Chomsky* (pp. 35-54). London: Routledge & Kegan Paul.

Deacon, T. (1997). *The symbolic species. The co-evolution of language and the human brain.* London: Penguin.

Doughty, C., & Williams, J. (Eds.). (1998). *Focus on form in classroom second language acquisition.* Cambridge: Cambridge University Press.

Faw, B. (2000). Consciousness, motivation, and emotion: Biopsychological reflections. In R. D. Ellis & N. Newton (Eds.), *The cauldron of consciousness. Motivation, affect and self-organization* (pp. 55-90). Amsterdam: John Benjamins.

Goleman, D. (1995). *Emotional intelligence. Why it can matter more than IQ.* London: Bloomsbury.

Hecht, K., & Green, P. S. (1992). Grammatikwissen unserer Schüler: gefühls- oder regelgeleitet? *Praxis des Neusprachlichen Unterrichts, 39*(2), 151-162.

Hörmann, H. (1976). *Meinen und Verstehen. Grundzüge einer psychologischen Semantik.* Frankfurt: Suhrkamp.

Kaplan, R., & Bresnan, J. (1982). Lexical-functional grammar: a formal system for grammatical representation. In J. Bresnan (Ed.), *The mental representation of grammatical relations* (pp. 173-281). Cambridge: MIT Press.

Kempen, G., & Hoenkamp, E. (1987). An incremental procedural grammar for sentence formulation. *Cognitive Science, 11*, 201-258.

Krashen, S. (1985). *The input hypothesis: Issues and implications.* London: Longman.

Levelt, W. J. M. (1989). *Speaking.* Cambridge: Bradford/MIT Press.

Long, M. H. (1988). Instructed interlanguage development. In L. Beebe (Ed.), *Issues in second language acquisition: Multiple perspectives* (pp. 115-141). Cambridge, MA: Newbury House.

Long, M. H. (1998). Focus on form: Theory, research, and practice. In C. Doughty & J. Williams (Eds.), *Focus on form in classroom second language acquisition* (pp. 15-41). Cambridge: Cambridge University Press.

MacWhinney, B. (1989). Competition and teachability. In M. L. Rice & R. L. Schiefelbusch (Eds.), *The teachability of language* (pp. 63-104). Baltimore: Brookes.

Multhaup, U. (1999). The construction of knowledge: Its conditions and causes. In B. Mißler & U. Multhaup (Eds.), *The construction of knowl-*

edge, learner autonomy and related issues in foreign language teaching: Essays in honour of Dieter Wolff (pp. 91-108). Tübingen: Stauffenburg.

Paradis, M. (1994). Neurolinguistic aspects of implicit and explicit memory: Implications for bilingualism and SLA. In N. C. Ellis (Ed.), *Implicit and explicit learning of languages* (pp. 393-419). London: Academic Press.

Piaget, J. (1980). The psychogenesis of knowledge and its epistemological significance. In M. Piattelli-Palmarini (Ed.), *Language and learning. The debate between Jean Piaget and Noam Chomsky* (pp. 23-34). London: Routledge & Kegan Paul.

Pienemann, M. (1984). Psychological constraints on the teachability of languages. *Studies in Second Language Acquisition, 6*(2), 186-214.

Pienemann, M. (1998). *Language processing and second language development. Processability theory.* Amsterdam: John Benjamins.

Pinker, S. (1989). *Learnability and cognition: The acquisition of argument structure.* Cambridge, MA: MIT Press.

Swain, M. (1985). Communicative competence: Some roles of comprehensible input and comprehensible output in its development. In S. Gass & C. Madden (Eds.), *Input in second language acquisition* (pp. 235-256). Rowley, MA: Newbury House.

Timm, J.-P. (Ed.). (1995a). *Ganzheitlicher Fremdsprachenunterricht.* Weinheim: Deutscher Studien Verlag.

Timm, J.-P. (1995b). Die „Fuzziness" der Sprache als Begründung für einen ganzheitlich-funktionalen, erfahrungsorientierten Grammatikunterricht. In J.-P. Timm (Ed.), *Ganzheitlicher Fremdsprachenunterricht* (pp. 120-148). Weinheim: Deutscher Studien Verlag.

Wolff, D. (1994). Der Konstruktivismus: Ein neues Paradigma in der Fremdsprachendidaktik? *Die Neueren Sprachen, 93*, 407-429.

Spoken discourse: From linguistics to pedagogy

Christina Lausevic

Auf der Satzebene wird Sprache in Lehrbüchern bereits sehr gut dargestellt und kann so modellhaft beim Erwerb von Strukturen und Redemitteln genutzt werden. In diesem Kapitel geht es speziell um gesprochenen Diskurs. Obwohl in jüngster Zeit viel unternommen wurde, natürliche Sprache in Hörverstehenstexte zu integrieren, ist es nötig, dass wir das Potential echten gesprochenen Diskurses im Klassenzimmer weiter untersuchen, sowohl im Hinblick auf die direkte Verwendung mit den Lernern als auch auf die Einbettung in Lehrbuchdialoge. Erkenntnisse nicht-pädagogischer Disziplinen wie Diskurs- und Konversationsanalyse lassen sich noch konzentrierter in Sprachlehrmaterialien und *Taskdesign* nutzen. Die Integration der Diskursorientierung in die gegenwärtige Praxis ist dabei nicht nur ein weiteres Zusatzdesiderat, sondern stellt sich vielmehr als Möglichkeit einer Verbesserung der kommunikativen Kompetenzen auf allen Ebenen dar. Der „Quantensprung" von der Linguistik zur Pädagogik ist jedoch keineswegs einfach. Viele der Anliegen zur Verwendung realen gesprochenen Diskursmaterials mit Lernern werden in diesem Beitrag aufgegriffen, und es wird gezeigt, wie gerade Entscheidungen über zu verwendendes Material von den pädagogischen Zwecken abhängen.

Language at sentence level is already well represented in textbooks to provide models for mastery of grammatical structures and functions. This chapter focuses specifically on spoken discourse and argues that, whilst much has been done to incorporate natural speech into listening material in recent years, we need to explore the potential role for real spoken discourse in the classroom – in terms both of its direct use with learners and also how it might feed into spoken input such as textbook dialogues. Insights provided by such non-pedagogic disciplines as discourse and conversation analysis can feed into language teaching materials and task design in a more focused way. Integrating a discourse approach into current practice is not simply seen as a desirable add-on, but rather as a way of enhancing learners' communicative competence across the board. The leap from linguistics to pedagogy, however, is by no means simple. Many of the concerns about using real spoken discourse with learners are addressed and it is shown how decisions about *what* to use with learners depend entirely on pedagogic purpose.

1. Introduction

On the occasion of the 1994 Eurovision Song Contest in Dublin, the compère asked a non-native spokeswoman for one country's jury (her image projected via satellite onto the screen):

> Could we now have the results of the X jury?
> *To which she responded:*
> Yes. *(pause)*

This met with roars of laughter from the mainly Irish audience, whereupon, once the laughter had died down, the bewildered spokeswoman proceeded with the results of her jury.

This exchange mirrors a common source of native-speaker humour, whereby the respondent, often a cantankerous child, deliberately ignores the intended meaning of an utterance and responds instead to a function more commonly associated with its surface structure (which is sometimes less demanding to deal with!). This is the case in the following mother-daughter exchange, where the mother is forced to use a more direct request for action which leaves no doubt as to her original intended meaning.

> Mother: What's this doing here? (indicating dustpan and brush on stool)
> Daughter: Sitting there.
> Mother: Well, will you move it?
> (Own data, 1996)

In the Eurovision example, by contrast, the non-native respondent initially seems to genuinely misinterpret the compère's polite request for action (or directive) as a real factual question or elicitation. Whilst the spokeswoman can be in no doubt as to what action she is there to perform (i.e. to provide the results of her jury), the pause following her affirmative suggests she is either expecting a second, more direct request for action or that she is unaware that the preferred response to such requests is the performance of the actual action itself (in this case the reporting of the results). This highlights the difficulties people who are otherwise highly proficient in English as a second language can have when confronted with real language use. Whilst textbooks do a good job of teaching direct and indirect requests at single utterance level (including the type used in the first example), there seems to be little opportunity for learners to see how speech acts such as requests unfold in real spoken discourse over several utterances. Linked to this, it is also worth considering how much opportunity learners are given to observe possible distance between surface linguistic forms and underlying meanings in samples of discourse.

Here we are in the realms of pragmatics and how meanings are interpreted not only from the actual language used but also from the context and situation of the discourse. Authors such as Swan (1985) have implied that pragmatic competence does not need to be taught because it is universal. He gives the example of the two burglars who, as victims of the structural syllabus, fail to recognise the illocutionary force behind their friend's warning "The policeman is crossing the road"[1], and subsequently get caught red-handed. The context, he argues, provides enough information for anyone with a modicum of common sense to decipher underlying meanings. Whilst pragmatic competence is clearly part of learners' normal development in relation to their L1, the question arises, however, to what extent the realisations of the expression of intention differ in the L2.

Presumably learners from cultures where indirect speech acts are less common may have more difficulty interpreting indirectness[2] in the L2, even with all the available contextual information to hand. The same applies to the ways in which signals and mechanisms of conversational discourse are used to structure talk. Although such signals will exist in all languages, the actual manifestations of these are likely to be overlooked in the L2 unless learners' attention is drawn to them in some way. My observations of discourse-processing problems of German students during my five years working in German higher education provide some anecdotal evidence for this. Towards the end of tutorials my use of pre-closing signals (discourse frames such as "okay" and "right" with falling intonation and followed by a silent

---

1 This is a criticism of Widdowson's claim that this utterance cannot be interpreted correctly by learners if they know only its propositional meaning (1978, p. 19).

2 There are clearly degrees of indirectness which are not captured by Searle's definition of indirect speech acts as those performed by another illocutionary act (Searle, 1979). Relating this to my second example, "Will you move it?" would in fact be classified as indirect by Searle as it uses a question (secondary illocutionary act) to perform a request ("Please move it"). However, it would be difficult to interpret this utterance (along with the "Would you mind..." type) as anything other than a request for action (see Tsai, 1994). In many cases, such as in "What's this doing here?" the boundaries between elicitation and requests for action are less distinct.

pause) were not recognised by my German tutees, thus forcing me to adopt more explicit pre-closing statements such as, "We'll need to finish there as there's someone else waiting outside." Interestingly, students who had returned from their study or work periods in the UK or the USA, had no problems interpreting and even using such signals.

The fact that learners have already developed pragmatic and discourse competence in relation to their mother tongue is clearly no guarantee that they will be able to recognise and interpret pragmatic and discourse phenomena correctly in the foreign language. The question is: How do we provide exposure and draw learners' attention to such phenomena in the EFL classroom? Unlike some of the extremists' views criticised by Cook (1998), I am not proposing that real unadulterated language such as CANCODE[3] data should replace current language teaching materials and the study of the formal aspects of the language system. I am suggesting, however, that we need to investigate the possible roles for real spoken discourse in the classroom, and re-evaluate existing textbook input in the light of this. The main focus of this chapter is to present an appraisal of the issues relating to the use of real spoken language with learners, and to investigate the relationship between *what* we use and *how* we use it.

2. The "real" language issue

After much dismissal of classroom language as somehow not part of the real world and therefore inauthentic, we are starting to recognise that simplifying language for learners (accommodation) through teacher talk and scripted language samples in textbooks, for example, is a perfectly natural and therefore authentic activity. In fact, not to do so and to talk to learners as if they were native speakers would be inauthentic (van Lier, 1996). However, it is also recognised that learners will benefit from exposure to the wide variety of expression which

---

3 CANCODE (Cambridge and Nottingham Corpus of Discourse in English) is a computerised corpus of spoken English, currently consisting of about five million words. The data are collected from real-life conversations in a wide variety of contexts in Great Britain. See Carter and McCarthy (1995) and McCarthy and Carter (1995).

native speakers engage in. This has little to do with authenticity[4] and more to do with providing learners with a variety of input and challenge. Ironically, through acting authentically and accommodating to audience demands, we may be depriving learners of this very variety and challenge (ibid.). The task facing textbook writers and teachers is not to choose between one or the other, but to strike a balance between both concerns.

No one would deny that we have made huge strides in the last 30 years in making both written and spoken input more natural for learners. Real texts (written mode) have long been incorporated into coursebooks or brought into classrooms by teachers and learners. Use of real spoken language data is, however, much rarer, and dialogues (still the basis for oral communication skills training in most textbooks) do not contain many of the features of real spontaneous discourse. Before considering how real data might either be used directly in the classroom, or at least feed into spoken input, it is necessary to address the very real concerns which exist about using such data with learners.

2.1 Real versus textbook dialogue

To consider the issues involved in using real spoken discourse with learners, let us take a look at a sample. The following dialogue is taken from data collected on a university campus by Scotton and Bernsten (1988) to compare recordings of direction-giving in American English with the textbook equivalent (see below). The rather abrupt opening is due to the instructions given to the direction seekers always to start with the question "How do I get to the vet clinic?".

1. Real dialogue

S1 How do I get to the vet clinic?

S2 The Vet Clinic? Oh man, it's a haul (pause) Uh, okay. Go up to the bridge, and that's on Farm Lane. And you want to go right all the way up until you pass – um. Do you know where-um. Are you familiar with the campus?

S1 Pretty much.

S2 Do you know where the (pause) uh Agriculture Hall is?

---

4 We still need a label to distinguish accommodated from non-accommodated language. From now on, for the sake of clarity, language produced for real communicative purposes outside the classroom will be termed "real".

S1 Yeah, I know.
S2 Okay. When you see the Agriculture Hall, it will be on your right hand side. You want to go left again down towards Akers. Then the Vet Clinic should be on that road, and it says Vet Clinic.
S1 It does?
S2 Yeah. You can't miss it. It should be just past the intersection of Bogue Street and the street you'll be on (rising intonation).
S1 Okay.
S2 All right.
S1 Thank you very much.

2. Textbook dialogue (Ferreira, 1981, in Scotton and Bernsten, 1988).
S1 Excuse me, how can I get to the post office from here?
S2 Cross University Avenue. Turn right. Walk straight ahead along University Avenue for three blocks. Turn left at Church Street. Walk south for two blocks. Turn left at Bridge Avenue. The post office is the big building on the corner of Bridge Avenue and Church Street.
S1 Thank you for your help.

2.2 What are the concerns about using real spoken data in the classroom?

At first glance most teachers might find it hard to see how real data with its false starts (self-repair), interjections ("Oh man" and "uh"), fillers ("um") and pauses could have any application to language learning. Unlike the textbook dialogue, there are many features in the real data which are not directly part of direction-giving and seem to have little or no semantic meaning or propositional content. Apart from the above, there are, for example, backchannel signals such as "yeah" to keep the conversation going, confirmation checkers (lines 4 and 7) and topical boundary markers or frames such as "okay" (lines 2 and 9) marking a change in the focus of the discourse (here signalling the start and end of an aside). Textbook equivalents are, by contrast, tidy, concise, information-rich and easy for learners to follow.

The textbook dialogue may also be more appealing to teachers as, unlike the first, it consists entirely of complete sentences. Because of the demands of on-line processing, natural speech often consists of a series of chopped-off utterances as speakers modify what they want to say as they are saying it (false starts).

This brings us to a third related factor which may lead many to reject the use of authentic speech in the classroom. Whereas textbook dialogues such as the one above are based on the written form of the language, i.e. sentences consisting of words selected and ordered according to the rules of written grammar, spoken discourse is concerned with coherent use of language for communication. The rules of grammar are rather treated as a resource, with native speakers conforming to them, where necessary, or ignoring them (Cook, 1989, p. 7). The following example demonstrates this very well:

> You can run a hou- whatcha- now whatcha you can - ran a house- you can run a- and *do* the job, which is important, y' can't y- a man can't do it himself, and a woman can't do it himself w- if y' want it to be successful. In most cases. (Schiffrin, 1994, p. 25).

Schiffrin's data reinforces concerns about the quality of some spoken data, which in Cook's terms can be "inarticulate, impoverished and inexpressive" (1998, p. 61). Just because a feature occurs frequently does not make it a good model for language learning (ibid.). Indeed, learners, like native speakers, may value language which is lexically rich and original, rather than language which is recycled and marked by dysfluencies.

When we consider such impoverished language samples, it is not surprising, perhaps, that authors such as Hedge (2000) reject real spoken discourse as a vehicle for teaching grammar. Her argument is that, for acquisition, learners need exposure to language demonstrating idealised grammar rules. Real speech, it is implied, does not provide learners with models of complete grammatical utterances, often because the information contained in the shared context makes explicit use of language unnecessary (hence the use of ellipsis as in "Want a cup of tea?"). The absence in real data of a one-to-one correlation between form and function, such as in the examples at the beginning of this chapter, is also seen as an obstacle to using discourse to teach grammar (ibid.). In other words pragmatic meaning is seen as a hindrance.

Another concern relating to casual conversation, where topics emerge from talk rather than being the reason for talk, is that the topics will be so peculiar to the speakers and the specific context they may fail to engage learners' interest. All real language is also culturally loaded, unlike the more neutral textbook versions. A native-speaker model may not be the most appropriate in the EFL context when the majority of English speakers in the world are non-native speakers.

To summarise, many of the concerns about spontaneous spoken discourse relate to characteristics of incompleteness or imperfection, and at the same time specificity of context (including culture – primarily that of the British or American native speaker). All of these make such language less comprehensible and more difficult for learners to produce, although production in itself might be seen as a questionable goal for the very same reasons.

2.3 Why use real spoken data in the classroom?

At the heart of the concerns about imperfection and culture is the unchallenged assumption that real language samples would be used as a model for production. Despite all the research which shows that learners do not learn what we teach, in relation to spoken discourse it seems to be assumed (and indeed feared), that learners will uncritically turn input into output and start using native-like discourse without fully understanding the implications. I am proposing that we need to distinguish between two uses of discourse – discourse as a model for production (DAMP) and discourse as a stimulus for critical awareness (DASCA). Whereas for the latter it would be appropriate to use a wide variety of real spoken data, some method of simplification would be necessary for the former.

2.3.1 Discourse as a model for production (DAMP)

Textbook dialogues play an important role in presenting learners with neutral core language which is comprehensible and reproducible. There has, however, been much criticism of them for presenting learners with an over-simplified and somewhat distorted view of language.

Many textbook dialogues tend to stress adjacency pair sequences (question and answer strings), and are usually very short, focusing on one topic at a time. It is perhaps not surprising therefore that learner-native speaker interaction is marked by abrupt topic shifts and pauses, with the native speaker adopting the role of interviewer and the non-native providing few follow-up moves (Holmen, 1985). Textbook dialogues prepare learners for minimal phatic or transactional exchanges but do not provide practice in topic handling and turn-taking strategies, strategies for keeping the conversation going and dealing with communication problems (including cultural differences). The distinction between semantics and pragmatics is crucial here. Whilst the non-propositional language found in the first direction-giving dialogue may be semantically poor, it is *pragmatically* rich – in other words these utterances perform a function in the discourse (for example, to hold the floor, signal topic shifts, or to keep the conversation going). Textbook dialogues, which are designed to exist as independent units, are pragmatically poor and unlikely to prepare learners for pragmatically intensive discourse. As Bygate (1987) remarks in relation to social talk, the freedom of topic choice typical of social talk will represent a challenge for the unpractised language learner.

Carter (1998) also argues that more could be done to make spoken production models reflect what linguists are discovering about differences in spoken grammar (e.g. the frequent use of ellipsis). Grammatical choices (forms) at discourse level are affected by context, including interpersonal factors. For example, the bald imperative, favoured by textbooks for direction-giving, accounted for fewer than half of all directives in Scotton and Bernsten's research. They also found that direction-giving is not a one-way transaction, as implied by many textbook dialogues, but also involves the direction seeker in responding to confirmation and orientation checkers. Although purely transactional language is very rare in real data (McCarthy, 1991), many textbook dialogues only prepare learners to transact.

Simplifying real dialogues, whilst maintaining the natural discourse features (modelling) has been suggested as a way of providing more realistic practice models. One method of modelling is to use a discourse framework model (e.g. based on a description of the moves performed) to write a new parallel dialogue following the same move structure (Beaumont, 1993). Using four of the five moves proposed by Sinclair and Coulthard (1975) (I=Initiation; R=Response; F=Follow-up; Fr=Frame – marking boundaries in discourse), we can apply this to the direction-giving dialogue. In the new dialogue in the right column, I have changed vet clinic (an American term) to the more culturally neutral and familiar post office.

S1	How do I get to the vet clinic?	**I**	S1	Excuse me. How do I get to the post office?
S2	The Vet Clinic? Oh man, it's a haul. Uh, okay. Go up to the bridge, and that's on Farm Lane. And you want to go right all the way up until you pass – um. Do you know where-um. Are you familiar with the campus?	**R** **Fr** **R** **I**	S2	The post office? Uh, it's a long way. Uh, okay. Go up to the bridge and that's on Prince's Street. And keep going all the way up until . . . Do you know the hospital?
S1	Pretty much.	**R**	S1	Yeah, I know it.
S2	Do you know where the (pause) uh Agriculture Hall is?	**I**	S2	Do you know the bank just after it?
S1	Yeah, I know.	**R**	S1	Yeah.
S2	Okay. When you see the Agriculture Hall, it will be on your right hand side. You want to go left again down towards Akers. Then the Vet Clinic should be on that road, and it says Vet Clinic.	**Fr** **R**	S2	Okay. When you come to the bank turn right. And the post office is on your right. It closes at 5pm.
S1	It does?	**I**	S1	Does it?
S2	Yeah. You can't miss it.	**R**	S2	Yeah, you should make it.
S1	Okay.	**F**	S1	Okay.
S2	All right?	**I**	S2	All right?
S1	Thank you very much.	**R**	S1	Thanks.

Most would agree that the new dialogue on the right is more natural than many textbook versions whilst remaining accessible to learners. Such dialogues are therefore likely to prove more effective at preparing learners for the cognitive and interactional demands of certain speech events such as direction-giving.

2.3.2 Discourse as a stimulus for raising critical awareness (DASCA)

A key role for real samples of spoken discourse is to engage learners in critical awareness-raising. With teacher and learners as joint observers and investigators of discourse, learners will be free to authenticate language for themselves and, with the guidance of the teacher, choose which language to incorporate in their own production for which purposes. Learners may or may not choose to sound like a British, American or any other native speaker, but to deny them the opportunity to investigate a range of discourse produced by different speakers in different contexts would be to stifle autonomy and freedom of choice. Van Lier's call to educators not to ignore any of the essential principles of authenticity (opportunities for authentication), awareness and autonomy are very relevant here. Learners need to develop sociocultural and sociolinguistic awareness through examining long stretches of contextualised language, but at the same time autonomy demands that they be free to choose whether to adopt what they observe for productive use (see Cook, 1989). By studying the relationship between contextual information (e.g. physical, social and psychological) and discourse, learners will learn how to encode and decode the intercultural and interpersonal aspects of language use, including interpersonal grammars (McCarthy and Carter, 1994).

Concerning the theoretical basis and methodology for using DASCA, recent research into the important role of "noticing" (conscious attention to form in the input) in facilitating second language acquisition is very relevant (see Fotos 1993, 1998). Given the limited exposure time in foreign language environments it is unlikely that learners will recognise discourse features unless their attention is drawn to them. A task-based approach can be used to allow learners to investigate and analyse the discourse functions of the choices made by speakers in various contexts, and to consider cultural similarities and differences. Learners could be given the task of comparing real discourse with textbook dialogues with similar functions, such as the ones presented in this chapter. Learners also need opportunities to select and test out appropriate conversational mechanisms for a variety of purposes. Learners may be asked to evaluate their use of such mechanisms in groups, e.g. turn-taking or their ability to introduce a new topic into the conversation. Discourse-related activities therefore involve critical awareness raising, opportunities for testing out and self-evaluation. Teachers have an important role in helping learners to understand the differences in the nature of the input they are exposed to, as well as the learning value of what they are asked to do with it.

3. Conclusion

In this chapter I have outlined two roles for real spoken discourse – the first is to feed into production models (DAMP) and the second is for raising critical awareness (DASCA). Transparency, in terms of learners being aware of how each of these types of input and the related activities can feed into their language learning, is crucial for authentication to take place and for learners to take charge of their own learning. Every area of language study can benefit from also seeing language as discourse, and learners' existing knowledge and competence in the L1 can be used to draw comparisons when interpreting data across a wide variety of contexts.

There are, however, a number of issues which need to be addressed. How can we make appropriate discourse samples more easily available to teachers? Whilst spoken corpus data will be more readily available in the future on computer and through books (such as Carter and McCarthy, 1997) there is still the issue of how we obtain good-quality recordings of real spoken discourse for use with learners. There is also the important question of learners' level: Could learners of a low language level be asked to investigate real language samples? Can the samples and tasks be graded to suit different levels? Should we distinguish between features for awareness (e.g. false starts) and those for use (e.g. topic-handling) at different levels? These are not reasons not to use spoken discourse in the classroom. On the contrary, they are reasons to experiment! There needs to be greater emphasis on helping teachers develop their own discourse awareness so they will have the confidence to explore alongside their learners. Teachers need to be aware however that, as there is no single and final interpretation of a discourse, their role is to facilitate discussion of the discourse from various perspectives and to raise awareness of the implications of various choices. Just as speakers have to work at negotiating meanings, learners need to develop strategies to analyse how meanings are realised in different speech events in the foreign language, and compare these to their mother tongue. Candlin puts it more succinctly when he states that

> . . . ways of teaching should shift from teacher-telling to learner-interpreting within a syllabus whose prime goal is the development of strategies for discourse processing, rather than an assembly of items" (Preface to Coulthard, 1977, p. xii).

Only once learners have started to look beyond the surface meanings of structures and developed discoursal insights will they evolve as conscious participants in spoken interaction able to select discerningly from the range of language choices at their disposal.

References

Bygate, M. (1987). *Speaking.* Oxford: Oxford University Press.

Beaumont, M. (1993). personal communication.

Carter, R., & McCarthy, M. (1995). Grammar and the spoken language. *Applied Linguistics, 16*(2), 141-158.

Carter, R., & McCarthy, M. (1997). *Exploring spoken English.* Cambridge: Cambridge University Press.

Carter, R. (1998). Orders of reality: CANCODE, communication, and culture. *ELT Journal, 52*(1), 43-56.

Cook, G. (1998). The uses of reality: A reply to Ronald Carter. *ELT Journal 52*(1), 57-63.

Cook, G. (1989). *Discourse.* Oxford: Oxford University Press

Coulthard, M. (1977). *An introduction to discourse analysis.* London: Longman.

Ferreira, L. (1981). *Notion by notion.* Rowley, MA: Newbury House.

Fotos, S. (1993). Consciousness raising and noticing through focus on form: Grammar task performance versus formal instruction. *Applied Linguistics 14*(4), 126-141.

Fotos, S. (1998). Shifting the focus from forms to form in the EFL classroom. *ELT Journal, 52*(4), 301-307.

Hedge, T. (2000). *Teaching and learning in the language classroom.* Oxford: Oxford University Press.

Holmen, A. (1985). Distribution of roles in learner-native speaker interaction. In E. Glahn & A. Holmen (Eds.), *Learner discourse.* Anglica et Americana 22, Department of English, University of Copenhagen.

McCarthy, M. (1991). *Discourse analysis for language teachers.* Cambridge: Cambridge University Press.

McCarthy, M., & Carter, R. (1994). *Language as discourse: Perspectives for language teaching*. London: Longman.

McCarthy, M., & Carter, R. (1995). Spoken grammar: What is it and how do we teach it? *ELT Journal, 49*(3), 207-218.

Searle, J. (1979). *Expression and meaning.* Cambridge: Cambridge University Press.

Scotton, C. M., & Bernsten, J. (1988). Natural conversations as a model for textbook dialogue. *Applied Linguistics, 9*(4), 372-384.

Schiffrin, D. (1994). *Approaches to discourse*. Oxford: Blackwell.

Sinclair, J. McH., & Coulthard R. M. (1975). *Towards an analysis of discourse.* Oxford: Oxford University Press.

Swan, M. (1985). A critical look at the communicative approach. *ELT Journal, 39*(1), 2-12.

Tsui, A. B. M. (1994). *English conversation. Oxford:* Oxford University Press.

van Lier, L. (1997). *Interaction in the language classroom.* London: Longman.

Widdowson, H.G. (1978). *Teaching language as communication*. Oxford: Oxford University Press.

Content and language integrated learning

Language awareness in content and language integrated learning

Sylvia Fehling

In dem folgenden Artikel wird eine Forschungsstudie zu Language Awareness bei „monolingual" und bilingual unterrichteten Schülerinnen und Schülern dargestellt. Zunächst werden die Begriffe „Bilingualer Sachfachunterricht" und „Language Awareness" näher erläutert. Anschließend wird das Forschungsprojekt vorgestellt und erste Ergebnisse diskutiert.

The following article focuses on a research project[1] on language awareness in content and language integrated learning (CLIL). First CLIL and language awareness are defined. Then the research project is described and first results are presented and discussed.[2]

1. Content and language integrated learning (CLIL) in Germany

Content and language integrated learning (CLIL) was introduced in a few German schools about 30 years ago, and plays an important role in German education today (Wolff, 2002). In CLIL subjects such as history, geography, politics and biology are taught in a language other than German, generally English or French. That is, a foreign language (FL) is used as the instructional language. While the FL is used to mediate understanding of subject-specific content and knowledge, the focus remains subject knowledge rather than facility in the FL. This means that the focus is on teaching the subject matter rather than on the mediating language skills (Fehling & Finkbeiner, 2002).

---

1 The project is the research of my dissertation. I am pursuing my Ph.D. at the Universität Kassel under supervision of Prof. Dr. Claudia Finkbeiner.

2 I want to thank Robert Raymond and Markus Knierim for their help and advice.

CLIL is mainly found in grammar schools.[3] Typically, students begin CLIL in grade 7 when most German students have had two years of English or French. In order to prepare the students more effectively for the higher language demands in CLIL, they receive one or two additional English/French lessons per week in grades 5 and 6.

In CLIL the regular curriculum is mandatory. Only some states like North Rhine-Westphalia and Rhineland-Palatinate have developed special curricula for CLIL which dovetail with the state-mandated curriculum in each state (Finkbeiner & Fehling, 2002; Schmid-Schönbein, Goetz & Hoffknecht, 1994; Sekretariat der Ständigen Konferenz der Kultusminister der Länder in der Bundesrepublik Deutschland, 1999).

1.1 Goals

The globalization of economic, ecological, political, social and communicative processes requires the ability to negotiate meaning in a number of different contexts in more than one language. CLIL places students in a position to communicate about their experience, but also about the target culture as well as culture-related and universal concepts such as, for example, human rights in the FL. Thus learners acquire not only content-specific language in the FL but they are also enabled to express themselves using the FL with conceptual clarity, subtle differentiations, and without error (Finkbeiner & Fehling, 2002; Mäsch, 1995, p. 339).

1.2 Code switching

An important prerequisite for success in CLIL is the alternation of the official classroom language (OCL), which is German, and the FL sequences during the learning process. It is crucial that students need to know key concepts of the subject content in German even though instruction may be delivered in the FL. It is not the goal of CLIL that students learn to talk about, for example, "climatic variation" only in

---

3 There are also other schools such as comprehensive schools, secondary modern schools and primary schools which offer CLIL (Finkbeiner & Fehling, 2002).

the FL while they are not familiar with key concepts such as the "greenhouse effect" in the OCL.

Classroom observations, which were conducted in several classes as part of the research, have shown that code switching is a very controversial issue: While some CLIL teachers use both the FL and German in the classroom, others use only the FL during the teaching process to provide the pupils with as much input in the foreign language as possible (Finkbeiner & Fehling, 2002).

2. Language awareness

Hawkins (1987), who was the first to implement language awareness in the curriculum, describes the aims of language awareness in the following way:

> It seeks to bridge the difficult transition from primary to secondary school language work, and especially to the start of foreign language studies and the explosion of concepts and language introduced by the specialist secondary school subjects. It also bridges the "space between" the different aspects of language education (English/foreign language/ethnic minority mother tongues/English as a second language/Latin) which at present are pursued in isolation, with no meeting place for the different teachers, no common vocabulary for discussing language (Hawkins, 1987, p. 4).

In the meantime, the aims of language awareness have been extended. Thus, foreign language learners' awareness and their perceptions of the process of language learning are now the main focus of language awareness (James & Garrett, 1991, p. 98).

However, the term language awareness has been used in a wide range of academic and pedagogical contexts, which has contributed to the fact that there is no clear and universally agreed upon definition. It is an umbrella term covering a whole range of issues and a cover term for anything related to language (James & Garrett, 1991, p. 3).

There are also a number of different terms which are associated with language awareness: knowledge about language, linguistic consciousness, metalinguistic awareness, linguistic insight, explicit knowledge, metacognition, and metacognitive awareness. That makes it problematic to clearly define language awareness.

In order to work with the concept of language awareness, the following definition by James & Garrett is used. James & Garrett (1991, pp. 12-20) differentiate five domains of language awareness:

- The *affective domain* is the emotional side of learning and can be specified in terms of "forming attitudes, awakening and developing attention, sensitivity, curiosity, interest and aesthetic response" (Donmall, 1985, p. 7, in James & Garrett, 1991, p. 13).
- The *social domain* aims at developing tolerance towards minority languages and can be utilized "to foster better relations between all ethnic groups by arousing pupils" awareness of the origins and characteristics of their own language and dialect and their place in the wider map of languages and dialects used in the world beyond" (Donmall, 1985, p. 8, in James & Garrett, 1991, p. 13).
- The *"power" domain* involves a critical awareness towards language, alerting people to the hidden meanings, tacit assumptions and rhetorical traps within language. It aims at developing sensitivity towards the manipulation of language (James & Garrett, 1991, p. 14; Fairclough, 1992).
- Developing awareness of patterns, systems, units, categories and rules of language in use forms the *cognitive domain* (James & Garrett 1991, p. 14; Donmall, 1985, p. 7).
- The *performance domain* is very ambiguous, since it is arguable whether knowing about language improves one's performance or command of the language. In other words, it is not yet fully understood whether a language learner who has a high level of language awareness has a better language performance (James & Garrett 1991, p. 14; Donmall, 1985, p. 7; Wolff, 1997, p. 515; Wolff 1993).

3. Research project

In my doctoral research project I examine the impact of CLIL on the development of language awareness. The language awareness of "bilingual" pupils participating in CLIL is compared with the language awareness of "monolingual"[4] pupils in conventional foreign language classes.

3.1 Research questions

The project focuses on the following research questions:

- Which domains of language awareness are fostered through CLIL?
- What are differences in language awareness at the beginning of grade 7 between pupils in "bilingual" classes and pupils in conventional foreign language classes?
- Which factors influence the development of language awareness (teaching methods, family background)?
- How does the verbal intelligence of pupils who take classes in CLIL differ from the verbal intelligence of pupils who take conventional foreign language classes?

3.2 Research methods, research participants, and research setting

In the research, which was conducted over two years from 1999-2001, both qualitative and quantitative methods were used to triangulate the research data (Finkbeiner, 1995; Finkbeiner & Schnaitmann, 2001).

In this longitudinal study, data from 193 pupils were collected. The research participants were pupils between the ages of 12 and 14 (grades 7 and 8) at four German secondary schools: one grammar school (*Gymnasium*) and three comprehensive schools *(Gesamtschulen).* Three of the schools are "bilingual" schools offering CLIL with English as the instructional language. The fourth school is a school which does not offer "bilingual" classes.

---

4 The terms "bilingual" and "monolingual" are used to differentiate the two groups of pupils compared in the research project. The term "monolingual" does not imply that these pupils speak only one language. Many "monolingual" pupils have two mother tongues (Turkish/German; Italian/German, etc.).

The data were collected within the following time frame:

- Testing period 1: September 1999 (T1)
- Testing period 2: March 2000 (T2)
- Testing period 3: September 2000 (T3)
- Testing period 4: March 2001 (T4)

In each school the following tests and questionnaires were used:

- *Kognitiver Fähigkeitstest*
- Questionnaire for pupils
- Language Awareness-Test
- Dictogloss (Fehling, 2002a)
- Questionnaire for teachers: Teaching methods
- Questionnaire for parents: Family background

In the following I present and discuss the results of the *Kognitiver Fähigkeitstest* as they relate to my research questions.

4. *Kognitiver Fähigkeitstest* (KFT)

The KFT is a standardized intelligence test used to evaluate the cognitive aptitude of 9- to 18-year-old students. It focuses on students' verbal, quantitative, and nonverbal aptitudes (Heller & Perleth, 2000, pp. 3-4).

In the research project the verbal part was used, which consists of exercises concerning vocabulary, word classifications, and word analogies. The test takes 45 minutes and was used at the beginning of each testing period.

4.1 Results of the KFT

In order to compare the "bilingual" and "monolingual" students' scores on the verbal part of the KFT the *Student's T-Test* was used (see Table 1) (Fehling, 2002b, pp. 65-66; Bortz, 1999, p. 133; Hartung, 1991).

Table 1. KFT verbal scores (Student's T-Test)

	Means			
	T1	T2	T3	T4
Bilingual	47.85	50.79	49.17	50.87
Monolingual	42.96	47.01	45.34	46.74
Statistical Significance	.000 highly significant	.002 very significant	.002 very significant	.001 highly significant

The results indicate that the "bilingual" classes have significantly better scores than the "monolingual" classes. It is striking that the "bilingual" groups score much higher than the "monolingual" groups already at the beginning of grade 7. These differences do not change within the two-year testing period.

The difference in KFT verbal scores may be related to the specific characteristics of "bilingual" groups. Most pupils taking CLIL classes do so because of their own and/or their parents' express desire. Furthermore, admission to a CLIL program is usually dependent on meeting a certain standard of achievement in grade 6. It can be argued, then, that "bilingual" groups may often be more competitive and achievement-orientated than "monolingual" groups.

5. Implications

The results of the KFT are very important for further data analysis and interpretation, since they can help to assess the students' achievements in the learning process. This means that increases in performance concerning language learning or especially language awareness may not only be influenced by CLIL, but by other factors as well. Thus it is very important in the data analysis to consider individual factors (such as verbal intelligence) and the linguistic background of the pupils (such as the mother tongue) to analyse and interpret further results of the project.

The results of the KFT are an important prerequisite for further analysis of the data. Nevertheless, they are only one part of the whole project. It would be inappropriate, therefore, to draw any early conclusions about the learning process and especially the development of language awareness in CLIL. Only the complete evaluation and analysis of all tests and questionnaires used in the research project will give a differentiated picture of the development of language awareness in CLIL.

References

Bortz, J. (1999). *Statistik für Sozialwissenschaftler* (5th ed.). Berlin: Springer.

Donmall, G. (1985). *Language awareness. NCLE papers and reports 6.* London: Centre for Information on Language Teaching and Research.

Fairclough, N. (1992). *Critical language awareness.* London: Longman.

Fehling, S. (2002a). Methodische Überlegungen zur Erforschung von Language Awareness. In S. Breidbach, G. Bach, & D. Wolff. (Eds.), *Bilingualer Sachfachunterricht: Didaktik, Lehrer-/Lernerforschung und Bildungspolitik zwischen Theorie und Empirie. Schriften zum Bilingualismus und bilingualen Sachfachunterricht. Volume 1* (pp. 161-172). Frankfurt/M.: Lang.

Fehling, S. (2002b). Language Awareness und bilingualer Sachfachunterricht: Bericht einer zweijährigen Evaluationsstudie. In S. Fehling & H.-C. Ramm (Eds.), *Mitteilungsheft des Fachverbandes Moderne Fremdsprachen Hessen e.V. Mitteilungsheft 17/März 2002* (pp. 62-68). Hannover: Schroedel.

Fehling, S., & Finkbeiner, C. (2002). Evaluation von Schulleistungen im bilingualen Sachfachunterricht. In C. Finkbeiner (Ed.), *Bilingualität und Mehrsprachigkeit. Modelle, Projekte, Ergebnisse* (pp. 22-32). Hannover: Schroedel.

Finkbeiner, C. (1995). *Englischunterricht in europäischer Dimension. Zwischen Qualifikationserwartungen der Gesellschaft und Schülereinstellungen und Schülerinteressen. Berichte und Kontexte zweier empirischer Untersuchungen.* Bochum: Brockmeyer.

Finkbeiner, C., & Fehling, S. (2002). Bilingualer Unterricht: Aktueller Stand und Implementierungsmöglichkeiten im Studium. In C. Finkbeiner (Ed.), *Bilingualer Unterricht. Lehren und Lernen in zwei Sprachen* (pp. 9-22). Stuttgart: Hampp.

Finkbeiner, C., & Schnaitmann, G. W. (2001). Darstellung und Diskussion der Lehr- und Lernforschung in der Jahrtausendwende. In C. Finkbeiner & G. W. Schnaitmann (Eds.), *Lehren und Lernen im Kontext empirischer Forschung und Fachdidaktik* (pp. 9-31). Donauwörth: Auer.

Hartung, J. (1991). *Statistik. Lehr- und Handbuch der angewandten Statistik* (8th ed.). München: Oldenbourg.

Hawkins, E. (1987). *Awareness of language: An introduction* (2nd ed.). Cambridge: Cambridge University Press.

Heller, K. A., & Perleth, C. (2000). *Kognitiver Fähigkeitstest für 4.-12. Klassen, Revision.* Göttingen: Beltz.

James, C., & Garrett, P. (1991). The scope of language awareness. In C. James & P. Garrett (Eds.), *Language awareness in the classroom* (pp. 3-20). London: Longman.

Mäsch, N. (1995). Bilingualer Bildungsgang. In K.-R. Bausch, H. Christ, & H.-J. Krumm (Eds.), *Handbuch Fremdsprachenunterricht* (3rd ed.) (pp. 338-342). Tübingen: Francke.

Schmid-Schönbein, G., Goetz, H., & Hoffknecht, V. (1994). „Mehr oder anders?" Konzepte, Modelle und Probleme des Bilingualen Unterrichts. *Der Fremdsprachliche Unterricht/Englisch, 28*(1), 6-11.

Sekretariat der Ständigen Konferenz der Kultusminister der Länder in der Bundesrepublik Deutschland. (1999). *Konzepte für den bilingualen Unterricht. Erfahrungsbericht und Vorschläge zur Weiterentwicklung. Bericht des Schulausschusses vom 04.01.1999.*

Wolff, D. (1993). Sprachbewußtheit und die Begegnung mit Sprachen. *Die Neueren Sprachen, 92 (6),* 510-531.

Wolff, D. (1997). Zur Förderung von Sprachbewußtheit und Sprachlernbewußtheit im bilingualen Sachfachunterricht. In G. Henrici & E. Zöfgen (Eds.), *Fremdsprachen Lehren und Lernen (FLuL). Themenschwerpunkt: Language Awareness* (pp. 167-183). Tübingen: Gunter Narr.

Wolff, D. (2002). Bilingualer Sachfachunterricht in Europa: Ein Überblick. In C. Finkbeiner (Ed.), *Bilingualität und Mehrsprachigkeit. Modelle, Projekte, Ergebnisse* (pp. 5-11). Hannover: Schroedel.

Teacher students practising task-oriented foreign language exercises

Heike Rautenhaus

Die meisten Lehramtsstudent/innen haben während ihrer eigenen Schulzeit einen eher „traditionellen“ Englischunterricht erlebt. Folglich lernen sie zwar schnell in den fachdidaktischen Veranstaltungen des Grundstudiums über Handlungsorientierung zu reflektieren, aber dieses Prinzip in Unterrichtspraxis umzusetzen, bleibt für sie problematisch. Es fällt ihnen außerordentlich schwer,

- sich von früher erworbenen Herangehensweisen und Erwartungen zu lösen
- die theoretisch akzeptierte Idee "Handlungsorientierung" bis in die Mikrostruktur konkreten Unterrichts herunter- bzw. kleinzuarbeiten.

Das Seminar, das von Hilbert Meyer und mir gemeinsam durchgeführt wurde, „Bilingualism and Task-Orientation in Foreign Language Teaching“, hat sich daher ein zweifaches Ziel gesetzt, nämlich sowohl in die Theorie von handlungsorientiertem Fremdsprachenunterricht einzuführen als auch die Studierenden entsprechende Übungen als Lerner erleben und als angehende Lehrer/innen selbst erstellen zu lassen.

In dem Aufsatz werde ich zunächst den theoretischen Hintergrund des Seminars aufzeigen und dann – exemplarisch – die Ziele und die vielfältig komplizierten Entscheidungsprozesse, die zur Entwicklung adressatenadäquater handlungsorientierter Übungen durchschritten werden müssen, beschreiben und die Wirkung dieser Übungen auf die Seminarteilnehmer an der Universität und auf Schüler/innen im Schulunterricht diskutieren. Ich werde dieses im Lichte eines humanistischen Ansatzes und im Kontext der wesentlichen Stichworte unserer Veranstaltung tun, nämlich: Authentizität, Lernerautonomie und bilingualer Sachfachunterricht.

During their own school days, most of our present students studied English as a foreign language the “traditional” way. This explains why it soon becomes easy for students to talk about task-orientation after the first introductory courses in didactics of foreign language teaching (FLT) at university, but why it remains a problem for them to put it into practice in the language classroom. It is hard for them

- to overcome deeply ingrained attitudes and expectations
- to understand the many decisions that have to be made on the long way from accepting the idea of task-orientation down to its implementation in specific situations (under various conditions).

Our seminar "Bilingualism and Task-Orientation in Foreign Language Teaching" therefore aimed at both conveying insights into the necessity, implications and structure of task-orientation in FLT, and also having the students experience and develop effective exercises themselves in the various contexts of bilingual education.

In this essay I will describe the theoretical background of the seminar and – exemplarily – the objectives and various stages in the development of task-oriented exercises. Furthermore, I will discuss their effects on students at university and on pupils at school level in the light of a humanistic approach and in the context of the key concepts of our seminar, namely authenticity, learner autonomy and bilingual teaching.

1. Why do we need task-orientation in foreign language teaching?

Task-orientation is neither based on a curriculum nor on an elaborate educational theory. Though its historical background can be found in the ideas of well-known pedagogues such as John Dewey, Georg Kerschensteiner, Adolf Reichwein, Célestin Freinet, Maria Montessori, Peter Petersen and others, none of these could be said to stand alone for the concept in question. The term, however, aims at a holistic and activity-centred concept of teaching with the following characteristics (Jank & Meyer, 1997):

- It uses the curiosity of the learner and involves the learner's head, heart and hands, that is, all his senses.
- It is holistic not only in reference to the learner, but also in reference to the contents to be acquired (no artificial fragmentation) and the methods applied. Classroom interaction is understood as a forum for negotiating meaning.
- Teacher and student follow an aim they agree upon. The intended product can be presented in various forms: a production on the (classroom) stage, a video recording, a picture, a model, a text, an experiment, an exhibition, a workshop etc. The intended product of the teaching-learning process determines the subsequent steps of the work in progress.
- It allows the students to discover, follow and develop their personal interests. If necessary and possible, the classroom is opened and extended beyond its physical limits.

- Cognitive elaboration and practical work must support each other.
- It expects neither the student nor the teacher to be perfect: everyone can make mistakes and learn from them.

Having said this, however, it cannot be denied that the teaching process at school remains artificial. It is determined by the inherent contradictions of teaching and learning: The teacher has reached his goal only when he has made himself redundant.

For the following reasons, a foreign language should be taught in a holistic and activity-centred way, that is, in a task-oriented manner:

- Theoretically, a language can be subdivided into its linguistic components. But in the communication process it functions only within the frames of given contexts that specify the "illocutionary force" of utterances (Austin, 1972; Searle, 1971).
- Language learning is dependent on comprehensible input; the learner learns by understanding. For full understanding he must be given the parameters of the situation.
- Language is a means of achieving things: By using language one gives and acquires information, solves problems, triggers emotions and causes attitudes, etc. This instrumental character of a language serves as the motivation for taking the trouble to study its system.
- The language competence a learner constructs in his mind is the result of joint mental processes that he and his communication partners have performed. Therefore the language learner needs social interaction in pursuit of concrete aims and the experience of applied communicative strategies.
- Linguistic and cultural skills are tightly interwoven and can only be acquired in close interrelation. Language transports thoughts, emotions, beliefs and attitudes and leads to practical activities. Therefore, whilst acquiring the language, the learner has to be involved in its culture with his head, his heart and his whole being.

So if students are to learn to perform meaningful, intentional activities by using a language (which is the ultimate aim of teaching a foreign language), they have to practise this in adequate factual and social contexts.

2. Task-orientation and bilingual teaching

To begin with, *bilingualism* is a state where a person is able speak more than one language. A long acquisition process has been triggered by various special community and family conditions which force the learner to communicate in different situations in two different languages. A balanced bilingual is someone who has equivalent competence in two languages while a dominant bilingual is someone whose competence in one of the languages is superior to his competence in another. More important is the difference between additive and subtractive forms of bilingualism. The first one means that "both languages and both cultures will bring complementary positive elements to the child's overall development" (Hamers & Blanc, 1989, p. 56), while the latter means that "two languages are competing rather than complementary; this form will evolve when an ethnolinguistic minority rejects its own cultural values in favour of those of an economically and culturally more prestigious group" (ibid.). *School-bilingualism*, however, as we experience it in German schools, is a different matter. Here we have only the problem of the stronger mother tongue interfering with the weaker target language.

At school, bilingualism is mainly an *aim*, to be understood as a step towards multilingualism. In bilingual education at school the subject taught in the foreign language determines the teaching contents and it is the criterion for success. The foreign language serves as the medium of communication. It is not the only and ultimate aim. We know that while bilingual education results in better second language (L2) fluency and a wider and more specified vocabulary, grammar skills tend not to profit from it (see, for example, Burmeister, 1997; Wode et al., 1996).

At school, bilingualism is also a *method*. In Germany, on the whole, neither total nor partial immersion is applied. For a relatively short amount of time the L2 is used as an instrument to transmit information, for thinking and problem-solving, and the principle of *aufgeklärte Einsprachigkeit* is applied. This implies that the technical terms of the special subject being taught are given in both, L2 and L1, because the learner is supposed to be enabled to speak about the topic in his mother tongue as well as in the foreign language. The principle also implies that code switching is allowed if necessary and that the negotiation of meaning is an integral (and productive) part of communication. The teacher tolerates linguistic errors and reacts on the contents of what the pupil said, before, if at all, he deals with the linguistic side of it.

So at school, bilingualism is a special opportunity. Provided the pupil can decide for himself whether or not to take part in bilingual education, he/she will regard this opportunity as a special challenge and be highly motivated to meet the expectations. If he/she is interested in the subject matter, his/her knowledge of it will strengthen his/her decoding processes and the relevance of decoding the material presented to him/her will deepen the intensity of the language learning process. There is a constant (mostly unconscious) interplay between working on his/her academic achievement in the subject matter and on his/her foreign language proficiency, as well as an interplay between conscious and intuitive language learning. Furthermore the pupil is given innumerable opportunities to use the foreign language in realistic and relevant authentic situations.

Of course, a good teacher makes some important adaptations to the teaching situation: she uses as much authentic material as possible, includes a maximum of visual aids and a variety of media. She follows the principle of didactic reduction and thereby helps the pupils to concentrate on the main points to be understood. She repeatedly trains her students in the use of subject-specific techniques because they go with special sets of words and phrases.

If one compares what has been said so far about bilingual education with the characteristics of task-orientation given above, it becomes clear that task-orientation is an adequate concept of teaching for bilingual education. Here the curiosity of the pupil, his/her interest in the subject matter, is the driving force behind his/her learning. Content and the means of its transmission are not separated. The pupil, too, is looked upon as a holistic entity who learns (a) how to deal with a subject matter and (b) how to use a foreign language successfully at the same time. Learning is seen as a process in which one needs to accept errors and to work on them.

Authenticity is extremely important for bilingual teaching. As far as authenticity of material is concerned, this would not seem to be new; bilingual teachers prefer to use language examples that are not constructed for the purpose of language teaching only but are genuine pieces of language with genuine functions within the L2 culture.

Equally important is the authenticity of interaction. Pupils do not "produce sentences" for the sake of linguistic exercise, but they interact with each other in pursuit of a practical communicative outcome, the purpose of which is transparent to all the participants. In this type of interaction, defective linguistic elements are "repaired" by the context or by the negotiation of the participants – that is, naturally – so that the subsequent discussion can go on unimpeded. The authentication process is the serious individual involvement of the user of the language.

Finally there is the authenticity of person, which is attained if the person using the language is a free agent and accountable for what he/she is saying. In bilingual education this means that he/she is responsible for the subject-based ideas he/she expresses. This self-determination is a precondition and a result of learner autonomy. This can be learned, but first of all the teacher should not be reluctant to grant her pupils teacher-independent learning situations, although this may seem rather difficult for her, since it is the opposite of what teachers are used to.

In bilingual education there is, however, also the danger of the learner being overwhelmed by his own, or the teacher's, expectations. Therefore, a humanistic approach is as important here as in any other language teaching situation. The teacher should

- sequence the items/activities for the pupils carefully
- formulate topics in such a way that the pupils can draw on their own experiences and their world knowledge
- provide the pupils with language material (vocabulary and discourse items) in context so that they can use them to discuss the topic
- allow for individual progress of the pupils
- offer assessment of the subject matter regularly so that the pupils can learn from their own success and failure in the course of time
- be clear about aims and priorities

- most importantly: create a climate of mutual trust and cooperation.

3. Task-oriented exercises in our seminar

From supervising teacher students during their practical work at schools, Hilbert Meyer and I knew that students, although able to talk intelligently about task-orientation in school, often cannot put that theory into practice. In our seminar "Bilingualism and Task-Orientation in Foreign Language Teaching", we therefore addressed both, conveying an insight into the necessity, implications and structure of FLT task-orientation (see above), and having the students experience and develop effective exercises themselves in the various contexts of bilingual education. This was aimed at helping the students

- to overcome deeply ingrained attitudes and expectations
- to understand the many decisions that have to be made on the long way from accepting the idea of task-orientation down to its implementation in specific situations under various conditions.

For each session of our seminar we planned a warming-up exercise. During the first two sessions we led these ourselves, for the following sessions the students had to take over. Since every teacher student of English also studies at least one other school subject, we asked the students to use their individual second subjects as the subject matter that should be taught and used for their individual warming-up exercises, which were to be performed in the seminar and evaluated later on. In order to let the students know what should be taught and demonstrated in their individual exercises every student was assigned to read certain pages on information or imagination gap exercises, on projection, interpersonality or process-evaluation exercises from *Process and Experience in the Language Classroom* (Legutke & Thomas, 1997).

The students tried to understand the precise assignment from the pages in Legutke and Thomas (1997) and developed a first draft for their exercise, which they discussed with me, in some cases in several extra sessions. The materials the students subsequently produced were supposed to meet the following criteria:

- The exercise was to meet the individual requirements set by Legutke and Thomas (1997) in the given pages.
- The degree of difficulty should be appropriate for the level of the students in the seminar.
- The material/requisites should be interesting and motivating.
- The tables and chairs should be arranged according to the social learning necessities.
- The introduction and any help to be given to their fellow students should be clear.

Warming-up exercises are normally understood as exercises that prepare the pupils for what is supposed to follow during the session. In FLT these exercises have the same function and are especially meant to help the pupils to switch over to speaking English during the next 45 minutes (to use their organs of speech adequately and give them confidence in their foreign language competence) and, in addition, to introduce the pupils to the subject matter they are going to deal with.

During the two introductory warming-up exercises Hilbert Meyer and I demonstrated the general rules that should be applied with regard to warming-up exercises:

- All participants should be open for new and unexpected experiences.
- Nobody should be forced to do anything he/she does not want to do.
- The groups should act undisturbed by any observer not involved in the simulation.
- The leader of the activity helps the players to feel comfortable.
- After the activity there is a discussion of the experiences made.

Each exercise developed and implemented by the students was evaluated in two ways:

- At the end of the seminar the participants filled in a questionnaire evaluating the effects of the warming-up exercises in general and of each individual exercise in particular.

- Each student responsible for a certain exercise wrote a seminar paper describing the stages of development of his/her exercise and evaluating it in the light of the theoretical concepts which the seminar had focused on and taking into account the criticism he/she had received.

In the following I will summarize the students' feedback given in the questionnaires:

- The question "Did you feel you had to *un*learn something by being involved in the exercises?" met with the following responses: "I had to learn that it is not so embarrassing and ridiculous to *play* in class as I always had thought", "I had to learn that I do not need to be the person that is dominating in the classroom and that I should give the pupils the chance to voice their own opinion". The statements reinforce our hope that the practical warming-up exercises helped the students to overcome some of their deeply ingrained attitudes and expectations (although it is impossible to gauge how long this will last).
- Responding to the question "What do you think is the most important thing you learned from the exercises?" the students point out the most important preconditions for successful task-orientation in FLT: The topics and exercises must be relevant to the personal situation of the pupils, the interactions must take place in natural situations and as natural, to a certain extent subconscious, processes. All this demands detailed preparations on the teacher's part.
- The questions "What is your overall view on warming-up exercises (a) in foreign language teaching and (b) in the bilingual classroom?" triggered responses in which the students especially point out the motivating, encouraging and individualizing power of warming-up exercises, their positive influence on a trustful and harmonious atmosphere in the classroom, and their usefulness for introducing the class to a new subject.

The answers show that the students understood the message of the seminar as well as the implications of warming-up exercises, especially for bilingual education. I hope the students will be more likely to put task-orientation into practice in their own future teaching. They have experienced the "feel of it"; they know the decisive points that have to be taken into account when preparing and leading such exercises.

4. Just one example

The positive results become even more obvious if one reads the individual reports (the term papers) of those students who developed, implemented and then evaluated one of the exercises. I select the most interesting one:

Martina Niebuhr's task was to develop a process-evaluation exercise (using Legutke & Thomas, 1997, pp. 142-150). Since her second subject was economics, she – after a long period of planning and rethinking – finally came up with the idea of simulating a section of an assessment centre in her exercise. This is a method used by companies to evaluate and select the "best" one out of a pool of hopeful applicants for a certain position advertised. Within an AP (=assessment centre) the applicants are confronted with authentic situations and problems which they have to master.

Martina assigned two different roles to the players: One set (numbered one to four in each group of six) represented applicants applying for a job and therefore participating in an AC. The others (numbered five and six in each group of six) represented employees of the department of the company organising the AC, whose task was the observation and evaluation of the applicants in the interest of the personnel department of the company in order to find the best applicant for the vacant position.

For both roles Martina developed a worksheet that explained the participants' tasks:

Worksheet for players numbered one to four, the "discussers": (1) a sales manager, (2) a chief financial officer, (3) a production manager, (4) a marketing director:

> You belong to the management of a medium-sized company. It is July 2000, and the company is distributing the yearly bonus for extraordinary work. The bonus for 1999 is £ 7,000. Each one of you has to try to push the interests of the employee of his/her department by persuading the others why his/her candidate deserves the bonus (or part of it). Try to come to a conclusion which satisfies each member of the management. The bonus must be spent completely. "Horse trad-

ing" as an instrument of discussion is not allowed. You have ten minutes to come to a conclusion.

Worksheet for players numbered five and six, the "observers":

You are working for the personnel department and you are looking for a good salesman for the company. The four members of the group discussion are applicants for this job. Observe the participants of the discussion and try to find answers to the following questions:

- Who opens the discussion?
- How are the conflicts solved?
- Who gives in and why?
- Who interrupts other people?
- Who gets the others to agree with him/her most easily and why do you think so?
- Does the group come to a conclusion?
- Is everybody satisfied with the results?
- So whom do you select as the "perfect" salesman for your company and why?

The third worksheet for all the players was a list with detailed information (name, position, qualification, age, date of entrance in the company, yearly salary, entrance salary, result of salary negotiation, reason for bonus proposal) about the employees to be pushed by (1) the sales manager, (2) the chief financial officer, (3) the production manager or (4) the marketing director.

In the seminar, after Martina had made sure that all her fellow students had understood the objective of an AC, she explained to them that now *they* were going to be the participants of such a discussion in an AC. She divided the class into groups of six, made the members in each group count from one to six, distributed the worksheets according to the numbers and made sure that the functions and consequently the worksheets for the players numbered five and six were not known to the others (numbered one to four). On the other hand the players numbered five and six received all the worksheets so that they would be informed about the task of those people they had to observe and assess.

After ten minutes of discussion within the groups, Martina asked the whole class to sit in a circle and to report on the results. She stressed that there could not be a right or a wrong outcome but every group should have reached a conclusion, which was the case. She also explained the task and function of those numbered five and six, the "observers", to those numbered one to four. The "observers" reported on their results, which they based on the questions on their worksheet, and a short discussion on the effects of an exercise like this followed. Martina asked her follow students to fill in a short questionnaire. Those numbered five and six were asked "How do you evaluate the process you observed?" In her term paper, Martina stresses the divergence and the autonomy of the answers: Some "observers" said that they had simply followed their guts, others had deliberately taken into account the variations in style, linguistically and in body language. Those numbered one to four were asked "Do you think the observers' evaluation is justified?" 15 out of 16 active "discussers" found the evaluation absolutely adequate; some of them gave reasons for it, one of them questioned if the "winner" really would be the best salesman in real life. The question "Did you like the exercise? Give reasons, please." produced answers which Martina summarized as follows: The exercise is motivating and interesting because of its realistic quality and task-orientation, it is an innovative example for bilingual teaching; it helps everyone (even the shyest participant) to express his/her own opinion. It was well prepared and well presented. All the participants answered the question "Do you think you could use a method like this in your future teaching?" in the affirmative.

In what way does this exercise fulfil the expectations of task-oriented bilingual teaching? In all its phases it was done in English. But the focus was subject content, in this case the *Sachfach* economics. In a realistic situation, students were using English as a means of communication, for gaining information, for solving a problem, for making decisions and for expressing their own feelings. The teaching material was not, strictly speaking, authentic since Martina had developed the idea and the worksheets according to the assignment given by Legutke and Thomas (1997) and was following the conditions given in the seminar. But the interaction was authentic and the students could accept the exercise and the material as realistic and highly transferable both to life as well as to practice in school.

References

Austin, J. L. (1972). *Zur Theorie der Sprechakte*. Stuttgart: Reclam.

Burmeister, P. (1997). Untersuchungen zum verstärkten Vorlauf in 5. Klassen deutsch-englisch bilingualer Gymnasialzüge in Schleswig-Holstein. In M. Wendt & W. Zydatiß (Eds.), *Fremdsprachliches Handeln im Spannungs-*

feld von Prozeß und Inhalt (Dokumentation des 16. Kongresses für Fremdsprachendidaktik der Deutschen Gesellschaft für Fremdsprachenforschung, Halle, Germany, October 4-6, 1995) (pp. 248-256). Bochum: Brockmeyer.

Hamers, J. F., & Blanc, M. H. A. (1989). *Bilinguality and bilingualism*. Cambridge: Cambridge University Press.

Jank, W., & Meyer, H. (1997). *Didaktische Modelle*. Frankfurt/Main: Cornelsen Scriptor.

Legutke, M., & Thomas, H. (1997). *Process and experience in the language classroom*. London: Longman.

Searle, J. R. (1971). *Sprechakte. Ein sprachphilosophischer Essay*. Frankfurt/Main: Suhrkamp.

Van Lier, L. R. (1997). *Interaction in the language classroom*. London: Longman.

Wode, H., Burmeister, P., Daniel, A., Kickler, K.-U., & Knust, M. (1996). Die Erprobung von deutsch-englisch bilingualem Unterricht in Schleswig-Holstein. Ein erster Zwischenbericht. *Zeitschrift für Fremdsprachenforschung, 7*(1), 15-42.

Wode, H. (1991). Formen und Leistungsfähigkeit mehrsprachigen Unterrichts. In A. Raasch, D. Herold, & C. Kiupl (Eds.), *Fremdsprachen lehren und lernen: Perspektiven für ein Europa nach 1992* (Saarbrücker Schriften zur angewandten Linguistik und Sprachlehrforschung 7) (pp. 35-46). Saarbrücken: Universität.

Wode, H. (1995). *Lernen in der Fremdsprache: Grundzüge von Immersion und bilingualem Unterricht*. Ismaning: Hueber.

Wolff, D. (1997a). Bilingualer Sachfachunterricht: Versuch einer lernpsychologischen und fachdidaktischen Begründung. In Amt für Schule Hamburg (Ed.), *Initiativen für den Fremdsprachenunterricht in Hamburger Gymnasien*. Fachtagung vom 23. bis 26. April 1997.

Wolff, D. (1997b). Content-based bilingual education or using foreign languages as working languages in the classroom. In D. Marsh & B. Marsland, & T. Nikula (Eds.), *Aspects of implementing plurilingual education* (Research and Field Reports No. 29) (pp. 51-64). Jyväskylä, Finland: University of Jyväskylä, Continuing Education Centre.

Project orientation in content and language integrated learning

Helmut J. Vollmer

In meinem Beitrag sollen die Möglichkeiten und Grenzen einer projektorientierten Arbeitsweise innerhalb des bilingualen Unterrichts untersucht werden. Dabei werde ich zunächst einige wesentliche Elemente des Projektlernens vorstellen und auf Prinzipien wie Erfahrungslernen, Lerner-, Prozess- und Produktorientierung usw. hinweisen. Sodann wird kurz auf Entwicklungen in der Fremdsprachendidaktik eingegangen, bevor gezielt die Vorzüge und Probleme eines projektorientierten Arbeitens im bilingualen Unterricht thematisiert werden. Insbesondere wird auf die spezifisch veränderten Handlungs- und Interaktionsanforderungen für Lehrende wie Lernende im Rahmen von Projektansätzen abgehoben (z.B. Beraterrolle des Lehrers, Möglichkeiten der Selbststeuerung und der Selbstevaluation auf Seiten der Lerner u.a.m.). Abschließend werden Überlegungen darüber angestellt, wie Projektarbeit besser im bilingualen Unterricht verankert und besser erforscht werden kann.

In my paper, I will first describe some of the basic elements of project learning and relate them to principles like learner and process orientation, experiential learning, holistic versus scientific approaches to learning, group work, collaborative learning, etc. I will then look at specific methodology issues in content-based education, focusing on the project approach. In particular, I will look at the relationship between the teaching traditions within certain subject areas (like geography or history) and what we know about successful foreign language learning and teaching. Basic principles of learner and process orientation, the teacher's role as a facilitator and a consultant and problems of (self-)evaluation will be dealt with in the context of project work. Finally, issues of how to better integrate project work into bilingual education and how to improve the research situation will be addressed.

1. Introduction

The idea of project work and project learning has been around in pedagogy for almost a century now (if not longer). For most proponents it was (and still is) *one* method among others to motivate students and organize classroom learning around topics or issues of the real world outside school. For others, like John Dewey (1916) or Kilpatrick (1918), the project "method" or approach was much more: they define a project as a type of planned activity which involves the whole person and which is embedded into a social framework supporting the development of democratic ways of thinking and attitudes. It was also seen as an avenue to social ways of learning and to democratic behaviour. This wider pragmatic perspective of project work (as expressed by the principle of *learning by doing*), was formulated similarly in other educational approaches, for example, in the concept of a "work school" (*Arbeitsschule*), in reform pedagogy or that of Freinet. As a matter of fact it is rediscovered regularly by each generation (e.g. Bastian & Gudjons, 1986; Chott, 1990).

Yet, up until recently, project work has never really been the centre of attention in mainstream scientific discourse, neither in the general educational sciences nor in pedagogical psychology nor in subject-specific theories of learning and teaching. Project learning was mainly discussed by critical groups and colleagues as an alternative to the traditional forms of institutionalized learning, namely those based on a transmission model with its statement of explicit learning objectives and the attempt to "cover" a certain syllabus; in particular the reduction of the learner to a mere recipient of information was severely questioned. In contrast to this, the learner was redefined as a partner or co-worker in this learning-teaching encounter and as the one responsible for his or her own learning progress in the long run (principles of *learner orientation* or *learner-centeredness* and *learner autonomy*). This general "attitude", which was not yet defined in terms of a coherent learning theory, has become influential within the last 20 years – without considering all the radical consequences necessary for putting it into practice, however.

In this perspective project work was seen as an effective form of education to activate learners, to have them participate in choosing the topic, setting the goals and in procedural decision-making, thus supporting the gradual development of autonomous learning. Projects were defined from rather limited activities (e.g. based on the study of texts and other documents, to be performed within the classroom) to very complex ones (e.g. encompassing field studies and/or data gathering of a genuine "research" type). Accordingly, they could just take the form of a thematic approach to foreign language learning, sometimes that of a role-play, a simulation or a holistic learning experience, sometimes they would link the classroom as a place of learning to life outside school or bring the outside world back into the classroom (see, above all, Fried-Booth, 1986; Legutke, 1988, 1996; Legutke & Thomas, 1991). Yet there was no substantial empirical research in this field, at least not on the micro level of individual learning processes and results; the relevant literature is dominated by sporadic reports and episodic evidence or, at best, by case studies, attempting to generalize beyond the personal experience level.

In Germany, the concept of project learning has entered the pedagogic repertoire, it has become a marginal but accepted part of school life, above all in the *Hauptschule* and *Gesamtschule* (cf. the so-called *Projektwochen*), less so in the *Realschule* and hardly at all in the *Gymnasium* (this is at least true for foreign languages; see Dietrich, 1995). Earlier attempts to introduce a thematic or project-based approach to the study of English in grades 7-10 (ISSUES by Langenscheidt-Longman) have failed. Similarly, in North America, project learning was best documented with "minority" groups of learners like adults and immigrants or in vocational training (Eyring, 1989) and only recently with "average" L2 learners in secondary schools (Beckett, 1999).

Ever since a more cognitive and constructivist view of learning has slowly been spreading, which stresses the need of an active learner in building up knowledge and in following his or her own inner agenda, the *role of project work has been changing*: it is about to move away from a marginal position (as an interesting method of classroom activity ensuring task variety and motivation) to becoming the most appropriate learning environment. Projects are seen as the best setting (at least in theory) for allowing learners to construct and acquire knowledge in a functional form, focusing on discovery procedures and on forms of self-directed learning. The impact of cognitive psychology and constructivism on foreign and second language learning has been demonstrated lately by Wendt (2000) and Wolff (2002), among others. The latter has convincingly argued for the central relevance of thematic project work as a focal point in place.

From here it is only a small step towards understanding why bilingual education as a content- and problem-based approach linked to the use of a second language would profit particularly from project work. I will argue that project orientation is one of the most appropriate forms of content and language integrated learning (CLIL), even if it is restricted to subject-matter issues and the development of subject-related concepts: it has the potential for arousing genuine interest and motivation, for posing adequate cognitive challenges, for developing systematic ways of thinking and proceeding, for linking school learning to scientific inquiry, and last but not least, to complement incidental language learning by focussed language support in L2 as much as in L1 (see Vollmer, 2000b).

2. Terminology

Generally speaking, in the area we are dealing with here, there is some fuzziness in the terminology – one of the main reasons being that the terms outlined above represent macro categories to describe organizational frameworks and sequences of learning activities, their sources and goals.[1] Based on my own (re)search and study of the relevant literature I will try and use the following terms in simple, but systematic ways.

A *project* then is a complex learning-teaching process/encounter comprising many activities and tasks all geared towards dealing with a certain (research) issue or problem by groups of learners or a whole class in order to study this issue more closely, to find out about it in detail and in systematic ways and to report on the findings.

Accordingly, I will use the term *project orientation* for a learning-teaching approach which will focus on working in projects or will organize a substantial part of the syllabus around projects. It is a superordinate category which comprises all types of theme-, topic- or problem-oriented classroom procedures, independent of subject-matter

---

1 There are many different concepts of learning and teaching in the respective literature which more or less explicitly relate to a project-oriented approach (see Kieweg, 1999). They reach from Open Education (e.g. by bringing native speakers and experts into the classroom or by documenting teaching and learning results for the outside world) via multisensory learning as a form of serving the different learner types down to enhancing learning by using the new media. Other concepts focus on collaborative efforts in learning (mainly group and pair work) or on content-based learning with authentic materials, with authentic tasks and with authentic interactions or they recommend the explicit teaching of learning techniques and learning strategies as a basis and prerequisite for autodidactic, self-responsible and autonomous learning (in the long run). Finally, approaches acknowledging the limits of school learning as opposed to real-life learning (Roth, 1998; Spitzner, 1996) also show resemblance to project orientation.

and institutionalization. The term *project work* relates specifically to the activities/interactions of the participating learners and the teacher to describe what is actually being done during a project.

Finally, the term *project learning* focuses on the specific ways in which learners engage in project work. These constructive activities have to be guided and built up by a teacher caring for his individual students and challenging them in differentiated ways. Therefore, the *role of the teacher changes dramatically in the project approach.* Whereas in traditional settings teachers are mainly expected to transfer systems of knowledge into the brain of the learners, they now have to facilitate and support the discovery processes of the learners, make suggestions (which can be accepted or not), provide orientation and models and, most importantly, help the learners develop the tools needed for tackling and solving problems on their own, on the spot and life-long. This new role has been characterized as one of *coaching* and *scaffolding.*[2]

3. Features and prototypical stages of a project

There are several frameworks describing the main elements and stages of a project. Their number largely depends on the refinement of the model, but otherwise most authors agree on the following six necessary steps (e.g. Bastian & Gudjons, 1986; Frey, 1993; Legutke & Thomas, 1991; see also Vollmer, 1998):

- Preparing or setting the ground: Creating the necessary orientation, conditions, prerequisites
- Thematic inquiry, deciding on a specific topic, formulating a (research) question
- Closer investigation of the topic, systematic inquiry, data gathering
- Analyzing the data, interpreting and evaluating the findings

---

2 There is not enough space here to elaborate on these important aspects in the teacher's changing self-definition (but see Vollmer, in press).

- Presentation of results, creating a product (per group and collectively)
- Reflection and evaluation of the project experience (process and product).

By way of comment, I would like to make the reader aware of the complexity of these stages.

(1) It seems to be necessary to develop a mental (or meta-cognitive) framework for project orientation, to reflect on the structure of a project in advance and to identify some of the demands and skills required by project work (and possibly provide lists of steps and skills already known) before starting the actual experience.

(2) The theme of a project could be taken from the curriculum (which normally reflects a systematically organized body of knowledge and abstractions of a scientific discipline, e.g. the *dinosaurs*) or it can be defined in cross-curricular terms (e.g. *migration*) or it is taken from the holistic experience and complexity of life outside school (like *water, energy, relationships*, etc.). Only if learners succeed in getting really interested in their specific topic (or subtopic) and formulate a real question, will they have the readiness and energy to follow it through and to involve themselves in this process of study, experimentation, reflection and evaluation; only then will experiential learning be possible.

(3) This will lead to a negotiated plan of action (or contract) in which the particular sub-groups, their issues, their possible procedures and their deadlines are spelled out. Only if such a plan of action exists, can it be checked again or renegotiated and evaluated at certain points.

(4) The learners not only participate in the definition of the topic and in formulating their own study/research question, but they also do their own planning for the realization of it. This can and will activate a wide sequence of procedures and learning forms, allowing them to bring in their specific interests, preferences, strengths, and skills – or to develop new ones on-line as they are required by working on the problem.

(5) Doing a project requires the willingness of the individual learners to co-operate with one another in pairs or in small groups. Through division of labour they have to be capable of taking over specific responsibilities (to which they agreed beforehand) and of organizing and coordinating their working process largely on their own (though the teacher will be in the background and available, if need be). This includes control of the group dynamics, of their individual and group-related learning processes and of their learning results. Each single member of a project group is accountable to all other members of the group.

(6) Project learning is above all discovery learning, experiential learning, learning by doing. The original project idea (the research question) can be modified, though, as a result of concrete observations, insights, reflections, etc. in order to be continued on a different level or with different means. In project work all of these steps and decisions should be consciously reflected upon and documented as much as possible so as to allow for an on-going evaluation of the steps and routes taken, the methods applied and the results obtained. In the end, the self-defined (research) question has to be "answered".

(7) The insistence on such an "answer" (or finding) is considered an integral part of the learning experience itself. In this sense projects are as much product-oriented as they are process-oriented. Whereas traditionally learning progress and achievement are defined and tested as an increase of knowledge in purely cognitive terms, the concept of "product" as a result of project work is of wider scope: products represent the learning process as much as the findings themselves, they can be expressed using all senses and skills, they comprise much more than just the cognitive segment of a learner's personality. Products are often the central goal towards which all project activities are geared, yet they are not an external part of the project. These products are also the basis for (self-)evaluation and for grading. This requires transparent criteria in advance (preferably developed with the students together) so that they can check against these standards during their work and particularly at the end. In doing so, there are chances of a more open and rational exchange on the assessment of learning outcomes and how they were achieved.

(8) Project results can be presented in many different forms. Normally learners share their expertise (questions, perceptions, procedures and findings) at least with their fellow students in class, often also with the wider public in school or even outside school, all of which happens in authentic communication. In this context a number of new skills (e.g. presentational techniques, mastery of modern technology) might have to be learned. This will again qualify learners beyond the specific project.

(9) Contrary to instructional models of learning, the project approach assumes that learning basically takes place within each and every individual learner, even when the teacher does not control all the task-centred activities. Each individual is genuinely equipped to follow his or her own learning agenda and to actively construct the relevant notions and conceptualizations (though sometimes guided and supported by the teacher). In order for this capacity to unfold and develop further it needs a learning environment like that of project work.

In summary, we can say that project learning means above all three things: first, negotiation about a theme or topic and formulation of a researchable question; second, active processing of the self-set task by way of collecting or creating data; third, the analysis of the data, formulating the findings and presenting them as project results. These are considered the core stages of any project. Each of them is very complex and demanding, requires flexibility and can involve many different (unforeseen) things, as has been proven in case studies (Fried-Booth, 1986; Eyring, 1989, Vollmer, 1998; Polman, 2000).

Project work can very soon reach the borderlines of disciplinary thinking and of traditional school organization (*Fächerschule*), but it can likewise be hosted within the limits of a specific subject-matter. It implies a re-definition of learning and teaching. It can lead to a liberation from traditional role models and thus to a new and surprising experience of content and process (as the two sides of the same coin), of interests, skills, competences and collaboration. For some people this looks like the end of measurable learning progress; for others it is an attempt to bring teaching in line with learning, to reconcile experience and academic thinking, to transform everyday notions into "scientific" concepts and understanding.[3]

4. Project orientation in foreign/second language learning

"No one would claim that project work offers some kind of magical remedy to all our problems in TEFL/TESL" (Maley, 1986). There is no final word on projects. But books like that of Fried-Booth (1986) or Legutke and Thomas (1991) bring together, in a coherent presentation, the principles underlying project work and the wealth of practical know-how on this subject. These perspectives are regularly updated in professional journals and introductory readers (e.g. Bach & Timm, 1996; Timm, 1998; *Der Fremdsprachliche Unterricht – Englisch*, 40, 1999).

The project approach is thought to make an important contribution to at least five critical areas in EFL/ESL teaching: topic-orientation, authenticity, group work, learner autonomy and motivation (Gardner, 1995). Project work provides students with opportunities for using the target language for real communication; however, the issues dealt with have to be substantial in the mind of the learners, because

---

3 Beside many advantages of project work, which are phrased differently by theoreticians and practitioners (for the latter see Arendt, 1999; Kieweg, 1999, pp. 6-7), there are of course also serious problems and risks involved in this approach which are mentioned in the relevant literature. For example, if the task definition is too complex, some of the learners may be overstrained so that they become discouraged and demotivated instead of the opposite. Then the complex task has to be broken down into smaller units, steps, feasible sub-tasks or manageable modules.

Group work allows for collaborative learning beyond the individual scope, but it could also provide opportunities for some learners to hide away. In this case working in pairs might be a solution. It is also stated that the individual learning process and its exact outcomes cannot be as finely observed and controlled as in traditional settings (this argument is questionable, however). Finally, the organizational investments for doing a project are considerable, sometimes even (too) high. Therefore, the relationship between *effort* (put into the preparation and administration of a project) and *effect* (in terms of learning outcomes in a wider sense) has to be weighed one against the other. Project work is not appreciated by everyone alike.

only then can they really identify and become involved. Coleman (1992, p. 36) found that "student choice of topic guarantees a degree of commitment and psychological involvement favourable to language acquisition". In the carrying out of a project, at least four types of authenticity will necessarily be present: authenticity of language input, of task, of event and of learner experience. It seems likely that the authentic "feel" of project work and the fact that the learners are brought face to face with their own learning, are important factors in the high levels of motivation observable in project-centred activities.

Project work also supports the unfolding of learner autonomy. By its very nature project work places the responsibility on the students, both as individuals and as members of a co-operative learning group. This is a big step forward, it requires practice and scaffolding. Autonomy becomes a "fact of life", so to speak (Beckett, 1999).

Finally, the language learning element of a project becomes transparent, less focused, less threatening: learners seem to be more successful in learning a foreign language when they are using it for purposes of information gathering and exchanging about it, rather than studying it as an end in itself.[4] In North America, this insight has led to the development of an approach called *content-based language learning* (CBLL), which seems to be most effective when it provides both meaningful communication about content and intentional language development. Thus, CBLL emphasizes the role of language as a vehicle for learning content and for organizing the learning process itself (both key concepts in bilingual education). As Richards and Rogers (2001, p. 208) have rightly observed: "This implies the centrality of linguistic entities longer than single sentences, because the focus of teaching is how meaning and information are communicated and constructed through texts and discourse".

Mohan & Beckett (2001) have recently claimed that functional linguistics offers a distinctive theoretical perspective and characterization of CBLL and addresses issues of advanced language development which are crucial when the second language is a medium of learning. They analyze the grammatical scaffolding by teachers and L2 learners related to *causal explanations* which form part of a project on the hu-

---

4 In this way learners become more relaxed about their use of the foreign language, which leads to a noticeable improvement in all communicative areas of coursework – an observation which is also true for bilingual education.

man brain. They show how the teacher has to be equipped for providing explicit language support on this level which links discourse structures and devices to cognitive moves and differentiation.

The strongest support for project work, however, comes from cognitive psychology and in particular from a cognitivistic view of learning and of language acquisition as language use. It has been argued convincingly that these are highly constructive activities of the human mind, just like all other forms of information processing, all other perceptions and mental conceptualizations. Within this frame of reference it becomes clear why the creation of an appropriate learning environment is so important: It is seen as the key factor for the unfolding of the necessary construction processes on the part of the learner. Wolff, for example, argues (2002, p. 355) that such a learning environment not only has to make these constructive processes *possible*, but that it has to make them *necessary*, even *force them upon the learners*. If they are not really authentically demanded, but just "put on stage" for motivational reasons (in order to instruct what was intended in the first place), the learners will quickly get suspicious, lose motivation and interest and only demonstrate "learning success" in a superficial way.

5. Project learning in CLIL

So far the methodology for bilingual education has been largely defined through the methods developed for the respective subject-matter areas, which are taught through the L2 as a working language. Projects are mentioned as one method among many others in almost all of the introductory books (as far as they were available to me) on *didactics* for the different subject-matters, for example, for geography or history, for social studies or art. But only in science education has project work really become prominent, with a clear focus on experiential or even experimental learning (see Polman, 2000).

As to the second language component in bilingual education, the insights and principles mentioned in the preceding section could be exploited much more. The reflection on the relationship between language and subject-specific conceptualizations is still very fragmentary, but at least it is growing (see Bonnet, Breidbach & Hallet, 2002). Nevertheless, important innovative considerations within foreign/second language teaching (e.g. CBLL or a constructivist view of learning) have not yet been adequately integrated into a common didactic framework. In order to arrive at a suitable methodology for content and language integrated learning, we need to combine subject-specific traditions (e.g. the specific forms of processing and analyzing expository texts) with functional linguistic theories (e.g. basic patterns of speech acts and discourse in relation to their cognitive equivalents) and with the insights of post-modern psychology and pedagogy. These have to be formulated within a cognitivistic and pragmalinguistic perspective, as much from the point of view of knowledge construction as that of second language acquisition (Vollmer, 2000a, 2002). Much of this task still lies ahead of us.

Fortunately, some of the practices in bilingual education are already embedded into general educational principles which are now thought to be indispensable for any type of learning in school, namely *learner orientation, action orientation, co-operative learning and the development of competences for life* (see Vollmer, in press, for an elaboration on these principles in content and language integrated learning). It may very well be, however, that other parts of the bilingual learning and teaching practice in Germany (and elsewhere) still follow a rather teacher-dominated approach, mainly focusing on the transmission of knowledge, although this would not be admitted. Nevertheless, first observations claim that a learner- and interaction-based approach to bilingual teaching leads to better learning results (Wode, 1995, pp. 152-153).

There is very little documentation, however, about the experience of bilingual teachers in using the project approach, about its systematic role or the possibilities of trying it out. An Internet search has brought some indication that it is a topic among certain groups of teachers, but rather a marginal one. The further development will depend (among other things) on how project learning is seen among curriculum planners, among materials developers or within the teaching profession itself. Is it identified as an approach to mediate between content and language learning or between subject-specific goals and educational goals of a more general nature?

As I have tried to show in my own case study on "Unemployment in and around Osnabrueck" (Vollmer, 1998, in press), the project approach seems absolutely functional for many goals of CLIL. Here are some of the strengths and advantages:

- Activation and application of prior knowledge and skills
- (Re-) Constructing knowledge in a negotiating way
- Mastering cognitive challenges, developing expertise
- Developing different working skills/techniques
- Experimenting with different data gathering and learning strategies
- Social learning through cooperation and collaborative dialogue
- Processing and using language for content and procedural analysis
- Reflecting on the social conventions of language use, comparing L1 and L2 as to their differences and similarities, presenting findings.

In particular, I have described how I went about the different issues and risks as they came up and how the end product (the oral and written presentations of the learners and the general discussion on the evaluation of the project as a whole) gave ample reason to believe that this project experience was a success.

One of the basic ambiguities of project work in bilingual education seems to be the unresolved tension between a curricular or disciplinary point of view and one which is more problem-oriented or even cross-disciplinary. Since most bilingual teachers define themselves as experts in a specific subject-matter (and not as experts in content and language integrated learning as yet) and since they feel obliged to fulfil certain curricular expectations, they are afraid that bilingual projects will take too much of the precious (and always limited) time or even distract them from covering the syllabus or from doing at least the core curriculum prescribed by the administration or other authorities. There is a hidden agenda in the mind of many bilingual teachers operating against acknowledging the difference between monolingual versus bilingual education: coverage versus reduction of content, combined with an intensified quality of learning. My own experience as a bilingual teacher has led me to include *one* project within *half a school year*. This formula seems to be feasible in other circumstances for other colleagues as well, if there is a wish to try out project work. In addition, I clearly decided to stay within the limits of the given subject (social studies), reconstructing part of it, adapting it to our own situation, our own interests and yet questioning its categories, procedures and explanations where necessary. This was well worth all the effort – the potential learning processes and the documented learning outcomes justified the many extra hours that learners and teacher alike invested in this experience. For me, project work looks almost like an ideal form to achieve many of these goals strived for in content and language integrated learning. It should therefore receive the attention it deserves and become a key element in any methodology for bilingual education. What we need above all is a comprehensive research strategy by which we can document the strengths of this approach (especially the cognitive and language-acquisition processes on the part of the learner) and also identify the problems more clearly.

6. Summary and perspectives

As I have tried to show, project-oriented learning is well feasible within bilingual education, although it implies a number of unknown factors, unsolved problems and risks. Some of these I have mentioned self-critically, others will have to be spelled out in more detail in the future. The basic elements of project-oriented learning can be incorporated into any content-based language learning approach, on all levels and within each type of school, as long as it is adapted accordingly. The interest and decision to try out project work is largely dependent on the attitudes and preferences of each individual teacher, but also dependent on prior information, competence and training. The more teaching experience with projects someone has, the more one will develop clear ideas and judgements about how to use this learning form in bilingual education and where its limits are.

By extending the bilingual approach into the lower levels (*Grundschule*) and other types of school (namely *Real*- and *Hauptschule*) the project method becomes even more important, because it involves active and differentiated learning, with all the senses and for a practical purpose, aiming at the development of competences needed in life. Learner activation and autonomy, action orientation as much as cooperative learning are general pedagogical principles which have to become elements of any methodology for CLIL. With a project learning approach there are better chances of linking content and language learning. Project orientation could help the classroom become again and again a place for integrated learning experiences, for critical inquiry and lively communication with a high relevance for understanding reality outside of school, for coping with it and for life-long learning.

References

Arendt, M. (1999). Projektunterricht? Ja, bitte – und immer öfter. *Der Fremdsprachliche Unterricht – Englisch, 40*, 10-16.

Bastian, J., & Gudjons, H. (Eds.). (1986). *Das Projektbuch. Theorie, Praxisbeispiele, Erfahrungen.* Hamburg: Bergmann & Helbig.

Bach, G., & Timm, J.-P. (Eds.). (1996). *Englischunterricht* (2nd ed.). Tübingen: Francke.

Beckett, G. H. (1999). *Project-based instruction in a Canadian secondary school's ESL class: Goals and evaluations*. Unpublished doctoral dissertation. The University of British Columbia, Vancouver, Canada.

Bonnet, A., Breidbach, S., & Hallet, W. (2002). Fremdsprachlichkeit als Spezifikum – Auf der Suche nach einer integrativen Didaktik für den Bilingualen Unterricht. In B. Voss (Ed.), *Fremdsprachenunterricht auf dem Prüfstand: Qualitätssicherung und Qualitätsverbesserung im Schul- und Hochschulbereich.* Berlin: Pädagogischer Zeitschriftenverlag.

Chott, P. (1990). *Projektorientierter Unterricht: Eine Einführung*. Weiden: Schuch.

Coleman, J. A. (1992). Project-based learning, transferable skills, information technology and video. *Language Learning Journal*, *5*, 35-37.

Dewey, J. (1916). *Democracy and education: An introduction to the philosophy of education*. New York: Macmillan.

Dietrich, I. (1995). Übungen und Arbeitsformen im Projektunterricht. In K.-R. Bausch, H. Christ, & H.-J. Krumm (Eds.), *Handbuch Fremdsprachenunterricht* (3rd ed.) (pp. 255-258). Tübingen: Francke.

Eyring, J. L. (1989). *Teacher experience and student responses in ESL project work instruction: A case study.* Unpublished doctoral dissertation, University of California, Los Angeles, USA.

Fried-Booth, D. L. (1986). *Project work*. Oxford: Oxford University Press.

Frey, K. (1993). *Die Projektmethode* (5th ed.). Weinheim: Beltz.

Gardner, D. (1995). Student produced video documentary provides a real reason for using the target language. *Language Learning Journal*, *12*, 54-56.

Kieweg, W. (1999). Projektbezogener Englischunterricht. *Der Fremdsprachliche Unterricht – Englisch, 40*, 4-9.

Kilpatrick, W. H. (1918). The project method. *Teachers College Record, 19* (4), 319-335.

Legutke, M. (1988). *Lebendiger Englischunterricht. Kommunikative Aufgaben und Projekte für schüleraktivierenden Fremdsprachenunterricht.* Bochum: Kamp.

Legutke, M. (1996). Szenarien für einen handlungsorientierten Fremdsprachenunterricht. In G. Bach & J.-P. Timm (Eds.), *Englischunterricht* (2nd ed.) (pp. 103-128). Tübingen: Francke.

Legutke, M., & Thomas, H. (1991). *Process and experience in the language classroom.* London: Longman.

Maley, A. (1986). Foreword. In D. L. Fried-Booth, *Project work* (p. 3). Oxford: Oxford University Press.

Mohan, B., & Beckett, G. H. (2001). A functional approach to research on content-based language learning: Recasts in causal explanations. *The Canadian Modern Language Review, 58*(1), 133-155.

Polman, J. L. (2000). *Designing project-based science: Creating learning through guided inquiry.* New York: Teachers College Press.

Richards, J.C., & Rogers, T. (2001). *Approaches and methods in language teaching* (2nd ed.). Cambridge: Cambridge University Press.

Roth, G. (1998). *Das Gehirn und seine Wirklichkeit.* Frankfurt/M.: Suhrkamp.

Spitzner, M. (1996). *Geist im Netz. Modelle für Lernen, Denken und Handeln.* Heidelberg: Spektrum Akademischer Verlag.

Timm, J.-P. (Ed.). (1998). *Englisch lernen und lehren. Didaktik des Englischunterrichts.* Berlin: Cornelsen.

Vollmer, H. J. (1998). Lerner- und Handlungsorientierung im bilingualen Sachfachunterricht. In L. Hermes & G. Schmid-Schönbein (Eds.), *Fremdsprachen lehren lernen. Lehrerausbildung in der Diskussion* (pp. 291-304). Berlin: Pädagogischer Zeitschriftenverlag.

Vollmer, H. J. (2000a). Bilingualer Sachfachunterricht als Inhalts- *und* als Sprachlernen. In G. Bach & S. Niemeier (Eds.), *Bilingualer Unterricht. Grundlagen, Methoden, Praxis, Perspektiven* (pp. 51-73). Frankfurt/M.: Lang.

Vollmer, H. J. (2000b). Förderung des Spracherwerbs im bilingualen Sachfachunterricht. In G. Bach & S. Niemeier (Eds.), *Bilingualer Unterricht. Grundlagen, Methoden, Praxis, Perspektiven* (pp. 139-158). Frankfurt/M.: Lang.

Vollmer, H. J. (2002). Leistungsfeststellung und Leistungsbewertung im Bilingualen Sachfachunterricht: Ein Desideratum. In S. Breidbach, G. Bach, & D. Wolff (Eds.), *Bilingualer Sachfachunterricht: Didaktik, Lehrer-/Lerner-Forschung und Bildungspolitik zwischen Theorie und Empirie* (pp. 101-121). Frankfurt/M.: Lang.

Vollmer, H. J. (in press). *Projektorientierung im bilingualen Sachfachunterricht.* Osnabrück: Universität.

Wendt, M. (Ed.). (2000). *Konstruktion statt Instruktion*. Frankfurt/M.: Lang.
Wode, H. (1995). *Lernen in der Fremdspache. Grundzüge von Immersion und bilingualem Unterricht*. Ismaning: Hueber.
Wolff, D. (2002). *Fremdsprachenlernen als Konstruktion. Grundlagen für eine konstruktivistische Fremdsprachendidaktik*. Frankfurt/M.: Lang.

Learning languages through songs and media

Elvis analysed

Willis Edmondson

Die Texte ausgewählter Elvis Presley-Lieder werden analysiert. Es wird dann argumentiert, dass solche Texte einen genauso berechtigten Platz im Englischunterricht wie literarische Texte einnehmen können.

Selected lyrics of Elvis Presley's songs are analysed. On this basis it is then suggested that such texts appear to be as relevant for language teaching purposes as literary alternatives. Lessons are therefore drawn.

Baby I don't care was released on Elvis Presley's *Jailhouse Rock* album in 1957. The title appears to suggest indifference, although the song is, of course, a love song. There is therefore a paradox to be resolved here: not caring has to transform into caring. This paradox reflects two issues centrally relevant to the commercial and musical success of Mr. Presley. The first is how it was possible to get countless young women from all walks of life in the fifties to believe that the singer cared about them, when he, the King, clearly existed on a totally different plane of reality, and at the same time to persuade countless young men to bow before the King, but also to identify with him. Presley and his managers were faced with the further problem of getting the parents of these young people to at least tolerate his music and records, as firstly the purchasing power of teenagers in the fifties was low, and secondly parents exercised, to some degree at least, authority over their offspring in that period, and rock 'n' roll was new, and perceived (correctly, as it happens) as essentially subversive. The dual problem was, then, how to make the transcendental human, and how to appeal to both Lucy and her mom. The lyrics of the songs, and the way they are delivered, are, I suggest, designed to address these problems.

It transpires that in the song *Baby I don't care* "he" is hip, while "she" is square[1]:

> *Baby I Don't Care*
> You don't like crazy music
> You don't like rocking bands
> You just wanna go to a movie show
> And sit there holding hands
> Baby you're so square
> Baby I don't care.[2]

After this first statement, the paradox whereby not caring is caring has apparently already been accounted for: the singer cares so much for the girl that he is able to overlook her lack of musical taste. But what of the more deep-seated paradox? If he is hip and she is square, how can she be attracted to him without feeling belittled? And what about mom? Of critical importance is the fact that in performance the last two lines are clearly separated via intonation and pausology. We are invited therefore as listeners to provide the semantic link ourselves. Is it, then, an adversive or a consequential link? Is it the case that you're terribly square, *but* I don't care, or are you so square *that* I don't care? The difference, I suggest, is crucial. In the first case, the link simply glorifies the King further. He asserts his greatness via his magnanimity. On the consequential interpretation, however, it is the degree of

---

1 When a song is performed, and especially when first and second person pronouns occur in the lyrics, one needs to distinguish between various "speaker" and "hearer" roles (Goffman, 1981, pp. 131-146; Edmondson, 1988). However, I shall designate these roles totally imprecisely, precisely because role ambiguity, overlap, and co-identification characterise Presley's lyrics, and such slipperiness is of course exploited. "He" is therefore both the first person narrator (or "singer") in the song, and also Mr. Presley, the "performer". Similarly, "she" may be both the "you" addressed and/or referred to in the song, listeners to the recording or live performance, and "overhearers", e.g. persons reading the lyrics in the confines of this paper, for purposes yet to be clarified.

2 The lyrics are reproduced without punctuation, and have been checked both with the records and various published sources, though slightly different versions of the lyrics are to be found in print. Particularly useful are the following websites devoted to Mr. Presley, offering songbook and/or discography:
http://www.geocities.com/SunsetStrip/Palladium/3234
http://www.elvispresleyonline.com/html/elvis_presley_online.html

squareness which works the transformation. She is responsible for his caring! There are, however, sexual overtones in the lyrics, which complicate the picture. The ambiguity discussed above is matched by the ambiguous implications of *just* in *You just wanna go to a movie show*. The implicit textual link can be read as *instead*, or as *moreover*. In the first case, then, holding hands is the *alternative* to rock 'n' roll. Hence, if we accept the reading whereby his not caring is a *consequence* of her squareness, her restrained entertainment preferences provide the reason. It is the good old-fashioned, small-town, pictures-on-a-Saturday-night romance that captures the King. On this reading, then, the King steps off his pedestal and becomes the boy next door. He cares for you *because* you are so square. Forget rocking bands, let's just get holding hands.

However, there is a *moreover* interpretation for *just*. On this reading, a propensity for popcorn and Doris Day is additional evidence of her squareness. On the first reading, *just* expresses an opposition between rocking bands and holding hands, but what about the second reading? Well, the opposition is between holding hands and – presumably – more adventurous modes of sexual expression. On this reading then, the song carried an implied identification between rock 'n' roll and sex[3], as opposed to Tin-Pan-Alley and romance.

So we can read the text both ways. We have the boy-next-door-meeting-Mary-Lou-down-at-the-waterhole Old World romance interpretation (cf. "Climb upon old Becky's back and let's ride to the picture-show" from *Movie Magg* by Carl Perkins, 1955). It's all good clean gingham. On the second interpretation, however, we have to reconstruct the hip alternative to just holding hands in the cinema, and the alternative is obvious – it's sex. The implication, then, is that the person addressed in the song not only fails to appreciate the King, but is also a virgin. The logical implication for the hearer is clear. Persons who are not square and are into crazy music express their sexuality.

Both interpretations – singer as boy-next-door and singer as King, the romantic and the sexual – co-exist, and both wreak their effect

---

[3] This identification of rock 'n' roll with sex was, of course, widespread in the fifties, when this musical form was new, and was often much more directly expressed than happens in Presley's lyrics (cf. for example Gene Vincent's *Baby won't you bop with me*, or, even more famously, Chuck Berry's *Baby let me bang your box*).

independently of their conscious appraisal (a thesis developed *inter alia* by William Empson; see Empson, 1956). In other words, these implications are not mutually exclusive alternatives. Thus, many young women listening to the song, and only indirectly addressed by the lyrics, presumably *do* like rocking bands – at least when Mr. Presley is lead singer, but might nonetheless be happy to identify with the romance of holding hands. Furthermore, of course, the romantic and the sexual themselves often go hand in hand. Young males listening to the song can, too, of course, share Mr. Presley's penchant both for crazy music *and* for holding hands and/or less square modes of togetherness. The point is that these different implications, connotations and interpretations are co-present, are interwoven in what have to be seen as semantically trivial lyrics, and are themselves triggered by language form and language expression.

Many of Presley's earlier songs deal with both starry-eyed romance and teenage sex, and succeed in packing both into a performance of often quite banal lyrical content. Consider the song *Don't* (song and music by Leiber/Stoller, first recorded by Presley in 1957). Interestingly enough, the title is again negative! Take this snippet of text:

> *Don't*
> Don't, don't, that's what you say
> Each time that I hold you this way.
> When I feel like this,
> And I want to kiss you, baby,
> Don't say don't.

The most immediate interpretation of the last line is that it is an appeal that she withdraw her negative response to the speaker's actions and/or his feelings. What, then, is going on? Maybe all he really wants is a kiss, a cuddle, and a continuation of holding hands in the movie show? Maybe. But note that she is not objecting to his "holding her", but rather his holding her *in a certain way*. Further, *feel* in line 3 is subtly ambiguous between an emotional and a physical happening. So we are poised once more between a romantic and a sexual interpretation of the circumstances of the song. Independently of the question how "heavy" the petting was, the most obvious interpretation of the stanza given here is that she is being coy, as a response to his attempted verbal seduction. However, this is of course not the whole story. The intonation and delivery of the "line" *Don't say don't* allows a quite different interpretation. The first occurrence of *don't* has strong stress, potentially terminal intonation, and is followed by a pause of two bars. We can therefore interpret the first occurrence of *don't* as a citation, rather than a prohibition, as is *no* in the following:

– He wants me to give up my career for the family.
– No! Say no!

Hence, just as we saw that saying *I don't care* may be evidence that I *do* care, so can saying *Don't say don't* be taken to mean *Do say don't*! In support of this line of reasoning, consider first of all the title (identical to what she says, and immediately followed by a quotation), and the continuation of the lyrics:

> If you think that this is just a game I'm playing,
> If you think that I don't mean every word I'm saying,
> Don't, don't, don't feel that way.
> I'm your love and yours I will stay.
> This you can believe:
> I will never leave you,
> Heaven knows I won't.

Here we have affirmations of seriousness, sincerity, devotion, loyalty, long-term commitment, and even a reference to the deity. In the light of this, the assumption that the title is a plea for sexual abstinence – a plea for "not going too far" – and not for sexual submission becomes highly plausible. Again, note that in this segment the repetition of *don't* is clearly reinforcing, i.e. it echoes the sexual abstinence interpretation of *don't say don't*. Further, the verb *feel* crops up once more, totally void of innuendo. So we can read the song both ways. Indeed, I suggest that at least subconsciously we have to read the song both ways, and language is the trigger.

Consider further *Baby Let's Play House* (song/lyrics Gunter, first released in 1955). "Playing house" is something children do and often involves babies – i.e. playing with dolls. This innocuous interpretation of the title is reinforced by the context of the song: Mary Lou is apparently leaving her lil' ol' home town, to go off to the evil world of college, where fools can be seduced by the attractions of pink Cadillacs. Staying home and playing house is apparently a much more wholesome alternative. Note incidentally the b-b-b-baby talk at the beginning of this song:

> *Baby Let's Play House*
> Oh, baby, baby, baby, baby baby.
> Baby, baby baby, b-b-b-b-b-b baby baby, baby.
> Baby baby baby
> Come back, baby, I wanna play house with you.
> Well, you may go to college,
> You may go to school.
> You may have a pink Cadillac,
> But don't you be nobody's fool...

On the other hand, it is hardly necessary to point out that playing house can be interpreted as a sexual metaphor (compare slightly outmoded euphemisms such as *living together* or *cohabitation*). That sexual games are involved in playing house is suggested by consistent innuendo, developed accumulatively in the song. Thus the emotional involvement of the singer is stressed:

> Now listen and I'll tell you baby
> What I'm talking about.

The game is described euphemistically as "doing what we did before" (why, if they were just playing house?), while a direct expression of sexual jealousy occurs later in the song:

> I'd rather see you dead, little girl,
> Than to be with another man.

Let us further focus on the central message: "I wanna play house with you". Linguistically, there is considerable sexual mileage to be gotten out of this expression. Clearly, *playing house* is a sub-category of *playing.* Consider then the ambiguity of

> I wanna play with you.

Is the verb *play*, or *play with*? Are you a co-player, as in *I wanna play cards with you*, or a plaything, as in *I wanna play with your yoyo*?[4] It is hardly necessary to point out that playing with a b-b-baby on the latter interpretation largely involves holding the baby, undressing it, and putting it to bed. Even if we accept the co-player interpretation, the sexual interpretation is not excluded. In this vein, we might ask

4 Aficionados will be reminded of another song by Chuck Berry, in which he played with his "ding-a-ling".

whether the use of a first person plural subject pronoun would lead to the paraphrase:

> "We can play with one another", or
> "We can play with each other".

In the first expression, the nature of the game is open – we both play something or other; in the second it is not – I play with you, while you play with me.

The shift between childhood innocence and sexual excitement which comes out in *Let's Play House* is equally obviously present in *Let me be your Teddy Bear* (Mann/Lowe, first released by Presley in 1957). The formulation in the title is surely marked – we are not confronted with a statement of personal volition such as *I want to be your teddy bear,* nor is there a plea for more attention, as might be formulated *Baby, love your teddy bear,* or something similar. Instead the speaker requests permission to assume a teddy bear role. Now one can only request permission to *do* something. Thus, while *being blond* would normally not be understood as an activity, if I ask your permission to be blond, the assumption is that I want to do something, such as dye my hair. On this argument, then, *be* in the title of the song is an activity verb. From this we deduce that this teddy is not always passive. It transpires that the tension between passive and active teddy roles mirrors the shift between a toy bear and a real one, and between childhood innocence and sexual excitement. In the first line, the teddy bear is "loving", but this active role is immediately constrained by the suggestion that the bear be chained. Note, though, that if we accept the idea that the bear is to be led around on a chain, we are handling a grizzly, not a passive plaything. So this chained teddy can be directly compared with lions and tigers. In rejecting these two roles (note the negation coming in now, together with the expression of personal volition), the hearer is both reassured (teddy is relatively harmless), but at the same time lulled into accepting a live, active bear as teddy. The first line in the last stanza reproduced here mirrors the title of the song, in that permission is again sought, and the verb *be* is used once more ("let me be around you every night"). The active implications of the use of this syntactic structure argued for in the analysis of the song's title hold here too, and are reinforced by the phrase *be around you,* which can have a physical (wrap-around) or a geographical (physical proximity) interpretation. Further, in pursuing a sexual interpretation here, one must point out that while running one's fingers through somebody's hair is conventionally innocuous when the recipient is human, bears in fact have relatively little hair on their heads, relative to other parts of their anatomy.

> *Let Me Be Your Teddy Bear*
> Baby let me be your loving teddy bear,
> Put a chain around my neck and lead me anywhere.
> Oh let me be (oh let him be) your teddy bear.
> I don't wanna be your tiger,
> 'Cause tigers play too rough.
> I don't wanna be your lion,
> 'Cause lions ain't the kind you love enough.
> Baby, let me be around you every night.
> Run your fingers through my hair,
> And cuddle me real tight.
> Oh let me be (oh let him be) your teddy bear.

So once more we have a rather primitive and lexico-syntactically highly simplistic text that is nonetheless woven into a complex of co-present meanings, without irony, paradox, incoherence or grammatical deviation resulting. Might lyrics such as these have a useful place in English language teaching programs? Maybe. It all rather depends on the purpose for which one might want to use them, I suggest. Do they offer useful exemplification of relevant features of the English language? Possibly. It rather depends on what one believes a specific group of language learners might usefully be made aware of. At least, as the above notes have shown, the effects reached in these lyrics are not in the least dependent on syntactic complexity, or the use of unfamiliar lexical expressions. The lexis is from the philologist's perspective embarrassingly banal. In other words, the language forms exploited will be familiar to all but the most elementary learners of English.

Before pursuing the issue of relevance, let us briefly explore some further themes illustrated in Presley's lyrics of the fifties that might be deemed potentially relevant to the concerns of teachers of English. Consider *Wear My Ring Around Your Neck* (Caroll/Moody, first Presley recording 1958). The interest here lies in the cultural interpretation of the title. In *Teddy Bear*, the girl was invited to *put a chain around his neck and lead him anywhere*. Now, however, it is the *girl* who is being invited to put his ring around her own neck! This gesture is, presumably, also a symbol of submission or bondage. Following a reference to *chains* and *necks*, in connection with wild animals, invocation of a *ring* possibly summons up the association of nose – and indeed in some cultures a ring in the nose is the accepted way of controlling a bear or a bull, rather than a chain around the neck. So is the title telling her to submit to his male ego? Maybe, but the alleged claim is that by wearing his ring, she would be advertising her love – the ring is a symbol of commitment:

> *Wear My Ring Around Your Neck*
> Won't you wear my ring around your neck
> To tell the world I'm yours, by heck?
> Let them see your love for me,
> And let them see by the ring around your neck.

In the context of boy/girl relationships, it certainly used to be more common to signal such a commitment by wearing a ring on one's *finger*, and while there are many non-European cultures in which the carrying of a large number of metal rings around one's neck is a sign of both beauty and social status, this was certainly not the case in the America of the fifties. So what is going on here? What sort of ring is involved, and how do you get it round your neck, by heck? The questions are rhetorical, but how widespread is knowledge of the relevant convention? How far can school or university learners of English deduce the social practice on the basis of linguistic proficiency?[5] Note that the formulation in the lyrics actively encourages the romantic associations suggested above, in that the verb *wear* is used. If I thread a certain key onto a piece of string, and tie the string around my neck, I may be said to *carry* your key around my neck, or even *keep* it there, but I could scarcely be said to *wear* your key in this way. In short, the practice of wearing a ring around one's neck appears to be culturally, geographically and historically specified. The practice takes on new meaning, too, in the light of current behaviour patterns in Europe. How far is it still culturally valid to assume that rings are worn on fingers? Given that piercing is a totally acceptable convention (at least among students and professors), how far do persons evidence their commit-

---

5 How many readers, for example, learnt of the practice and significance of hanging out yellow ribbons by virtue of a popular song, featuring such ribbons hanging on an oak tree? Consider, too, on the issue of cultural change, what would nowadays be signalled, if the ribbons were red.

ment to or liking of some other person by literally wearing his or her ring in their nose, their tongue, or indeed some less public part of their anatomy? The title of this song seems then to be a good instance of the links between linguistic expressions and socio-cultural practices, and illustrates how such practices may differ in space and time.

A different kind of interest is evoked by the title *I'm Left, You're Right, She's Gone* (1955). The lyrics essentially serve to justify and explain the word-play evidenced in the title. To this end, *two* women feature in the lyrics. One (you're right) had warned him about the other (she's gone). This relatively complex scenario leads to problems of closure, resolved when the narrator suddenly discovers that he has fallen for the woman who was right. This then is the background to the word-play indicated in the title. Three oppositions are played with on the basis of two meanings for *left*, and two meanings for *right*:

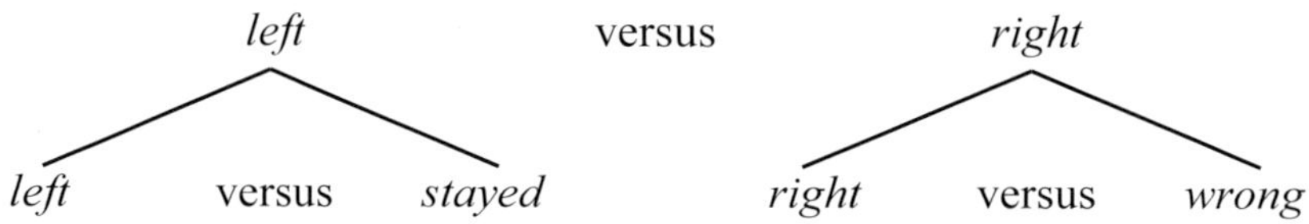

Thus, the singer believes it was wrong of "her" to have left him, and that "you" were right in foreseeing that this would happen, while he was wrong to believe in her faithfulness, and, moreover, wrong not to believe you. Further, of course, since she has left, he has been left alone. There are more subtle effects, too, in that the lyrics twice stress that the woman who turned out to be right told him *all along* how it would be, this consistency contrasting then with the fickleness of the lady who left. The happy ending also indirectly makes the point that the woman who was right turns out to be the right woman for him, too, apparently. A small sample of the text will suffice to suggest the tone:

> *I'm Left, You're Right, She's Gone*
> Well, you're right, I'm left, she's gone.
> You're right, and I'm left all alone.
> Well, you tried to tell me so,
> But how was I to know?

What is to be learnt from these analyses of a small sample of Presley material? The author has argued on several occasions that literary texts have no inherent special status in the business of language learning and teaching (Edmondson, 1991, 1993, 1997). That literary texts can usefully be exploited for purposes of language insight, awareness and motivation is of course true, but I claim that the same is true of practically any other kind of text as well. This is the point my analyses of Presley seek to make. Those who believe that literature has a special place in language classes often argue that literature exhibits unique features of language use and meaning. It surely follows, however, that such texts have in consequence no relevance for gaining insight into and command of non-literary language. I know of no arguments that invalidate this conclusion.[6]

Thus, I cannot accept the view that literary texts are particularly relevant for the purposes of language teaching and learning. I hold that *all* texts are potentially relevant, and that no particular genre can be given precedence, except of course for a specified group of learners. Therefore, I do not wish to argue that the songs of Mr. Presley are of especial relevance for the teaching of English in the German educational system, or indeed elsewhere. I do wish to claim, however, that such texts can be used to derive insight into language structure and use, culture, social norms and social change. Indeed, the analyses offered above might be deemed consistent with the goals of intercultural learning, language awareness, or even critical discourse analysis, though these are currently fashionable bandwagons I do not aspire to join.

The thrust of this paper is then consistent with Timm's demonstration that the lyrics of Bruce Springsteen or *The Police* can offer a good basis for language learning activities (Timm, 1998b). From my perspective, it is therefore appropriate that in Timm (1998a), *Englisch lernen und lehren*, the *Jubilar's* own contribution (Timm, 1998b) appears immediately after the chapter in the book focussing on literature – the chapter is entitled *Verfahren der Textbegegnung: Literarische und andere Texte*. We can, I suggest, be grateful for that rider.

---

6 Thus Widdowson (2000), despite his lucidity and stylistic joie-de-vivre, fails to escape this logical trap.

References

Edmondson, W. J. (1988). Speaker and hearer as discourse roles. In H. W. Ludwig (Ed.), *Anglistentag 1987. Tagungsberichte des Anglistentags. Band IX* (pp. 397-405). Gießen: Hoffmann Verlag.

Edmondson, W. J. (1991). Sind literarische Texte für den fremdsprachlichen Lehr-/Lernprozeß besonders geeignet? In K.-R. Bausch, H. Christ, & H.-J. Krumm (Eds.), *Texte im Fremdsprachenunterricht als Forschungsgegenstand* (pp. 53-60). Tübingen: Narr.

Edmondson, W. J. (1993). Literatur im Fremdsprachenunterricht – wozu? In J.-P. Timm & H. Vollmer (Eds.), *Kontroversen in der Fremdsprachenforschung* (pp. 275-284). Brockmeyer: Bochum.

Edmondson, W. J. (1997). The role of literature in foreign language learning and teaching: some valid assumptions and invalid arguments. *AILA Review, 12*, 42-55.

Empson, W. (1956). *Seven types of ambiguity* (3rd ed.). London: Chatto & Windus.

Goffman, E. (1981). *Forms of talk.* Oxford: Basil Blackwell.

Timm, J.-P. (Ed.). (1998a). *Englisch lernen und lehren. Didaktik des Englischunterrichts.* Berlin: Cornelsen.

Timm, J.-P. (1998b). Pop- und Rocksongs als „Lernschrittmacher". In J.-P. Timm (Ed.), *Englisch lernen und lehren. Didaktik des Englischunterrichts* (pp. 178-184). Berlin: Cornelsen.

Widdowson, H. (2000). Essay on literature and language teaching. An epistle to Dr. Edmondson. In C. Riemer (Ed.), *Kognitive Aspekte des Lehrens und Lernens von Fremdsprachen* (pp. 387-394). Tübingen: Narr.

Discovering Shakespeare: A media-integrated approach

Wilfried Brusch

Filmproduktionen der Stücke Shakespeares dürfen bei einem Vergleich mit Bühnenproduktionen nicht als zweitrangig angesehen werden. In ähnlicher Weise darf auch der Einsatz von Filmen bei der Behandlung von Shakespeare im Unterricht nicht als bequeme und schülerfreundliche Lösung diskreditiert werden. Die Auseinandersetzung mit Text-, Theater- oder Film-Version kann und muss als in gleicher Weise anspruchsvoll betrieben werden. Es werden fünf Strategien aufgezeigt, wie das Medium Film den Shakespeare-Unterricht bereichern kann:

1. Der Vergleich der Behandlung eines Themas in verschiedenen Stücken.
2. Die Gegenüberstellung einer alten und neuen Produktion eines Stückes.
3. Klassische Produktion und moderne Adaption im Vergleich.
4. Shakespearerezeption in einem zeitgenössischen Drama.
5. Visuelle Biographien: Von der Dokumentation zur fiktionalen Verarbeitung.

Am Beispiel der Eröffnungsszene von *Macbeth* wird gezeigt, wie Textlektüre, die dramatische Umsetzung im Klassenzimmer und der Einsatz unterschiedlicher Fassungen dieser Szene (aus verschiedenen Filmproduktionen) die Chance bietet, die Schüler für je unterschiedliche Interpretationen und künstlerische Konzeptionen dieser Szene zu sensibilisieren. Auf der Basis so einer intensiven, multimedialen Auseinandersetzung mit Shakespeare im Klassenzimmer kann eine Projektreise nach England mit dem Besuch der Shakespeare-Theater in Stratford und London ein unvergessliches Bildungserlebnis für die Lerngruppe werden.

Film productions of Shakespeare's plays must not be looked upon as inferior to stage productions. In a similar way using films for teaching Shakespeare in the classroom must not be looked upon as an easy option. Analysing a film can be as academically challenging a task as interpreting a text or discussing a "live" performance. Five strategies can be applied to integrate media material for teaching Shakespeare:

1. Comparing identical themes in different plays.
2. Comparing old and modern productions of the same play.
3. Comparing a "classic" production and a modern adaptation.
4. Discovering how Shakespeare is referred to in a modern drama.
5. From fact to fiction: visual biographies.

Taking the opening scene of *Macbeth* as an example, it is shown how reading, acting and viewing this scene can heighten the students' awareness of Shakespeare's art as a playwright. Shakespeare's plays have been produced more often than any other plays. A comparison of Macbeth, Scene I,1, as "done" in different productions, can heighten the students' awareness of the director's art. On the basis of this intensive and integrated Shakespeare experience in the classroom a visit to the Stratford and London Shakespeare theatres will be a unique contribution to the students' education.

1. Shakespeare's plays: as text, on stage and as media productions

Modern language acquisition theory tells us that a positive attitude (low affective filter) of the learner towards his learning task is of great importance for success (Krashen, 1985). When the study of Shakespeare's plays in school is based exclusively on reading and discussing the text, as still often happens, success-oriented motivation of the students may be difficult to achieve. Here is the statement of a pupil who does not understand why he has to study Shakespeare in this way:

> "I don't see why they give us this old-fashioned junk by Milton and Shakespeare and Wordsworth and all these has-beens," he protested. "Oh, I guess I could stand it to see a show by Shakespeare, if they had swell scenery and put on a lot of dog, but to sit down in cold blood and read'em – These teachers – how do they get that way?" (Lewis 1922, pp. 80-81)

This is what Ted Babbitt, an American high school student in Sinclair Lewis's novel *Babbitt*, published in 1922, says about reading Shakespeare in school (see also Brusch, 1996, pp. 41-42). When this statement and the ensuing discussion of the Babbitt family about the pros and cons of reading Shakespeare in school is discussed in advanced English as a Foreign Language (EFL) classes today, students invariably show considerable sympathy for Ted's attitude. In the 1920s there were indeed only the two ways of studying Shakespeare that Ted mentions: reading the text or watching it as a stage production. Today there is a third means of access: media production, be it television or video. And the day may not be far away when all media materials for the study of Shakespeare will be available on the Internet in every classroom, study or even living room (see also Walther, 1997).

Between 1978 and 1985 the BBC produced all 37 Shakespeare plays for television. The literary consultant for the Shakespeare project, John Wilders, called the Stratford playwright the most successful TV author of all time, although he wrote his scripts and produced his plays 300 years before TV and video were invented.

Kenneth S. Rothwell and Annabelle Henkin Melzer's international filmography and videography *Shakespeare on Screen,* published in 1990, strongly supports Wilder's statement. Rothwell and Meltzer (1990) supply information on media productions connected with Shakespeare's plays from 1899 until 1990. It comprises 747 entries.

Before the development of modern media the viewing of the plays of Shakespeare or of any other dramatist was the privilege of people who could afford theatre visits. Now film versions of all of Shakespeare's plays are available for everybody. In his essay "Shakespeare heute: Zwischen Wort und Bild" Gerhard Müller-Schwefe (1982) stated that as early as the 1960s one Shakespeare play shown on German television attracted almost as many people as all theatre performances per season in Germany put together: Franz Peter Wirth's *Hamlet,* with the main role played by Maximilian Schell, was shown on German TV in 1961, and 11 million people watched it. All theatre performances that year attracted an audience of 12.4 million people in Germany. Müller-Schwefe estimated that around 5% of all German theatre productions in those days presented a play by Shakespeare. In other words Shakespeare attracted an audience of 600,000 into the theatre that year, but almost twenty times as many people watched a single play on television.

Before we go on to show how media productions can be used for the study of Shakespeare one question has to be considered: Can media productions be regarded as a valid representation of a theatre play? On this issue Müller-Schwefe has this to say:

> Man wird daher auch kein Recht haben zu behaupten, daß eine Verfilmung eines Shakespeare-Textes prinzipiell dem Urtext ferner steht als eine Bühneninszenierung des 20. Jahrhunderts. Da der Shakespearesche Text grundsätzlich, um zur Wirkung zu kommen, einer medialen Umsetzung bedarf, ist nicht einzusehen, warum nicht im Zuge der Entwicklung neuer Medien auch das Hörspiel, der Spielfilm und die Fermsehversion als Möglichkeiten zur Umsetzung des Wirkungspotentials des Urtextes in Frage kommen sollen. (Müller-Schwefe, 1982, pp. 45-46)

John Wilders (1982) goes even further than Müller-Schwefe. He feels that television and video productions are closer to the Renaissance theatre of Shakespeare's time than our modern stage productions:

> Television can restore to Shakespeare's plays the unbroken flow and continuity they almost certainly achieved in the Renaissance theatre. ... Television performances can also be taken at a more rapid pace than is possible even in the most intimate of modern theatres. In the theatre the actor must ensure that his words, gestures, and the expression of his face are transmitted to many people, some placed at a considerable distance away, and he must therefore adopt a less than natural pace both of speaking and of physical expression. But a television actor, placed only a yard or two away from every member of his audience, can speak at a conversational rate and by the merest twitch of an eyebrow convey feeling. Not only does this speed of performance give to the plays a tighter unity, but it probably restores to them the pace and rhythm they achieved when they were first produced. The Globe Theatre, polygonal in shape, built largely of wood, rubble, and plaster, unencumbered by the sound-absorbing materials of carpeting and upholstery, was, I imagine, an acoustically lively place. The actor, in close proximity to his audience, could have rattled off his lines at a rate which made the "two hours' traffic of our stage" a fairly accurate description. (Wilders, 1982, pp. 61-62)

Certainly being present at a theatre performance, watching a play on video or reading the text are very different means of access to Shakespeare. Ideally reading, viewing and theatre-going should be integrated in order to achieve a meaningful study and enjoyable experience of a Shakespeare play. To achieve this in the classroom many teachers will have to overcome two culturally ingrained prejudices before they use these different means of access to a play. Peter Reynolds (1991b) points out:

> The act of reading continues to carry high status in contemporary culture despite its near-eclipse as a leisure activity among many young people. Watching television, especially in comparison to watching "live" performance, is a low-status activity. (Reynolds, 1991b, p. 189)

According to Reynolds, many teachers have a feeling of guilt when they use film material extensively in the classroom. They may be criticised by colleagues for taking an easy option. This attitude is unjustified and must be overcome, for film analysis can be just as challenging as text interpretation or the critical review of a theatre performance.

I would now like to do two things: Firstly I would like to give examples of how film productions and film material can extend and bring to life the study of Shakespeare. Secondly I would like to give an example of how the modern media can be used for a comparison of the interpretation of a single scene by several directors. Such comparison of different artistic concepts can help students develop their own independent judgement of the director's art.

2. Media material for Shakespeare study in the classroom

In this section examples will be given from the wealth of media material available for the study of Shakespeare in the classroom. English teachers will need to co-operate in the acquisition of the material and then make it available to each other in a video library in school. For further material see Antor's (1997) selected media library and videography.

Of course the way the media material described here can be used in the classroom can only represent a range of suggestions and must be adapted by individual teachers according to the needs and interests of their classes.

2.1 A thematic approach: The battle of the sexes. Branagh's opening of *Much Ado About Nothing* and Zeffirelli's finale of *The Taming of the Shrew*

The relationship and division of roles between men and women is a recurrent theme in many of Shakespeare's plays. It is a question that is still very much alive nowadays and also highly relevant for young people. In the two plays to be compared here the main characters, Beatrice and Benedick as well as Katherine and Petruchio, are engaged in a battle for power and dominance in their relationships. Video extracts of the opening of *Much Ado...* and of the end of *The Shrew* illustrate this.

Branagh (1993a) opens his film with the song *Sigh no more, ladies, sigh no more, / Men were deceivers ever,* which is found in Act II, Scene 3, lines 57-65 in Shakespeare's text. The song is made into a leitmotif for the entire comedy. Initially we see the lines of the song in white letters on a black screen, then music is added and the lines are recited. Next the Tuscany landscape is shown on an unfinished painting and eventually the following bucolic scene: Beatrice is sitting in a tree and reading the song to her picnic party. A messenger comes and announces the arrival of Don Pedro, Prince of Arragon, and his entourage returning from battle. At this news Leonato, governor of Messina, invites the prince to his house. Leonato's party of young ladies immediately start running back to the governor's mansion to get themselves ready for Don Pedro's reception. A striking example of functional visual choreography is the way Branagh contrasts the prince's line of men on horseback with the line of young ladies running down a hill.

In *The Taming of the Shrew* Shakespeare portrays a much more dramatic relationship between the self-willed Kate and Petruchio the macho. The play describes the power struggle between the two protagonists and ends with Kate's surrender: *Thy husband is thy lord, thy life, thy keeper / Thy head, thy sovereign;...*(Act V, Scene 2, lines 146-147). In this monologue Kate expresses submission after a long struggle – or does she not? There is no final answer to this question, as it is not possible to reconstruct Shakespeare's intention regarding the end of the play. Kate may only *pretend* submission in order to win the wager! In the final scene, Zeffirelli shows Petruchio enjoying the triumph of having tamed his wife and rightfully won the wager of 300 ducats. Yet when he looks around, Kate has disappeared. Petruchio seems to realise immediately what this may mean: he may only have won another battle and not the matrimonial war. He goes looking for his wife. The other people present are also aware of this and wish to follow. However Petruchio's servant blocks their way. He closes the door behind his master. In this way Zeffirelli leaves the central issue of the play open – open to interpretation and discussion in the classroom.

2.2 Comparing an older and a modern production of *Romeo and Juliet*

In 1968 the American director Franco Zeffirelli and in 1996 the Australian Baz Luhrmann produced *Romeo and Juliet.* To study and compare these productions is an attractive and challenging task. A group of students may be given the task of viewing and comparing these two versions at home and reporting back: Which version do they prefer? Why? The students may select one or two scenes to be shown and compared in detail. For this the scene with Romeo and Juliet's first meeting, Zeffirelli's balcony scene and Luhrmann's swimming pool scene, could be chosen. Zeffirelli's Juliet with her husky voice and "girly" mannerisms feels unnatural and even dated to young viewers today, whereas Luhrmann's Juliet and Romeo (Claire Danes and Leonardo DiCaprio) may be considered more natural in their behaviour towards each other. Zeffirelli's classical Italian and Luhrmann's modern Californian setting are very different and yet they both use Shakespeare's original lines and language.

2.3 Comparing a main stream production and a modern adaptation: *The Taming of the Shrew* (1967) and *Ten things I hate about you* (1999)

Zeffirelli's well known *The Taming of the Shrew* with Elizabeth Taylor and Richard Burton and a very light-hearted modern adaptation may be compared here. After a detailed study of the original text and the viewing of scenes from Zeffirelli's film, the comparison of these two films is a challenging and attractive task for an interested group of students and may be prepared at home. Gil Junger's *Ten things I hate about you* is an adaptation of the Shakespeare plot for an American high school comedy. The group will realise that Junger's film is light-hearted entertainment for teenagers with the occasional more serious message. If this film does not get the students interested in the original play, nothing else will. In how much depth the comparison can be made will depend on the interest of the students.

2.4 Background material for understanding a film production: The making of *Much Ado about Nothing*

This film *Chasing the Light* (Branagh, 1993b) about the making of Kenneth Branagh's *Much Ado about Nothing* is part of the Boxed Set edition of the film. The title alludes to the shooting of the final scene in the Tuscany location, where the cameras are moved right up above the scene to give a bird's eye view of the beautiful garden and the Tuscany landscape beyond. Branagh explains that only for a very limited time each day was there the right sunlight for this shot. *Chasing the Light*, as he has appropriately called this film, gives a lively impression of what film making is like. Branagh and his then wife Emma Thompson talk about their views on how to make Shakespeare's plays into successful films. Various actors such as Denzel Washington, Keanu Reeves and Robert Sean Leonard talk about their reasons for joining Branagh for this film. All of them are aware that Shakespeare films are rarely big box-office successes, but they give prestige to an actor on his way to stardom. Branagh admits that he has taken on these young American actors so that they may attract a young audience who have seen them in other productions and would otherwise never go to a Shakespeare production.

2.5 Shakespeare's *Macbeth* and the definition of tragedy in Willy Russell's *Educating Rita*

The classic definition of *tragedy* is worked out in a dialogue in Willy Russell's play *Educating Rita* better than any dictionary of literary terms ever will (Russell, 1981, pp. 27-29; Brusch, 1996, pp. 28-31). The play and the film (Gilbert, 1983) tell the story of Rita, a hairdresser, who takes part in an Open University course in order to complete her education. Frank, a university lecturer, is her part-time tutor for an "Understanding of Art" course. One day Rita decides to go to a theatre performance by herself for the first time in her life. It happens to be *Macbeth.* Rita is absolutely thrilled and next day visits Frank at the university to share her experience with him. Taking *Macbeth* as an example, Frank explains that the concept of tragedy, as used in classical drama, is entirely different from the everyday meaning of the word as sometimes found in a newspaper: tragic death – man killed by falling tree. Indeed, it would be advisable to read the text extract first and then show the film version. Students will notice that the text was originally written for a stage production with notes for the director at the beginning of each scene. In the film version however a natural location is used such as a university building and lecture room. Here something can be learned about both the limitations and opportunities involved in stage and film productions.

2.6 Visual biography: *The Life of William Shakespeare* (1995)

This is excellent background material on Shakespeare and his time together with comments by Stanley Wells, director of the Shakespeare Institute, and Robert Smallwood, deputy director of the Shakespeare Centre in Stratford. There is also an interview with Brian Blessed on what it is like to be an actor in the Royal Shakespeare Company. He also comments on *Macbeth*. Blessed explains that for him *Macbeth* is more than a drama about the life and death of a villain. In *Macbeth* Shakespeare describes evil not as the deeds of a(n) (in)human monster but as the temptations and weaknesses of a human being like you and me. This interpretation may lead to a discussion about evil in general or the misuse of power in politics. If not, the latter could be provoked by a statement like this: "Macbeth could no longer happen today, as all modern societies have democratically elected and controlled governments. The public in these societies is sensitive to the misuse of power, reacts immediately and knows how to defend and safeguard democracy." It will be interesting for the teacher to see how the students react and what examples of modern dictatorships they come up with (e.g. Hitler, Milosevic or the Taliban regime).

2.7 Malcolm Hossick: *William Shakespeare. A Concise Biography* (1991)

In contrast to the film discussed above with its comments by scholars and actors on Shakespeare's art, this video (Hossick, 1991) gives a good impression of what there is still to be seen of Shakespeare's life and times in modern Stratford. It would be very useful for preparing the class for a trip to the Warwickshire town and its theatres.

2.8 Biographical fiction: John Madden's *Shakespeare in Love* (1999)

"Shakespeare falls in love with Gwynneth Paltrow and as a consequence writes *Romeo and Juliet.*" This is the tongue-in-cheek summary of the plot of this film given by a well-known British linguist recently in a lecture at Hamburg University. Although the trivial plot of this film has nothing to do with historical facts, the film can give students a vivid impression of what Shakespeare's London, its theatres and the life of theatre owners, playwrights and actors in those days might have been like.

3. Integrating the three means of access: *Macbeth I.1*

In the above chapter examples were given of the type of media material available for use in the classroom. Now I would like to show in detail how the reading and acting of a scene and the viewing of different media versions of this scene can be integrated into a study of Shakespeare in such a way that his art is better understood and made more enjoyable.

Macbeth is by far the most frequently chosen play of Shakespeare's for study in German advanced EFL classes. The famous opening scene with the dialogue of the three witches in this most tightly constructed of Shakespeare's plays creates an ominous and foreboding atmosphere without giving away the central issues of the play. When Friedrich Schiller in 1801 wrote an adaptation of *Macbeth,* he made the witches tell the audience that they were about to watch a play where an honest man is led into temptation (lines 25-26):

> Strauchelt der Gute und fällt der Gerechte,
> dann jubilieren die höllischen Mächte.

Schiller added about two dozen lines in which he clarified the central issues of the play the audience was about to see. When his friend Körner criticised him and said that he preferred the original version for the fact that nothing is given away, Schiller answered that clarity is necessary, "weil die Masse des Publikums zu wenig Aufmerksamkeit hat und man ihr vordenken muß" (Schiller, 1949, vol. 13, p. 386).

Producing the scene remains a daunting task for every director of *Macbeth,* as it sets the tone for the entire play. To make students aware of this keynote effect of the opening scene a comparative study of different media versions is ideal. Before we can do this, it would be good for the students to have "hands-on" experience of the play by acting out this scene themselves.

This approach is also suggested by Rex Gibson (1963) in his Cambridge school edition of *Macbeth*:

> The best thing to do with the opening scene is to act it out. It doesn't take long to learn the lines. Present it as dramatically as you can. Prepare sound effects – thunder, rain, battle sounds, cats, toads – and anything else you think you'd hear in such a fearful place. Use your imagination … Electrify your audience. (Gibson, 1963, p. 2)

Get off the page onto the stage. Reynolds (1991a) seems to follow here his colleague Gibson's advice: learning by doing. One scene acted out will make students aware that a Shakespeare text can only be properly understood from the reality of a theatre performance. After the students have taken turns in acting this scene and then evaluating each other's efforts, they will be interested in finding out how different directors and actors have "done" this scene.

As already mentioned, Shakespeare is doubtless the author who has attracted more theatre and media directors than any other writer. In Rothwell and Meltzer's (1990) Shakespeare filmography there are 62 entries for *Macbeth*. The following four versions may be enough to show different approaches:

3.1 Roman Polanski's *Macbeth* (1971)

Contrary to tradition, Polanski (1971) did not choose an open heath but a lonely beach as the location for the opening scene. The three witches walk along, stop and dig a hole in the sand to bury a cut-off human arm, a dagger and a noose. They sprinkle blood from a golden chalice over this and then cover everything with sand. During this ritual they speak the opening lines as an incantation. The morning sky is red and blue. It does not need a highly developed sense of artistic awareness to realise that Polanski is here making natural phenomena take on symbolic meaning.

3.2 Jack Gold's *Macbeth* (1988)

In contrast to Polanski's naturalistic version Gold's (1988) is a studio version produced by the BBC. The witches are at first indistinguishable from the stone slab of a giant barrow they seem to have slept on overnight. Through thunder and lightning they slowly come to life and then enact the scene. This is very much a "mainstream" production.

3.3 Orson Welles' *Macbeth* (1947)

Shot in just 21 days in 1947 at a small Hollywood studio, this is a black and white production of high intensity and obviously still very much influenced by the disaster of the Second World War. The initial scene shows horse riders in costumes that make them look like Huns. It is followed by a silent cauldron scene in which an effigy of a human being is created out of wet clay. After this the witches' dialogue is spoken with a strong Scottish accent.

3.4 Serebryakov's *Macbeth* (1992)

This animated version is part of a series of six Shakespeare plays that were created in a joint venture in a Moscow and a Cardiff studio. Animation is a very different medium with its specific possibilities and restrictions. This production condenses the play to 30 minutes and can be used as a visual summary of the play. In the opening scene a speaker from the off summarises the historical situation in which the drama of *Macbeth* is about to take place. Initially students may find this medium a challenge. The witches' dialogue is shown unabridged and there is even an element of comic relief in the way the animated figures of the witches appear, float around in a circle of incantation and then disintegrate.

After showing these four versions of the opening scene, the obvious question is: "Which version do you find most convincing?" It should be made clear by the teacher that there is no such thing as the "best" or the "right" version. Just as every director has "his" or "her" version the students should be encouraged to criticise and, "in the theatre of the mind's eye" (Reynolds 1991b, p. 191), create their own version.

The possibility of comparing four or even more media versions of one scene is exclusive to Shakespeare studies simply because there are so many productions of his works. Video technology makes Shakespeare's plays instantly available, literally at your finger tips. Above all, a comparison of different directors' artistic concepts of a scene is a unique way of heightening students' artistic awareness and appreciation.

This comparative in-depth study of one scene with the help of different video productions can be done, according to the students' interests, with other key scenes of *Macbeth* or indeed any other of Shakespeare's plays, provided that the different media productions that exist are available in the school's video library.

4. Finally

The intention of this paper has been to show how the study of Shakespeare's plays in the English language classroom can be made much more interesting and enjoyable by integrating media productions into the reading and critical discussion of a play. However, there can be no doubt that being present at a theatre performance in Germany, or, better still, taking the class to Stratford or the Globe Theatre in London, as some Hamburg English teachers do, will be the climax of English language education at school. It must be remembered that a living play is

> more than actors on the stage interpreting a text: it is a communal event in time, an occasion created by actors and audience together. (Müller-Schwefe, 1982, p. 38)

Clearly after reading, discussing, acting and viewing a Shakespeare play as suggested here, students will enjoy a performance in a theatre and should be encouraged to develop their own independent critical judgement. Language education in school, indeed education generally, can have no higher aspiration.

References

Antor, H. (1997). Shakespeare Alternativ. Auswahlbibliografie. *Der Fremdsprachliche Unterricht. Englisch, 31*(30), 10-12.

Branagh, K. (Director). (1993a). *Much Ado about Nothing* [Film]. (Available from Samuel Goldwyn Company)

Branagh, K. (Director). (1993b). *Chasing the light. The making of 'Much Ado about Nothing'* [Film]. (Available from Samuel Goldwyn Company as part of the *Much Ado About Nothing* Boxed Set)

Brusch, W. (1996). *Discovering Shakespeare. Student's book and teacher's notes.* Stuttgart: Klett.

Castle Communications (1995). *The life of William Shakespeare* [Film].

Gibson, R. (1963). *The Cambridge School Shakespeare: Macbeth.* Cambridge: Cambridge University Press.

Gilbert, L. (Director). (1983). *Educating Rita* [Film]. (Available from Acorn Pictures)

Gold, J. (Director). (1988). *Macbeth BBC Shakespeare* [Film]. (Available from BBC Enterprises)

Hossick, M. (Director). (1991). *William Shakespeare. A concise biography.* [Film]. (Available from Wonderland Entertainment)

Krashen, S. D. (1985). *The input hypothesis: Issues and implications.* New York: Longman.

Lewis, S. (1922). *Babbitt.* London: Jonathan Cape Ltd.

Luhrmann, B. (Director). (1996). *Romeo and Juliet* [Film]. (Available from Twentieth Century Fox Home Entertainment)

Müller-Schwefe, G. (1982). Shakespeare heute: Zwischen Wort und Bild. In W. Habicht (Ed.), *Deutsche Shakespeare Gesellschaft West. Jahrbuch 1982* (pp. 36-55). Bochum: Kamp.

Polanski, R. (Director). (1971). *Macbeth* [Film]. (Available from Playboy Productions and Columbia Pictures)

Rothwell, K.S., & Melzer, A. H. (1990). *Shakespeare on screen. An international filmography and videography.* New York: Neal-Schuman Publishers.

Reynolds, P. (1991a). *Practical approaches to teaching Shakespeare.* Oxford: Oxford University Press.

Reynolds, P. (1991b). Unlocking the box: Shakespeare on film and video. In L. Aers & N. Wheale (Eds.), *Shakespeare in the changing curriculum* (pp. 189-203). London: Routledge.

Russell, W. (1981). *Educating Rita. A comedy.* London: Samuel French.

Schiller, F. von. (1949). *Schillers Werke. Nationalausgabe* (Ed. H. H. Borchardt). Vol. 13. Weimar: Hermann Böhlaus Nachfolger.

Serebryakov, N. (Director). (1992). *Shakespeare. The animated tales. Macbeth* [Film]. (Available from Island World Video)[1]

Walther, M. (1997). Shakespeare – die etwas andere Art. *Der Fremdsprachliche Unterricht. Englisch, 31*(30), 56-57.

Welles, O. (Director). (1948). *Macbeth* [Film]. (Available from Republic)

Wilders, J. (1982). Shakespeare on the small screen. In W. Habicht (Ed.), *Deutsche Shakespeare Gesellschaft West. Shakespeare Jahrbuch 1982* (pp. 56-62). Bochum: Kamp.

Zeffirelli, F. (Director). (1967). *The Taming of the Shrew* [Film]. (Available from Video Collection International)

Zeffirelli, F. (Director). (1968). *Romeo and Juliet* [Film]. (Available from Paramount Pictures)

[1] The accompanying books in this series are published by Heinemann Young Books.

Are pop and rock songs "simple forms"?

A genre study with some implications for the process-oriented approach to foreign language learning

Wilfried Gienow & Karlheinz Hellwig

Die Gattungsstudie bietet eine textuelle und praktische Auswertung rezeptiver und produktiver Verarbeitungsprozesse, bezogen auf Fremdsprachenlernen. Semiotisch gesehen erfasst der Begriff „Text" die *plurimediale* Struktur von Songs, d.h. ihre sprachliche, musikalische und – wie bei Videos – ihre bildliche Schicht von Textualität. W. A. Kochs *Encyclopaedia of Simple Text-Types* (1994) ordnet Pop- und Rock-Songs den „Einfachen Formen" zu. Wird diese Zuordnung dem Grundverständnis des Fachbegriffs gerecht? Der erste Teil des Artikels diskutiert diese Frage und prüft die Ergebnisse der Diskussion. Der zweite enthält eine kurze prozessorientierte Interpretation zweier Songs – einer davon ein „Musik Video Clip" – und vermittelt einige wesentliche Erkenntnisse für prozessorientierte Arbeit mit Pop- und Rock-Songs beim Fremdsprachenlernen. Die mediale Übermittlung der Songtexte in Audio- oder Video-Form ist von unterschiedlicher Wirksamkeit im Lernprozess. Darum sind ins Bildliche übertragene Songs nicht *per se* mehr oder weniger wirksam als Audio-Songs oder umgekehrt. Wichtig ist z.B., dass die Songs *subjektive* Verstehensweisen in jungen Leuten anregen. Der dritte Teil empfiehlt Lernwege für die Unterrichtspraxis, die dazu beitragen, „die eigene Identität zu finden", und – beispielhaft – die individuelle Suche nach dem Selbst entfalten zu können.

The genre study presents textual as well as practical evaluations of receptive and productive processing in the context of foreign language learning. The term "text" – semiotically – covers the plurimedial structure of songs, i.e. their verbal, musical and – as in videos – their visual layers of textuality. W. A. Koch's *Encyclopaedia of Simple Text-Types* (1994) classifies pop and rock songs as *Simple Forms*. Is this classification justified according to the basic understanding of the term? The first part of the article discusses this question and evaluates the results of the discussion. The second part offers a short process-oriented interpretation of two songs – one being a "music video clip" – and gives an impression of some essential findings for a process-oriented work with pop and rock songs in foreign language learning. The medial transmitting of the song texts in audio or video form is of differing effectiveness in the process of learning. That is why pictured songs are not *per se* either more or less effective than audio songs or vice versa. It is important, f-or instance, that the texts stimulate subjective interpretations in young people. The third part of the article recommends practical ways of learning, which contribute to the topic of "finding one's identity" and exemplify the individual search for one's own self.

Our understanding of process-oriented learning – not too far away from a non-radical constructivism – has been integrating different approaches of innovation, such as "learning through action" ("Handlungsorientierung" according to Bach & Timm, 1989), but also creative and the individual learner's autonomous activities. This concept of integrative innovation has become essential to Johannes-Peter Timm – in particular in his programmatic and progressive "guide" *Englisch lernen und lehren* (1998a).

The authors of this article have verified "their" learner orientation specifically based upon meaningful content material as well as on adequate learning and teaching strategies referring to individual *and* general mental processes (see, for example, Gienow & Hellwig, 1999). That is why we have selected a topical and interesting theme concerning two "eminent texts" which offer language combined with only musical or musical and visual presentation: "pop and rock songs" (*p a r s*) (Timm, 1998b). We are going to discuss them with reference to their structure and themes, their appeal to learners and strategies and activities of learning.

1. Pop and rock songs as structures and genres

First we have to consider some genre theory. Even under the basic aspect of semiotics, the general theory of signs, the fundamental structural level of *p a r s* is that of language: In general the creation of them begins with writing or referring to their lyrics; moreover all pre- and, much more, close understanding of "textual" structures are linguistically bound (Gadamer, 1965).

According to the "hidden thesis" of this article we have to look at a specific chapter of genre theory: Under the influence of Cassirer's "philosophy of symbolic forms" (developed in the 1920s and summed up 1944/1972), Jolles (1930/1958) coined the term "simple forms" ("Einfache Formen"; see also Hellwig, 2000, pp. 139-158). The original term denotes a meaningful principle of structure, which is "simple", less complex than highly differentiated literature, but already indicates art *in statu nascendi*, in form of a basic structural pattern, a strongly appealing "gesture of discourse" ("einzelne Gebärde der Sprache"; Jolles, 1930, p. 45) which can and has been varied in their historical development and has also influenced "great" literature. Originally applied to five individual types of folk literature – orally transmitted in the past, but also today (e.g. riddles, proverbs, jokes, fairy tales) – , these simple forms have developed increasingly to a considerable number of types up to now. Probably therefore they deserve attention and interest, in particular for didactical reasons. Accordingly they have been rediscovered and revisited (Hellwig, 1971, 1985; Koch, 1994). Koch and his team have discussed *p a r s* with respect to the "evolution" of literary forms and have come to present and describe 45 text-types, among them "pop and rock songs" (Beal, 1994).

The term "evolution" in itself hints at the fact that all literary genres are not fixed, but undergo modification and diversification – handled by the creativity of their writers and recipients. This is true for simple forms, too. Beal (1994) talks about *p a r s* as simple forms and sees them as *one* genre. He describes them referring to "the music", "the audience" and "the intentions of the composer and the singer". (Sometimes there is potentially more in them than their producers and performers intend. Why does he not speak about the writers of the *lyrics*?)

The music may – "textually" and appealingly – be dominant, but Beal almost forgets about the linguistic basis of the songs. Nevertheless he cannot but list some thematic aspects of rock songs: "youth, freedom, bohemianism, authenticity through live performances, anticapitalism and artistry" (ibid., p. 210). Several more themes could be mentioned, specifically personal identity, loneliness and being together, love and sex, the intercultural experience, racism, violence, the anti-war or peace perspective, surrealism and humour (Donnerstag, 1989; Thaler, 1999). Often the themes are mixed and intermingled in the songs – themes which touch key problems of our times (Klafki, 1996). Beal also considers the linguistic structure of *one* song (not worth quoting):

> The lyric itself could hardly be more simple or repetitive. … Looking beyond its sound and rhythmic patterns the language of our example is remarkable for the absence of complex, distinctive or unusual grammatical structures of figurative language. … The rhymes are banal and hackneyed and the words themselves occur in numerous popular songs. … As in … many songs there is a speech situation in which a fictional "I" adresses a fictional you … Like other minimalist pop song genres [now plural! Author's note] … the purpose of this song is not to convey information, not to progress from a beginning through a middle to an end …, but by its circular, atemporal nature to create social identities, provide dance rhythms, create and sustain fantasies and celebrate urban street culture. (Beal, 1994, pp. 212-214)

Is *some* simplicity of *one* text enough proof to identify *p a r s* as *a* Simple Form? The songs' often basically narrative and sometimes monologically reflective structures (internal monologues), show that sub-genres of language forms have come into existence (some lyrics are song-like, *liedhaft*, others come close to ballads), and styles of music (country folk, blues, rap, reggae, etc.) have also produced sub-genres. The problem is more differentiated than Beal suggests it is – calling *p a r s* a Simple Form. His "genre" covers, as the whole article shows, a "collection" of language and music sub-genres. Didactically the principles of repetition, duplication and parallelism are of importance, because they allow and recommend individual remakes, rewriting and inventive composition in easy language by the learners, even the relatively poor and weak ones (Siedtmann, 1998, pp. 247-251).

Although *p a r s* tend to be linguistically simple, it in fact depends on *the individual song* whether there is mere simplicity of content and form or more. Often they are not reduced to just *one* "gesture of discourse" (Jolles, 1930/1958). Therefore, didactically, all depends on selection according to the learners' language competence, their interests and needs, also guided by textual quality, as far as possible. Donnerstag (1989), like others, sees rock songs as the more artistic and relatively *complex* type of texts (Donnerstag calls them "textually demanding", *textintensiv*; p. 170) compared to pop songs. His monograph – based on reader-oriented approaches of literary science and aiming at learner-oriented didactics – takes mainly rock *lyrics* into account in order to come to ways to develop adequate reading strategies in the learners. The lyrics, according to their appealing (linguistic) "codes" and layers of potential meaning (*Isotypieebenen*; ibid., pp. 180-182), are classified under three categories: structures with

(a) rather a simple code and little poetic expression,

(b) a more open, anticipating ambiguous code and

(c) an almost complex and fairly poetic code – hence a differentiatingly demanding listening, reading and understanding potential.

These are criteria of textual quality. At least type (c) is often far beyond simplicity. That is to say, all depends on the individual "text" and the ways of reception. Can they not be considerably beyond simplicity and trivial mass media with druglike effects (cf. the differentiated analysis in Thaler, 1999, and Blell, in press)? Musically and verbally they are often not reduced to *one* "gesture of discourse" (Jolles, 1930/1958).

We have selected two texts only, advised by members of the young generation, one – a pop song – created as early as 1982, and another – a rock song – presented as a current music video clip.

1.1 Paul McCartney & Stevie Wonder: "Ebony and Ivory"[1]

The song became a hit and was "in the charts" for a long time. Indeed it still is a popular piece of music (frequently to be found on the Internet). It has become a "classic" in the tradition of the Beatles, who began their career in the early 1960s. Written and composed – and in its presentation strongly influenced – by Paul McCartney, the creative head of the Beatles, it would appear to be a promising text for didactic purposes.

As it is the music which attracts in the first instance we begin the analysis with the song's sound track.[2] The interpreters are a white and a black man – fitting the song's metaphorical title. It may be true that Stevie – a blind man with a highly developed sensitivity – *and* his background of black culture have contributed a lot to the composition with its striking soul impact and, much more so, to the interpretation. In the end, the song appears to be the joint creation of two befriended men.

The music is performed naturally *and* electronically, it is real and virtual music:

the singers with their voices and clapping hands	the fundamentally smooth rhythm produced by a bass guitar, a synthesizer, the piano and the drums	the synthesizer imitating a chorus sound of wood-wind and brass instruments	another guitar – sounding like a banjo – and a vocoder imitating a chorus of singing voices

It seems to be a studio production performed by the two artists only; however, they certainly used some electronic aids.

The composition, its soul character, and the vocal interpretation make the harmonious music smooth, appealingly pleasant and melodi-

1 EMI R 6054; George Martin: Parlophone, 1982.
2 Sound-only (i.e. "karaoke") versions for singing are easily available.

ously insinuating. It begins with a short introduction, almost sounding like a (small) big band, which is repeated later. The passages of singing are interspersed with kind of banjo soli, maybe to stimulate some dancing. In fairly regular repetition – being connected with the chorus – there are emphatic accentuations in the soloists' singing like rises or upswings, additionally underlined by a lengthening of the vowels in stressed syllables. These accents go with important words and expressions of the lyrics, such as "together", "harmony", "side by side". The music with the singers' voices *and* the words are linked closely.

> CHORUS: Ebony and Ivory
> Live together in perfect harmony
> Side by side on my piano keyboard
> Oh Lord, why don't we?
>
> We all know that people are the same
> Wherever you go
> There's good and bad in everyone
> We learn to live, we learn to give each other
> What we need to survive
> Together alive
>
> CHORUS: Ebony, Ivory, living in perfect harmony
> Ebony, Ivory, ooh
> We all know…
>
> CHORUS: Side by side on my piano key board
> Oh Lord, why don't we?
> Ebony, Ivory, living in perfect harmony
> Ebony, Ivory, living…

An intense and idealistic plea for peace and harmony between the races, offered in the Beatles', Soul, Blues and Gospel tradition. A pleading song of soft political agitation. The singers address their audience directly and repetitively. The language counts in an "eminent" pop song. The singers perhaps aim at a global and intercultural identity – being far ahead of mankind's development. The singers widen their relationship including all who listen in their "we". Are we, actually, "all … the same"? In spite of "good and bad in everyone" Paul and Steve try to teach "learn(-ing) to live" and "to give each other / What we need …". The dominant metaphor of the beginning, the poetic key pattern of the song, is repeated again and again "to rub the message in".

1.2 Creed: "With arms wide open" 1999/2000[3]

In music video clips (mvc) the pictures are immediately striking to the eyes of a watcher, and moreover his/her ears hear "the additional something". Does this really lead to understanding (Thaler, 1999; Blell, in press)? Let us follow this aspect of the text first and then add some impressions of the music.

From a dark, gloomy sky – promising a thunderstorm – the camera shifts to a landscape of green hills and soon focuses on a young man from below, the singer and "hero", first with a medium long, then a close-up shot. On the one hand he seems to be highly concerned (about what?), on the other almost "radiant", perhaps even happy. A corresponding gesture goes with his facial expression. He is singing intensely and beseechingly, accompanied by a regular two beat rhythm with a strong stress on the first beat. He begins to walk, while the bass player appears for a moment, and so does the drummer. Suddenly fire balls hit the ground around the singer. Why are they aimed at him? Nevertheless he finds his way to a tower. Inside a big bell falls down and breaks one of the floors. The singer jumps through the hole and now stands in front of a whirling well. The camera shows light from the top. After a moment of praying the singer dives into the well, soon after emerging from the depth in a rapidly flowing river. Now the drummer accompanies the climax with a wild and aggressive beat. Has the singer survived experiences of initiation? Very soon after, the camera shows him standing close to a coastline and somehow tracks him to the top of a mountain. There, in the distance, he spreads out his arms widely. It is not only *this* ritual action, which is obvious, also his praying etc. ... A Jesus gesture? Rather a gesture of freedom and joy, perhaps even triumph. The sky has cleared up showing some red above the horizon. Is it the colour of dawn or dusk? Surrounded and tempted by the four ancient elements and their ambivalent powers he has survived situations of danger and seems to be reborn. In a shifting montage of settings the "hero" goes through a sequence of rather mental than real situations of difficulties, troubles and danger.

Most of the clip is presented as open and ambiguous. It is the lyrics, finally, which convey a good deal of clarity: It is everyday lan-

---

[3] Singer: Scott Stepp; album "Human Clay"; lyrics available on the World Wide Web: http://www.letssingit.com

guage, in its syntactic structure rather anaphorical. It is easy language. But in its *clip* version the song corresponds rather to type (b) than to type (a) of Donnerstag's "codes" (see above). It presents the singer's monologue about himself (not his girl). He has "just heard" from her that they are going to have a child – a piece of news full of joy and hope, but he also has doubts about himself, in particular whether he will be able to take care of his family. He promises to do his best in order to master the new situation. The film not only illustrates his feelings and his ambivalent internal situation, but also anticipates his overcoming of (all) difficulties and mastering (all) challenges. All? – It ends as the title and the chorus repeatedly suggest full of hope and confidence: "With arms wide open". Despite its only gradual clarity, which leaves much open, the clip gives rise to associations, questions and comments and individual interpretations.

With arms wide open (Creed)

Well I just heard the news today
It seems my life is going to change
I close my eyes, begin to pray
As tears of joy stream down my face

With arms wide open
Under the sunrise
Welcome to this place
I'll show you everything
With arms wide open
With arms wide open

Well I don't know if I'm ready
To be the man I have to be
I'll take a breath, I'll take her by my side
We stand in awe, we've created life

With arms wide open
Under the sunrise
Welcome to this place
I'll show you everything
With arms wide open
Now everything has changed
I'll show you love
I'll show you everything
With arms wide open
With arms wide open

I'll show you everything
Oh yeah
With arms wide open
Wide open

If I had just one wish
Only one demand
I hope he's not like me
I hope he understands
That he can take this life
And hold it by the hand
And he can greet the world
With arms wide open

With arms wide open
Under the sunlight
Welcome to this place
I'll show you everything
With arms wide open
Now everything has changed
I'll show you love
I'll show you everything
With arms wide open

With arms wide open
I'll show you everything oh yeah
With arms wide open
wide open

2. On pop and rock songs from a process-oriented perspective

A fundamental idea of process-oriented foreign language learning is to look at the existential foundations of communicative language use and embrace the findings for the learning process. In general it can be assumed that language learning is part of the development of the learner's personality. This means among other things that at least aspects of the learning matter should be suited to the learners' personal situation, their expectations and needs, previous experience and knowledge.

> We understand process orientation as a complex-integrative concept, supported by findings in cognitive- and learning-psychology, psycholinguistics, and neo-hermeneutic text-theory – a concept that aims at intensifying and deepening foreign language acquisition by constantly stimulating subjective learning processes. (Gienow & Hellwig, 1999, p. 66)

P a r s in their wide variety of types (see Thaler, 1999) can contribute to the learner-oriented approach to foreign language learning: There is no doubt *p a r s* are "youth culture". The songs are obviously in tune with certain thoughts and feelings of young people, that is, they are full of "meaning" to them. They help suppress the "ugliness" of circumstances and the dictates of the real world, above all, they give the young a feeling of happiness.

Should teachers therefore not even be supposed to find out if the songs are suitable for learning?

2.1 Components of the songs and their effectiveness in foreign language learning

However, today it is not enough to deal with the song texts, although the verbal text remains most important in foreign language learning. "The verbal text is only one code within a whole bundle of semiotic codes, which carries meaning and each of which interacts with the other" (Hodge, 1985, p. 121; as cited in Koch, 1994, p. 211).

The widespread use of music video clips (mvc) requires a look at the verbal text as well as at the music- and the picture text. Thaler (1999) refers in this context among other things to his classroom experience in working on audio songs, which was noticeably accompanied and influenced by the pupils' mvc-reception, which is why the rejection of the visual level increasingly appeared as a methodical anachronism.

Recent research on *p a r s* with advanced learners of English showed that pictured songs (mvc) *per se* are neither more nor less effective than audio songs or vice versa. The illustration of the two songs does not necessarily show any supporting effect with regard to the motivation of language production. The sound-only versions give more creative reasons (Blell, in press, p. 10).

The result confirms a general finding of process-oriented work with media in foreign language learning, according to which the forms of media are of differing effectiveness in different phases of the learning process. Audiovisual perception is of a different quality than "pure" listening or watching. An important question is, for example, what scope for personal thoughts and ideas and the development of language abilities and action is given by either the medium's or the lesson's structure. The differentiated use of mvc and audio songs as well as their medial components takes among other things into account that the perceptive capacity and the powers of imagination show functional similarities. The act of visual recognition, for example, is affected by the activation of visual images, audio recognition by a concurrent audio imagination (Gienow, 1987, p. 79).

Another interesting feature of mvc is how the visual and the audio channel interact (see, among others, Thaler, 1999). In this respect, the individual viewer's relationship toward the mvc turns out to be a crucial factor, which would clearly necessitate a learner-oriented approach. The approach to complex mvc is mainly affective-emotional and strongly influenced by the interest in the singers/bands, which also seems to be decisive for being ready to deal seriously with the mvc during the foreign language lesson at all (Blell, in press, p.10).

2.2 On the potential of the songs and music video clips for the learning process

Both songs analysed above are open for linking up foreign language activities with personal feelings and assessments. They show a particular potential for identification.

In "Ebony and Ivory" the music with the singers' voices and the words of the song are closely linked. "Harmony" is *the* key word of the song and, moreover, all the components of the pop song (the tune, the singers, their singing and words) are in "perfect harmony" with each other. The idea is rather obvious and clear and should be widely accepted for a meaningful discussion in class. The wish for harmony is relatively strong in young people (Gienow, 1994). Based on their needs and individual situations the learners will be able to establish a relation between the main idea of this pop song and their inner selves. The binding of topic aspects to learners' knowledge, experience, expectations and perspectives is essential for real interaction with the learning-matter. "Ebony and Ivory" with its popular content aspects and its clarity will certainly help towards a better understanding of cultural similarities and differences in our world and provoke the learners to question their own views on interpersonal harmony.

The rock song "With arms wide open" is more open to different interpretations than the pop song "Ebony and Ivory". Even the verbal text, "which conveys a good deal of clarity" (see above), causes uncertainty. The line "I hope *he*'s not like me I hope *he* understands" raises questions, for example: Who is *he*? What is *he* to understand? Why should *he* be different from the singer? The mvc pictures provoke many more questions, for example: Where do the fire balls/shells come from? Why are they aimed at him? What is the meaning of this? Is he to overcome his uncertainty and ever new problems of his changing life in a threatening world? The chorus "with arms wide open", the equivalent pictures of the singer with his arms spread out, and the strong, emotional, moving two-beat rhythm of the mvc give the viewer reason to believe in the "hero's" self-confident future.

The three sides of the medial text (music, words, pictures) interact with each other and modify the meaning of the components and the medial text as a whole. This makes the text especially open to subjective associations and characterises its potential for individual interpretations, which, in their turn, influence the continuously developing process of finding one's own personal identity.

Performance videos as well as *narrative* ones with their relatively narrow, partly matching sound-picture relations are just right for the beginning phases of learning with mvc. They should, to a certain degree, guarantee the efficient reception and processing of the different codes (music, pictures, words). However, performance and narrative videos could also be used legitimately in a following, advanced process phase, if the perspectives of the mvc are in tune with the learners' previous experience.

Under certain conditions *concept videos* with their more separate, rather split-up components and their openness to individual associations seem to be more suitable for the creative foreign language discussion. A decisive condition for stimulating language activities still remains – besides the general acceptance of the open form of presentation – that the medial text as a whole and/or in its components should be on roughly the same level with the learners' general and language knowledge. The learners also have to acquire appropriate strategies and techniques to enable them to grasp the meaning of the different related semiotic codes of the *p a r s* and deal with them in a meaningful way – strategies and techniques which they could use separately or in combination while working on a simple or rather complex form of a song.

3. Some practical advice on the process-oriented approach to pop and rock songs

The obvious thing to do would be to offer the learning-matter in such a way as to involve the learner's knowledge and personal experience. Since the young are usually well acquainted with the current songs, their presentation does not necessarily come first.

Let us begin with the more complex text. If we think of the mvc "With arms wide open" the following approach – here in outline – should be possible. It is designed to stimulate and to foster the learner's sense of identity:

(1) "With Arms Wide Open": Gathering images, ideas, expectations.
What comes to your mind when reading this line?
Where and when did you read/hear these words?
Do you remember anything in particular?
What do you personally associate with the phrase?
A film's title is "With arms wide open". What pictures, text, music or sounds would you expect? (Give preference to one aspect.)

(2) Presentation of the mvc: completely, in parts and/or the audio version.

Did the video/song meet any of your expectations? Which?
Did you notice anything particularly good or bad?
Why did you like or dislike the above-mentioned sequence or passage?
What impressed you most about the film?

(3) Working in small groups on your impressions and ideas.
Choose a topic and select a number of appropriate ideas:
Which video sequences, passages of the song text, and musical impressions are you going to interpret?
What are your personal links to the selected sequences or passages?
How are you going to publish your work? (Make up a dialogue, a scene, a collage ..., write and pin up a text, create a new song, exchange some information via the Internet ...)

(4) Editing/publishing and discussing the work.
What is your opinion on the matter presented?
Present and defend your opinion in a discussion.
Make suggestions as to how the publication might be improved.
Find new topics based on your previous experiences and your current expectations of life.

Mutual components such as nearness and distance determine personal identity to a remarkable degree. That is why song texts or mvc, too, are not only noticed with sympathy, but also with antipathy, at least partly. They affect the watchers/listeners in a pleasant or an unpleasant way. The people agree or disagree with what is on offer. The teacher, whose job is to provide learning-matter, should pay attention to the interaction of similarity and difference. They play a noticeable part in developing one's own identity.

The pop song "Ebony and Ivory" has become a kind of "classic" among the generations, and therefore and for its musical and verbal qualities it has been used frequently in the foreign language classroom. It fits the context of many learning units such as "Music unites the races", "Friendship between 'black and white'", "Overcoming racism", "'Good and bad' in everyone?", "Intercultural experiences and creation", "Global harmony?". The following learning steps – most of them process-oriented and contributing to widening the learner's identity – would lend themselves to a group in their fifth year of English:

(1) After some thematic introduction, a "mind opening", the learners listen to the "karaoke" version only and give their spontaneous reactions (likes/dislikes, other statements, questions; if necessary with guiding stimuli by the teacher, e.g. "Does the music 'ring a bell' with you? Does anybody know the song/the singers? What is/could it be about?"; activating pre-knowledge, guessing; "is there anything striking for you in the music – instruments, passages, which re-occur, which can be sung easily?". The teacher answers the learners' questions. If necessary a second playing of the "karaoke" track.

(2) Before the second presentation of the song text the teacher distributes the lines of the script (a cut transparency). While the learners are listening to the song version they put line by line on the overhead projector so that the lyrics are reconstructed. Questions about unknown words and expressions. Classmates (if necessary the teacher) answer the questions.

(3) Discussing the song: The discussion may begin with reference to some important statements of questions by the learners (see step 1). Possible stimuli might be: "What is the song about?" – "And the music? Does it go with the themes? – Why, why not?" – "Does it remind you of a specific musical style?" – "What about the singers' relationship?" – "What are the song's key words and lines in your opinion?" – Additional task: "Find your own title for the song." – Discussion of the titles.

(4) Creative writing: "Either write your own 'Ebony and Ivory' lyrics or a brief comment on the question 'O Lord, why don't we live in perfect harmony?' or a letter to Paul McCartney about his and Stevie Wonder's song." – Presentation and discussion of the learners' texts. (The teacher tolerantly corrects the written texts, makes suggestions for revision and demands a final version.)

(5) Perhaps singing the song (plus rhythmic movement or dancing) using the "karaoke" version.

4. Conclusion

The genre discussion and these exemplary analyses of the two texts go to show that there are *two different genres*, namely pop *and* rock songs. They differ mainly in their language, their literary structures and verbal expression and, hence, in their differently complex and ambiguous appeal to their listeners. Therefore, although both genres are thematically linked, it is ultimately the individual test which proves them to be a simple or rather a complex form. The real importance of a pop or rock song with regard to foreign language learning remains a sufficient meaningful potential in content and form that can stimulate a particular learning process. The multi-medial structure and the multidimensional way of reception largely contribute to place them beyond simplicity – at least didactically.[4]

References

Bach, G., & Timm, J.-P. (Eds.). (1989). *Englischunterricht.* Tübingen: Francke.

Beal, D. (1994). Pop and rock song. In W. A. Koch (Ed.), *An encyclopaedia of simple text-types in lore and literature* (pp. 209-226). Bochum: Brockmeyer.

Blell, G. (in press). Musikvideoclips im Englischunterricht: „medialer Himmel" oder „mediale Hölle"? In H. Decke-Cornill (Ed.), *Fremdsprachenunterricht in medialen Lernumgebungen.* Frankfurt a.M.: Lang.

Cassirer, E. (1972). *An essay on man. An introduction to a philosophy of human culture.* New Haven: Yale University Press. (Original work published 1944)

Donnerstag, J. (1989). *Rezeptionstheorie und Literaturdidaktik. Literarische Lesestrategien und* rock lyrics *im Englischunterricht.* Essen: Die Blaue Eule.

Gadamer, H.-G. (1965). *Wahrheit und Methode. Grundzüge einer philosophischen Hermeneutik* (2nd ed.). Tübingen: Mohr.

Gienow, W. (1987). *Audiovisualität und Fremdsprachenerwerb: Untersuchungen zu Grundlagen, Realisierung und Wirksamkeit audiovisueller Veranschaulichung im Englischunterricht.* Habilitationsschrift. Potsdam: Pädagogische Hochschule.

Gienow, W. (1994). Verständiger werden im Englischunterricht? Beispiele prozeßorientierten Medieneinsatzes, mögliche Wirkungen und Begründungen. In W. Gienow & K. Hellwig (Eds.), *Interkulturelle Kommunikation*

---

[4] The authors are most grateful to Anneliese von Thadden-Schmidt for her linguistic advice, to Ingo Carboch and Friedemann Hellwig for their help in selecting the texts, to Friedemann also for all musical advice and his final computer processing.

und prozeßorientierte Medienpraxis im Fremdsprachenunterricht (pp. 77-93). Seelze: Friedrich.

Gienow, W., & Hellwig, K. (1999). Process orientation – an integrative concept of foreign language learning. In *Acta Universitatis Wratislaviensis No. 2127* (pp. 63-78). Wrocław: University.

Hellwig, K. (1971). *Englische Volksmärchen. Literarisch – kulturhistorisch – soziologisch.* Bonn: Bouvier.

Hellwig, K. (1985). Versuch einer Grundlegung zur Didaktik „Einfacher Formen“ am Beispiel „Rätsel“. *Die Neueren Sprachen, 84*, 530-555.

Hellwig, K. (2000). *Anfänge englischen Literaturunterrichts. Entwicklung, Grundlagen, Praxis. Primarstufe – Jahrgangsstufe 11.* Frankfurt a. M.: Lang.

Jolles, A. (1958). *Einfache Formen.* Darmstadt: Wissenschaftliche Buchgesellschaft. (Original work published 1930)

Klafki, W. (1996). *Neue Studien zur Bildungstheorie und Didaktik* (5th ed.). Weinheim: Beltz.

Koch, W. A. (Ed.). (1994). *An encyclopaedia of simple text-types in lore and literature.* Bochum: Brockmeyer.

Thaler, E. (1999). *Musikvideoclips im Englischunterricht. Phänomenologie, Legitimität, Didaktik und Methodik eines neuen Mediums.* München: Langenscheidt-Longman.

Timm, J.-P. (Ed.). (1998a). *Englisch lernen und lehren. Didaktik des Englischunterrichts.* Berlin: Cornelsen.

Timm, J.-P. (1998b). Pop- und Rocksongs als „Lernschrittmacher“. In J.-P. Timm (Ed.), *Englisch lernen und lehren. Didaktik des Englischunterrichts* (pp. 178-184). Berlin: Cornelsen.